RURAL RESISTANCE IN THE LAND OF ZAPATA

TANALÍS PADILLA

Rural Resistance in the Land of Zapata

THE JARAMILLISTA MOVEMENT AND

THE MYTH OF THE PAX PRIÍSTA,

1940–1962

Duke University Press

Durham and London

2008

© 2008 Duke University Press

All rights reserved.

Printed in the United States of America on acid-free paper ∞

Designed by C. H. Westmoreland

Typeset in Warnock Light with Pabst display by Achorn International

Library of Congress Cataloging-in-Publication Data appear on the last printed page of this book.

An earlier version of chapter 4 appeared in "'Por las buenas no se puede': Rubén Jaramillo's Campaigns for Governor of Morelos, 1946 and 1952," *Journal of Iberian and Latin American Studies* 7 (2001): 21–48. An adaptation of chapter 7 appeared in "From Agraristas to Guerrilleros" The Jaramillista Movement in Morelos." *Hispanic American Historical Review* 87 (2007): 255–92. Some information from chapter 1 also appears in this article. The material is reprinted with the permission of each journal.

The Office of the Associate Dean for the Social Sciences of Dartmouth College provided a subvention toward the publication of this book.

CONTENTS

ACKNOWLEDGMENTS

I would not have been able to complete this book without the help, support, and encouragement of numerous people. As such, it represents a collective effort. I am especially grateful to Michael Monteón, my adviser at the University of California, San Diego, for guiding the dissertation upon which this book is based and for the time he has continued to devote to me after I finished at UCSD. I am deeply indebted to my other graduate school professors, David Gutiérrez, Ramón Gutiérrez, Christine Hünefeldt, Ramón E. Ruiz, Rosaura Sánchez, and Eric Van Young, for their time and the intellectual rigor they demanded.

Throughout the years that I have worked on this project, several institutions have provided generous funding. UC MEXUS and the Center for U.S.-Mexican Studies supported much of the research and writing for my dissertation. A postdoctoral fellowship from the Ford Foundation enabled me to spend a year at Yale University undertaking the first revisions to transform my dissertation into a book manuscript. Likewise, the Dickey Center at Dartmouth College funded and organized a seminar that brought together several of my Dartmouth colleagues, as well as Jeffrey Gould and Adrian Bantjes. The seminar was exceptionally helpful, and I am grateful to Lisa Baldez, Judi Byfield, Doug Haynes, Annelise Orleck, Marysa Navarro, Misagh Parsa, John Watanabe, and Christianne Wohlforth for taking the time to read my work and for the sparks of insight generated by their discussion.

To Jeff and Adrian I extend my heartfelt gratitude for making the trip the Hanover and for their invaluable feedback. I thank Dartmouth College for consistently supporting my research.

Throughout my research and writing I have relied on numerous people whose comments, guidance, and insight fueled my passion for this work. Cindy Forster read and commented on numerous incarnations of this manuscript, offering meticulous feedback that has enriched its texture. Through work, travel, and activism Cindy has been an inspiring historian, a wonderful friend, and the clearest example of what it means to be a committed scholar. To my other undergraduate professors, colleagues, and friends Sid Lemelle, Victor Silverman, and Miguel Tinker Salas, I owe the desire to be a historian, the good humor with which to confront difficult times, and the comfort of knowing I can always turn to them. Across the years I have been blessed with other wonderful colleagues and mentors. From the beginning Barry Carr enthusiastically encouraged me to pursue this topic at a time when few ventured beyond the 1940s. My conversations with him and his comments on portions of this manuscript have greatly enriched this work. Gil Joseph, with his characteristic generosity, read and commented on the entire manuscript. For this and his gracious mentoring while I was at Yale, I am indebted. I thank Enrique Florescano whose lively discussions and encouragement will stay with me. Avi Chomsky, John Hart, Christina Jiménez, John Lear, and Louise Walker have also read and contributed invaluably to this study. I am grateful to the staff at Duke University Press, especially Valerie Millholland, for taking an interest in this project and for her insight and guidance through the publication process. I would also like to thank Duke's anonymous readers for their extensive and constructive feedback, and Kathryn Litherland for her keen editing work.

My colleagues at Dartmouth College have been a wonderful blessing. I have been continuously amazed at how my fellow members of the History Department go out of their way to support my research and teaching. I am especially grateful to Judi Byfield, Joseph Cullon, Annelise Orleck, Celia Naylor, and Craig Wilder for their encouragement, affection, and extreme generosity of spirit. Their smiles and good humor brought me much-needed warmth during those long New Hampshire winters. I also thank Miguel Valladares for seemingly performing miracles by locating and bringing key sources for me to use in Hanover. Over my years of teaching I have had several memorable students, but Claudia Rueda brought special joy to life inside and outside the classroom. Her sensitivity and enthusiasm give me hope.

Returning to Mexico has been one of the most wonderful aspects about researching and writing this book. There I have found myself surrounded by incredible scholars, amazing friends, and inspiring activists who show an unwavering commitment to social justice. Since the beginning of this project my conversations with Javier Villanueva have nourished me in so many ways. His comments on my work and his gentle, poetic voice always filled me with a sense of possibility. Luis Hernández Navarro read and commented on several portions of this work, bringing to it important insight. Several chapters bear the imprint of our discussions, in which he framed so many issues with a passion that is contagious. I am grateful to Carlos Montemayor, who years ago took an interest in my work and commented on several chapters. His own work on guerrillas highlights their significance to the current situation in Mexico. I thank Armando Bartra, who gave me access to valuable newspaper articles housed in the Instituto Maya. I would also like to extend my gratitude to the staff at the Archivo General de la Nación, who were always so kind and helpful in locating the documentation I needed.

Several people in Morelos played a crucial role in making this manuscript a reality. I am especially indebted to Plutarco Emilio García for granting me access to his personal collection of Jaramillista documents and interviews. I am deeply grateful to him and hope that this work honors the trust he has shown in me. Over the years Guillermo Peimbert has been a true friend, always providing a place to stay, wonderful conversation, and much-needed comic relief. Aura Hernández shared key sources with me. I am ever grateful for her generosity. I also thank Guadalupe García for providing important documents on women Jaramillistas, and Florencia Ibarra, who opened her home to me in Cuernavaca and was always so warm and wonderfully supportive. Victor Hugo Sánchez Reséndiz shared with me his insight on Morelos, taking me to some of its most beautiful towns. A state known for its tourism, language schools, and water parks, the trails I explored with Victor Hugo gave me a different view of the state, one far more wonderful. From the villages that diligently celebrate their religious festivals, to bustling markets alive with vibrant smells and colors, to communities organized against ever-encroaching neoliberal projects, Morelos continues to be a site of resistance. It is in these places where Jaramillismo most came alive.

I am grateful to my family, especially my mother Eva, who has always encouraged me to pursue my passions. During my numerous stays in Mexico City, my aunt and uncle Hilda Moreno and Arturo Padilla have opened their home to me and provided support, company, and wonderful home-cooked meals. Enrique Dávalos has been an inspiring and compelling friend whose good nature and work inside and outside the classroom is a source of inspiration. It is difficult to do justice to the role Bobby has played in this work. From the very first stages he has accompanied me in all aspects, enduring my roughest of drafts and worst of moods. With his characteristic sweetness, patience, and humor he helped me push through difficult times and in the most crucial moments provided the much-needed voice outside myself. His love and tenderness are a consistent source of strength.

Most of all, I am indebted to the Jaramillistas, the men and women and their families who took me into their homes and shared their life stories with me. It is difficult in these times to remain hopeful, but in those moments when I feel pessimism's cold edge I remember the words of campesino and campesina Jaramillistas as they related the reasons for their struggle. This work is dedicated to them with the hope that, in some way, it does justice to their history.

INTRODUCTION

In the early afternoon of May 23, 1962, two military trucks, two jeeps, and a civilian car, together carrying about sixty soldiers and several armed civilians, surrounded the home of Rubén Jaramillo, a prominent agrarian leader in the south-central state of Morelos. Captain José Martínez, who led the operation, shouted for Jaramillo to step out and accompany them, or else they would machine-gun his home. Jaramillo emerged from his small adobe home but refused to comply with the men's orders to get in the car. When Filemón, one of Jaramillo's stepsons, displayed the official pardons given to Jaramillo and his wife, Epifania Zúñiga, by President Adolfo López Mateos (1958–64), Captain Martínez put them in his pocket and told Filemón not to complicate matters. In the commotion, Raquel, Zúñiga's oldest daughter, slipped out of the house and went to seek the help of Tlaquiltenango's municipal president Inocente Torres. He told her everything was in order; the soldiers and civilians had an arrest warrant issued by the attorney general's office. When Raquel returned, Rubén, her mother, and her three brothers, Enrique, Filemón, and Ricardo, were all gone. A few hours later, the bullet-riddled bodies of the five family members were found on the outskirts of the Xochicalco ruins, an archeological site near Cuernavaca.[1]

As word of the quintuple murder spread, so too did the shock about this crime committed by government officials. While government repression was hardly new in rural Mexico, its manifestations were typically more subtle.

The state had targeted agrarian leaders in the past but usually did not murder entire families like this. What's more, the military tended to reserve its show of force for popular mobilizations, not for executing specific leaders. Government officials delegated such jobs to hired gunmen or ordered them carried out under the cover of darkness. The audacity of this act left the "Xochicalco massacre" etched in public memory for decades to come, often overshadowing the 24-year-long trajectory of the Jaramillista movement itself.

The Jaramillista struggle began two and a half decades earlier in the southern region of the state of Morelos, the homeland of Emiliano Zapata. During the Mexican Revolution (1910–20), peasants from this small state fought for land and community autonomy with such determination that even though their political project was defeated, their right to land became enshrined in the constitution. When President Lázaro Cárdenas (1934–40) carried out a massive agrarian reform in the 1930s, he was, in part, fulfilling the land aspirations of the rural poor who had fought in the decade-long civil war. Cárdenas's successors, however, would come to honor agrarian reform more in the breach and land hunger continued throughout the twentieth century. The legacy of the Zapatista struggle, in turn, remained alive through memory, legend, and myth and permeated rural consciousness throughout Mexico. Zapata became both a symbol of campesino struggle and the moral barometer by which to judge popular leadership. It is no surprise that when Jaramillo began to speak out in the name of the poor, campesinos in Zapata's homeland simply referred to him as another Zapata.

Although Jaramillo and many of those close to him had fought under Zapata, he represented another generation of agrarian struggle. Rather than fight for land and community autonomy, this generation sought the state support necessary to make the campesino economy viable in a rapidly modernizing nation. The Jaramillistas demanded credit, technical assistance, better prices on their products, and basic state services such as schools and hospitals. Unlike the Zapatistas, whose locus of organization had primarily been the peasant community, the Jaramillistas incorporated a broader cross-section of the Morelos population. Drawing their strongest support from the sugar- and rice-producing zones along the southern contours of the state, their ranks included subsistence farmers, seasonal laborers, migrants, sugar-mill workers, and even a few rural schoolteachers. Despite this diversity, they identified themselves as campesinos, "a distinct social group united by a shared set of political and economic interests as well as by a collective history of oppression."[2]

As with most poor people's movements, the Jaramillistas came to depend heavily on their leader, who articulated, and in some respects embodied, the complex dynamic of the Morelos countryside. Born in 1900, Jaramillo joined the Zapatista forces at the age of 15. Himself a farmer, in the 1930s he became an outspoken defender of rice and sugar cultivators. When attention to the countryside began to dwindle after 1940, he mobilized campesinos in southern Morelos to preserve the revolutionary gains. For this he earned the wrath of caciques (local strongmen), politicians, and in time, the federal government, who sent the army in his pursuit. Undeterred, Jaramillo relied on the Zapatista legacy of armed struggle and, together with other revolutionary veterans, fled to the mountains in self-defense. From there he continued mobilizing the local population, launching proclamations that denounced the government's betrayal of the constitution.

In many respects, Jaramillo represents a classic example of the Gramscian organic intellectual. Having received no formal education (it is said that his first wife, Epifania Ramírez, taught him how to read and write), he spent hours studying the Mexican Constitution and especially agrarian law. Like leaders who headed struggles in other countries under dramatically different contexts, Jaramillo fashioned an eclectic ideological mix that ranged from reformism, to communalism, to class struggle, to anti-imperialism. In this respect, his unclassifiable political philosophy is reminiscent of Augusto Sandino, who not long before had led a small band of rebels against the United States's occupation of Nicaragua.[3] As did other less famous Central American leaders who committed their lives to speaking out in defense of the poor, Jaramillo both drew elements from the dominant ideology (in Mexico's case, revolutionary nationalism) and translated complex theoretical paradigms, including Marxist ones, into simple categories.[4]

Jaramillo led mobilizations in the late 1930s, but the group known as the Jaramillistas emerged in 1942 at the Zacatepec sugar cooperative, where workers and campesinos mounted a joint strike to assert their rights against management's abusive power. When the manager hired gunmen to target strike leaders, a group of campesinos, led by Jaramillo, unearthed the rifles they had preserved from the revolution and fled to the mountains. But they remained underground for only a year, and in 1943 the federal government issued them an official pardon. In 1946 the Jaramillistas mounted an electoral campaign backing Jaramillo for state governor. Despite the agrarian leader's popularity, he lost the elections to the official party candidate. In what would become standard practice throughout the twentieth century, the Mexican Revolutionary Party, later the PRI (Institutional Revolutionary Party), handled the Jaramillista electoral challenge through a combination of fraud and repression, forcing Jaramillo into clandestine action and initiating the second armed uprising of his group.[5] In 1951, however, the Jaramillistas again put down their weapons and—in alliance with a national party formed by disenchanted members of the PRI—participated in the following year's elections. This campaign was much larger than the one six years earlier and involved the far more visible participation of women. The government's fraudulent and repressive tactics grew accordingly, forcing the Jaramillistas to once again turn to armed struggle. During the six years in which this third uprising unfolded, the Jaramillistas became more radical, attempting to take over some municipalities and issuing proclamations whose tone revealed an increasing lack of faith in legal channels. But their militancy notwithstanding, a small, localized rebel group was in no condition to take power from a solidly entrenched ruling class. So in 1959, when the state once again pardoned Jaramillo, campesinos under his leadership initiated a campaign to settle some vacant land on the Michapa and Guarín plains in western Morelos. Although the government initially decided to concede this land to the Jaramillistas, the army soon came to remove the settlers. Shortly thereafter, another army unit kidnapped and killed Jaramillo, his wife, and their three sons, most likely under orders from the national government.

The Jaramillista movement—with its varying tactics and seeming contradiction between militancy and reformism—presents us with an intriguing set of questions. What, for example, was the relationship between campesinos who came together under Jaramillo's leadership and the Zapatistas who a few decades earlier fought in the revolution? How were these movements different? To what extent can we attribute such differences to rural dwellers' experience under Cárdenas? Why did the Jaramillistas go back and forth between armed tactics and reformist strategies such as electoral politics? Why did the government continue to pardon Jaramillo? Why did Jaramillo continue to accept these pardons? What is the legacy of the Jaramillista struggle? And what does it tell us about the current situation in Mexico?

The answers reveal important aspects about the Jaramillista movement in particular, and about twentieth-century Mexico more generally. When the revolutionary war ended in 1920, the triumphant Constitutionalists, led by northern bourgeois reformers, set about to consolidate their hold on power. They could do this only by heeding the demands of those who during the revolution had stubbornly fought for broader social reforms such as land and labor rights. Indeed, these provisions had already been incorporated into the constitution drafted in 1917 when various revolutionary factions attempted to reach an agreement that might put an end to the fighting. But the fighting continued for at least three more years and would ultimately entail the murder of Zapata in 1919. Perpetrated by the Constitutionalists at a meeting in which he was invited to parley, this betrayal has not been forgotten by Morelos's campesinos.

The agrarian leader's assassination was a devastating blow to the Zapatistas, but the new government knew that the *Morelenses* could not be pacified through force alone, and in the 1920s President Plutarco Elías Calles (1924–28) implemented an extensive land reform in the state. Even so, Zapata would not die easily, and his struggle began to acquire mythic proportions, serving as a reminder that the new ruling group had not come to power with the interests of the poor in mind. The state thus attempted to appropriate Zapata's image and, duly cleansed of his rebellious spirit, place him in the pantheon of Mexico's founding fathers. Once celebrated and spread by the government, however, Zapata's image was a double-edged sword. "Far from enabling it to manipulate opinion, the state's somewhat sudden and clumsy embrace of Zapata merely helped it open lines of negotiation," notes Samuel Brunk.[6] "After a decade of warfare in which most of Mexico's administrations had labeled the Zapatistas bandits, their leader was now being acknowledged, in public ritual as well as national policy. . . . The state was admitting that the Zapatistas had been right in their struggle all along."[7] This, in part, helps explain the official pardons issued to Jaramillo. Given the government's claim over Zapata, an armed campesino group operating in his homeland and invoking the legacy of Zapata did not sit well with a state party claiming itself to be revolutionary. The government may have had the physical force, but the Jaramillistas possessed the moral legitimacy.

The legitimacy of campesino demands was further reinforced in the 1930s, when President Cárdenas finally implemented the land, labor, and educational reforms mandated by the 1917 constitution. Land redistribution constituted a centerpiece of his policies, and, throughout Mexico, campesinos received ejidos (collective landholdings), credit, and technical support. In addition, Cardenista reforms included the creation of industrial projects, structured as cooperatives, to help modernize the countryside. In Morelos, for example, Cárdenas built the Emiliano Zapata sugar refinery, in which a campesino-worker council, headed by Jaramillo, was to act as the mill's highest authority, overseeing even the manager. Such actions won Cárdenas the strong allegiance of the rural poor, seemingly demonstrating that, in the right hands, the state could serve to protect the interest of the marginalized. Inspired by this experience, the Jaramillistas sought to become part of the government structure by running Jaramillo for governor of Morelos. This action represented a key difference with Zapata, who never recognized the legitimacy of the Constitutionalists' laws.

But if Cárdenas had opened the door to campesino leadership, he also re-inforced the wielding of presidential power and the consolidation of an offi-cial party that would hold office for seventy-one years. Cárdenas encouraged the mobilization of popular sectors, but only within separate state-sponsored unions and federations. Moreover, Cárdenas used this populist structure towards fortifying executive power. State-sponsored reforms would thus continue to depend on the goodwill of whoever held the presidential office. The Jaramillistas lived this contradiction firsthand in the Zacatepec mill. The cooperative structure not withstanding, it was Mexico's president who appointed the mill's manager, and Cárdenas's successors—less sympathetic to the needs of the countryside—chose figures who cared little about sugar growers.

But rather than succumb to management's will, the Jaramillistas orga-nized a strike to assert their rights. While their actions elicited a repres-sive response from local power holders, they also provided the basis for broader alliances. It was at the Zacatepec mill that Jaramillo first devel-oped a relationship with important labor leaders, some of them Marxists. These connections broadened Jaramillista ideology, leading them both to form common cause with workers and to consider tenets of socialism. This more radical vision emerged in the written proclamations the Jaramillistas made during their armed incursion. Thus, while the Jaramillistas had ini-tially drawn on the Zapatista legacy of armed struggle, state repression also caused a gradual, but noticeable, radicalization.

These shifting tactics became a hallmark of the Jaramillista movement and foreshadowed a process of radicalization that would mark subsequent guerrilla groups, who showed no such faith in reformism. When the Jaramillistas sought to settle the vacant lands in western Morelos between 1959 and 1962, not only were they operating with a history of reformist demands truncated by a repressive state, but their struggle became infused with the possibilities for social change catalyzed by the triumph of the Cuban Revolution in 1959. Across Latin America, Castro's Cuba spoke to the possibility of profound social change, igniting the hopes of the masses and the fears of the elites. The Cuban Revolution thus instilled struggles across the Americas with new elements. The United States reacted with hostility toward the island and feared additional Cubas; Cold War politics thus quickly intensified throughout the continent and increasingly shaped government responses to social protest. It was in this context that the state dealt its decisive blow against the Jaramillistas, assassinating their leader and his family on May 23, 1962, a date Morelense campesinos still commemorate.

Although he was a powerful symbol among Morelos's organized campesinos, the legacy of Jaramillo has not yet registered within the accounts of Mexico's midcentury history. Traditionally hailed for its political stability and rapid economic growth, the period between 1940 and 1968 actually witnessed a steady progression of social unrest. Sparked by material demands, such struggles rapidly turned into larger political clashes—to which the state invariably responded with force. The Jaramillistas are representative of this process. Their movement stands as a popular expression of some of the most important developments in twentieth-century Mexican history and deepens our understanding about the complex relationship between Mexico's enduring one-party system and the citizens over which it presided. Not only does it reveal a less-than-stable political landscape, but it also demonstrates the extent to which state terror undergirded Mexico's "perfect dictatorship."[8] Movements such as the Jaramillistas challenge conventional notions that 1968—the year the army massacred hundreds of civilians peacefully demonstrating in Tlatelolco's plaza—was the key turning point for the postrevolutionary regime.

Long before 1968, campesinos, teachers, and rail and oil workers had mounted powerful protests against the government. While not organically related, these movements shared a common characteristic: they fought to preserve the social clauses mandated by the 1917 constitution. That such reformist demands were threatening enough to elicit a repressive response indicates the extent to which the PRI had institutionalized its own political control and after 1940 increasingly implemented an economic order that privileged business interests and foreign investment. Popular groups fought this process every step of the way, drawing not on "weapons of the weak"—a form of resistance based on subtle defiance and minor acts of sabotage—but by consistently challenging the state, at times more militantly than others.[9] The Jaramillistas—who twice engaged in electoral struggle, on three occasions took up arms, explicitly organized around women's rights, spearheaded a massive land takeover, and attempted to forge alliances with groups at the national level—are one example of the scope and depth of this resistance. The Jaramillista struggle had its origins in Zapata's agrarianism, took form with Cárdenas's populism, and was transformed with the renewed hope for radical change inspired throughout Latin America by the Cuban Revolution. It provides a conceptual link between movements rooted in the revolution and those that would emerge throughout the twentieth century and, in the dawn of the twenty-first, show no signs of abating.

In this way, the Jaramillistas speak to the nature of contemporary peasant movements. Peasant revolts of the colonial and nineteenth century generally had the community as their locus of action. In the twentieth century, in the context of increased capitalist penetration, the broader-reaching powers of modern states, and rampant urbanization, the nature of rural uprisings changed. The Jaramillistas—whose diverse composition included day laborers, smallholders, communal land proprietors, migrants, workers, and rural schoolteachers, and whose varied modalities of struggle ranged from electoral politics, to campesino-labor alliances, to land invasions and armed struggle—exemplify some of these transformations. Campesino movements did not decline as Latin America became more urban, but rather broadened their demands and expanded their ties with other groups, factors which have deepened their political consciousness.[10]

Rethinking the Miracle

Traditionally considered Mexico's "golden age," the decades from 1940 to 1968 saw unprecedented growth of the economy, urban centers, and the nation's infrastructure. A supposedly nationalist government sought foreign investment, especially from the United States, gave generous concessions to private enterprise, and promoted tourism. During these decades the economy grew at an average rate of 6 percent. Mexico held elections regularly, was governed by civilians, and experienced apparently orderly transitions of power, in contrast with the turbulence that characterized many other Latin American nations. The PRI justified its hold on power at the local, state, and national level with the notion that, as the party of the revolution, it best encompassed the interests of all sectors of Mexican society. The official rhetoric of this period celebrated a national character whose tenets included, on the one hand, modernization, middle-class prosperity, and consumerism, and on the other, traditional values such as commitment to the family and female domesticity. This duality was especially evident in the images of "cosmopolitan splendor and folkloric charm" Mexico sought to project abroad.[11]

But there was a darker side to this picture. While the economy grew, income distribution actually worsened. In 1950, for example, the poorer half of Mexican families received 19 percent of national income. By 1975, their share had dropped to 13 percent. In that same year, the top fifth of the population received 62 percent of national income. Mexico's economic inequality was among the highest in Latin America.[12] As Jeffrey Bortz put it, the high levels of industrialization after 1940 "modernized the country without lifting it from underdevelopment."[13] And this underdevelopment manifested itself not only through the continued existence of poverty, but through the deterioration of living standards for a significant portion of the population, especially in the countryside. This outcome was hardly inevitable. It resulted from an official practice that equated a pro-business policy with industrialization. President Miguel Alemán (1946–52), for example, gave generous concessions to the private sector—including businessmen who often occupied prominent government positions. Through an alliance with foreign enterprise there began to emerge a group of millionaires, including Alemán himself, whom *Fortune* magazine listed as one of the world's richest men.[14] But concessions to private enterprise came at a heavy cost to workers, from whom the government demanded discipline, and from campesinos, whom the state abandoned in favor of agribusiness. The effect on the countryside, which subsidized urban development by means of price controls on basic commodities, was especially devastating.

Popular protest accompanied the government's every attempt to abandon social reforms. As rural dwellers fought to preserve or make good on the agrarian mandates of the revolution, urban laborers battled official unionism, one of the lynchpins of PRI control. Additionally, teachers, who were intended to cement the state's power throughout the country, in many areas became organizers of resistance to it.[15] Teachers fought to preserve the social reforms of the 1917 constitution, in which public education figured as a key to progressive victory. The radical potential of their demands and their organic links with rural communities (a great number of teachers were themselves of campesino origin) can be especially seen in the high proportion of teachers who later joined or led armed movements.[16] By 1958, the teachers' mobilizations began to coincide with massive railway workers' strikes, and the state increasingly used force against them, disbanding marches, firing strikers, dislodging sit-ins, and jailing leaders. The railway workers succeeded in rekindling the labor movement in the later months of 1958, when their union managed to break from official control. This victory was especially significant because a decade earlier the government's imposition of an official party loyalist, nicknamed *el charro*, had seemed to signal the defeat of labor as an independent force. So decisive was this intrusion that the term *charro* is still applied to company unions. But the 1958 victory was short lived. In the early months of 1959 the government implemented a virtual state of siege, dispatching the army that, machine gun in hand, ordered conductors to reinstate service.[17]

The railway workers' movement had been so massive, and its possibilities for fracturing PRI corporate control so great, that its defeat sparked an important polemic regarding the revolutionary potential of Mexico's labor movement. The Mexican Communist Party (PCM), specifically, came under fire for its dogmatism and blind adherence to the Moscow line.[18] Part of this dogmatism included the passive involvement of party officials, who allowed peasants and laborers to take the greatest risks. Indeed, though Jaramillo would join the PCM in 1961, he expressed strong skepticism towards its leadership, stating, for example, "The people there are too fancy, like Dionisio [Encinas, the PCM's general secretary from 1940 to 1959]; I have talked to him, and he already fancies himself a rich man . . . he has more hope in the politicians than in the common people."[19] While the PCM played an important role in popular mobilizations throughout Mexico, it did so almost in spite of itself. From its ranks emerged key labor and campesino leaders, usually those expelled from the party. These "dissidents," Barry Carr writes, "were often the first men and women to break with sterile orthodoxy and attempt a reconciling of the socialist tradition with changing realities of Mexican society."[20] Such defectors also played a role in the Jaramillista movement and were especially important in the land invasions that took place between 1958 and 1962 in the northern states of Sinaloa, Baja California, Nayarit, and Colima, where the government too sent the army to contain the mobilizations—a sign of the critical situation in the countryside.

With the intensification of the Cold War after the Cuban Revolution, the Mexican government began to see communists everywhere, as though the presence of Marxists explained the widening opposition to the PRI's rule. Having killed Jaramillo, crushed the teachers and railroad workers, and in the mid-1960s put down a major doctors' strike (an indication that discontent had reached the middle class), the government, under President Gustavo Díaz Ordaz (1964–70), would unleash the army on the student movement in Mexico City. This bloody crescendo took place under the world's gaze, only a few weeks before the 1968 Olympic Games were to be held in Mexico City. The exact number killed on October 2 is still unknown, but estimates range from two to five hundred. Hundreds more were beaten and imprisoned.[21]

The year 1968 currently stands as a watershed in Mexican history, in large part because the state's use of force at Tlatelolco was so concentrated, flagrant, and massive. Moreover, while the movement included the participation of numerous sectors of the working class, Tlatelolco is remembered primarily as a student massacre. The shock of the attack is thus compounded by the middle-class origins of many of its victims.[22] The student movement may have seemed far removed from the events in Morelos six years earlier, or even from the labor movements which in the 1950s shook the capital. But the legacies of those struggles found expression in the 1968 marches, which drew from a wide sector of society and gave voice to long-held grievances. Participants were conscious of the PRI's long trajectory of repression. Luis González de Alba, a prominent member of the strike committee, for example, recalled, "With our footsteps we were somehow avenging Jaramillo, his pregnant wife, both murdered, his dead children; we were avenging years and years of cowardly crimes, crimes that had been carefully covered up, crimes resembling those committed by gangsters."[23] The student movement would be another link in the repression, however, not the liberating moment he and so many had hoped for.

The particularly long-lived nature of the Jaramillista struggle, its location in a rapidly urbanizing state so close to the nation's capital, and the significance of Morelos as the homeland of Zapatismo allow us to discern in the Jaramillistas certain trends encompassed more broadly by the extensive social militancy of these decades. The Jaramillista strike at Zacatepec in 1942 provided an early indication of the limitations in Cardenismo. The subsequent Jaramillista mobilization in the Zapatista tradition showed the politicization of the country's rural population directly resulting from the revolution. Likewise, Jaramillista efforts to link the struggles of workers and campesinos during their electoral campaign and their mobilization to demand land at Michapa and Guarín, where participants included a substantial number of migrants from other states, not only shared certain parallels with land invasions elsewhere in Mexico but also foreshadowed a radicalization that would emerge in subsequent decades. More significantly still, the last episode of the Jaramillista struggle took place at a time of massive labor unrest, during which the Mexican government confronted the powerful rail workers' and teachers' strikes. That these movements would suffer the same fate as the Jaramillistas reveals that the Mexican state, long before 1968, was willing to make massive show of force to curtail social activism. When the 1968 student protests signaled that earlier labor unrest had moved to the middle classes, the government reacted even more violently, symbolic of an increasingly desperate clench on power. And yet, as had been the case of the Jaramillistas, the state's violent repression would elicit even more militant responses, as guerrilla groups began to dot the Mexican landscape.

This extensive social protest, and the government's repressive reactions against it, reveal a new picture of the postrevolutionary period. No longer can we speak, as official historians once did, of a Pax Priísta, an economic miracle, and a process of modernization that slowly but surely reached the most remote corners of Mexico. The 1968 Tlatelolco massacre brought that image to a crashing end. The slowdown in the high levels of growth that had characterized Mexico's economy for almost thirty years was another nail in the coffin of the country's golden age. As scholars began to fully consider both the PRI's repressive measures and the social consequences of its economic policies, a different view of Mexico and the revolution that spawned its modern state came into focus. Revisionist historians now saw the decade-long civil war not as a social revolution whose overthrow of the dictator Porfirio Díaz (1876–1910) brought about a socially conscious, albeit strong, state, but as a popular struggle hijacked by a politically ambitious elite whose new system of rule stood as a mere form of modernized authoritarianism.[24] In this light, Cárdenas's land and labor reforms had not liberated workers and campesinos, but rather anchored them as clients of the state, the president, and the PRI.[25]

With the emergence of regional case studies, however, this revisionist view slowly gave way to more-nuanced interpretations of the process by which the revolution unfolded. Postrevisionist scholars have investigated the ways in which popular agency limited the elite's hegemonic project, arguing for the negotiated nature of state formation in the two decades after the revolutionary war.[26] Not only has the slow and beleaguered course of state consolidation become increasingly manifest, but the process by which the state accommodated and incorporated the myriad forms of popular culture has elicited a whole new body of literature focusing on everyday forms of resistance.[27] In these studies, hegemony, and its corollaries of culture and identity, have become the primary locus of analysis, with state formation conceived as "above all a *cultural* process."[28] Scholars have turned away from institutions and their mechanisms of imposition to take a decentered approach to power in an effort to "understand the relation of local culture and agency to regional and national processes."[29]

The historiography on the revolution has influenced scholarship on the era after 1940. As Alan Knight asserts, "The Revolution embodied and, in turn, recast certain established themes in Mexican history. It was both a product and producer of that history—as its protagonists, regularly invoking the past, were well aware."[30] Not only did assessments of the revolution shape scholars' views on subsequent decades, but the revolution itself acted as a magnet for twentieth-century historians. The scant historical literature that currently treats the decades after 1940 falls into two general camps. One is dominated by North American scholars, who, in the postrevisionist tradition, focus primarily on popular culture.[31] By studying aspects of consumer culture, comic books, music, television, and tourism, these scholars seek to understand how Mexicans developed their identities during the proclaimed golden age. The "politics of culture," contends a recent anthology on the subject, "constitutes one of the keys to understanding Mexico after 1940" and provides "the best and *sometimes the only* window onto crucial aspects of the post 1940 Mexican experience."[32]

A different window into this period is provided by an earlier generation of Mexican scholars, who, since the 1970s, actively sought to counter official history and the perspective of the press that, with few exceptions, was more a mouthpiece for the government than a source of information.[33] Written mostly by activists and public intellectuals, these narratives recount some of the major popular struggles that took place during the Mexican Miracle, including the railway workers' strikes of 1948 and 1958, the teachers' movement of the 1950s, the agrarian mobilizations in northern Mexico, the guerrilla groups in Guerrero and Chihuahua, and the 1968 student movement. Their accounts serve as important reminders of the major social battles that took place during Mexico's supposed golden age. Given the emphasis these studies place on the power of the state and their casting of history within the framework of a bourgeois revolution, most of these works fall within the revisionist camp.

The history of the Jaramillistas confirms the picture these revisionist scholars have drawn concerning the PRI's authoritarianism and demonstrates the party's scant commitment to the principles of social justice. But, by emphasizing the way in which Morelense campesinos used the legacy bequeathed by the Zapatistas' revolutionary struggle, this book explores a new side of the "miracle." State violence and popular resistance emerge here as an escalating dialogue: each act of state repression was answered by popular organizing and militancy. While the present study falls into the post-revisionist camp, it shifts our gaze from culture and identity to the process of sustained struggle that marked the supposed Pax Priísta. Rather than a process of negotiation, movements such as Jaramillismo illustrate the extent to which the political transformations spearheaded by the PRI between the 1940s and the 1960s were accompanied by massive popular protest seeking not some radical alternative, but the fulfillment of the 1917 constitution. It was only when the state responded with repression that these groups became radicalized. While this book incorporates some of the methodology inaugurated by scholars of popular culture—for example, by analyzing the way Jaramillistas refashioned political projects such as Cardenismo with elements of the local tradition of Zapatismo—it emphasizes the process of sustained confrontation that marked the postrevolutionary period before the widely acknowledged 1968 crackdown. Moreover, the PRI's continued undermining of the constitution, its use of co-option to quell protest, and its consistent use of force against sectors that threatened to fracture its political machine help us better understand recent political developments in Mexico. Seen in this light, the electoral defeat of the PRI in 2000 was not the maturing of a political system from a one-party state into democracy, but a partial rupturing of the old state apparatus, which—as the continuing violence in Chiapas, Guerrero, and Oaxaca demonstrate—is still capable and willing to repress popular movements.

It is crucial to acknowledge these militant challenges and the state's repressive response because, as Greg Grandin argues, "the prerequisite for the rapid economic restructuring that took place throughout the Americas beginning full throttle in the 1980s—lowering tariffs, deregulating capital streams, reducing government social spending, weakening labor protections—had as much to do with the destruction of mass movements as it did with the rise of new financial elites invested in global markets."[34] While Grandin excludes Mexico (along with Costa Rica and Ecuador) from this assessment, there are indeed some important parallels. Although Mexico's revolution—which took place decades before the Cold War—and the state that emerged from it significantly tempered the violence that characterized other Latin American countries, there has been a sustained battle against leftist elements. It was this process that, not only in Mexico, but throughout Latin America, paved the way for the imposition of a neoliberal system which has precipitated a drastic deterioration in the standard of living for the majority of the population.

If we listen to the voices of those who fought against the power of caciques, refused to give up their land, formed independent unions, fought for genuine democracy, and battled the corruption of state agencies, the extent to which official violence was standard practice becomes painfully clear. The Mexican government's dirty war against such mobilizations (especially in the 1970s) is only now coming to light, exposing the use of torture, disappearances, the destruction of entire villages, and the disposal of bodies from airplanes in mid-flight—some of the same tactics employed by the most repressive Central and South American dictatorships.[35] This history is still one in desperate need of telling and depicts not the golden age the PRI sought to project at home and abroad but a modernization dependent on the rollback of social reforms, a population fighting to preserve them, and a political machine whose wheels were greased through repression.

Methodology and Sources

The story told here is one guided by the words of the movement's participants, contextualized within the larger sociopolitical forces of the time. My
analysis appears embedded in a narrative that attempts to capture the experience of the Jaramillistas as they sought to make history in circumstances
not of their choosing. They did so by acting on the Zapatista legacy, appropriating tenets of Cardenismo, and engaging with international events,
especially the Cuban Revolution. While acknowledging the importance of
conceptual specificities such as discourse, symbol, and memory analysis,
my study privileges the notion of historical process—one of the casualties
of cultural or linguistic reductionism.[36] Rather than battle over meaning, the
Jaramillistas sought to hold the government to its part of the compromise
that ended the revolutionary war in 1920. Instead of appropriating official
rhetoric, the Jaramillistas challenged the government to adhere to its own
laws and legitimizing discourse, much of which originated in notions of justice stemming from the social aspects of Mexico's revolution. Many of these
ideals, moreover, the government had appropriated from popular movements such as the Zapatistas. The Jaramillistas were clear about government hypocrisy, leading one campesino to remark, "The law is hardly ever
followed here, especially when it favors us."[37] Other campesinos were simply
conscious that their rights had been hard won and their preservation demanded vigilance. Stated José García, "We have gone voluntarily to defend
our rights as Zapata put them down in writing. For example, we are united
to defend what he wrote about the ejidatarios' right to land and water. If ever
we don't defend them, the government takes more from us."[38]

To reconstruct events that marked the course of the Jaramillista movement, this study draws from five principal types of sources: correspondence
between Jaramillistas and government officials; manifestos, pamphlets, and
speeches produced by participants in the struggle; memos reporting on the
group's activities from state agents to the minister of the interior; newspaper
articles; and oral history. Letters and petitions from Jaramillo and the people
close to him reveal the ways in which the Jaramillistas related to the state
and how they framed their demands. Pamphlets, manifestos, and political
leaflets shed light on the movement's goals and ideology. Newspaper reports
serve as a useful source to confirm names, places, and dates. Likewise, they
aid in reconstructing events such as armed confrontations, elections, and

public meetings between the Jaramillistas and government officials. Given the extent to which newspapers were controlled by the government during this period, media reports at once show official attempts to discredit the movement and the way elite circles viewed the Jaramillistas. Significantly, in the early 1960s, two alternative newspapers emerged. One was the weekly leftist magazine *Política*, and the other a Morelos newspaper published in Cuernavaca entitled *Presente!* Both these sources were sympathetic to the Jaramillistas and thus offer a glimpse into how urban supporters perceived the movement.

Reports from agents to the minister of the interior and oral testimonies are key sets of sources, in essence laying out official and popular versions of events. The files of the Dirección General de Investigaciones Políticas y Sociales (Agency for Social and Political Investigations) in Mexico's national archive contain hundreds of boxes of uncatalogued state department reports. These virtually untapped sources proved to be a gold mine, yielding key information about the Jaramillistas and providing an important perspective on the government's intelligence apparatus. Documents declassified in 2002 from the Dirección Federal de Seguridad (Department of National Security) add an additional layer revealing the origins of Mexico's dirty war. Most of these sources consist of reports on public acts, while others were from agents searching the Morelos countryside and hot on the trail of Jaramillo. These accounts are often imprecise and convey only a superficial assessment of the situation. Furthermore, they tend to exaggerate the threat of the group they were charged with tracking. This common practice served to justify the agents' existence, increase their allocated funds, and garner praise from superiors for a job well done.[39] Despite these limitations, these sources are valuable for two reasons. First, as the eyes and ears of the state, the sum of the views of these agents often determined official policy. Second, it is possible to glean campesino voices from these documents, as infiltrators reproduced speeches, reconstructed meetings, and detailed action plans. Indeed, despite their nature as official sources, they are, as Gilbert Joseph noted, "a window on peasant consciousness," since the information was "gathered to assist the state in controlling diverse forms of social protest."[40]

But the voices of participants emerge clearest in the oral testimonies themselves, their memories revealing the layered framework permeating rural consciousness. Like all sources, these testimonies are constructed, fragmentary, and partial, though not necessarily more difficult to work with than written texts produced at the time. As with newspaper and government sources, exaggerations are obvious, facts subject to verification, and contradictions self-evident.[41] But the words of the participants are invaluable in their ability to provide a picture of the past unrecorded by written documentation—a glimpse into the way the dispossessed experience, interpret, and combat their condition of poverty. Hearkening back to some of the pioneering Latin American studies of oral history, these testimonies, rather than memory in the form of textual narratives, are the primary subjects of analysis here.[42] This approach does not imply the uncritical use of participants' words and takes into account that people's memories are structured by events in the present. Rather than a limitation, changing memory patterns can be particularly revelatory as they access information long silenced. As discussed below, for example, Jaramillista veterans were far more explicit about the indigenous component of their movement in the 1990s—after the Zapatista Army of National Liberation (EZLN) launched its rebellion in Chiapas—than they were in testimonies recorded in the 1970s and 1980s. "Oral sources," as Alessandro Portelli stated, thus "tell us not just what people did, but what they wanted to do, what they believed they were doing, and what they now think they did."[43] This self-reflection arises through the links speakers make with other historically significant events or figures. It becomes possible, therefore, to analyze the significance Jaramillistas assign to their actions, thus expanding the information we may glean from past events.

The oral histories gathered for the present study emerge from three distinct historical moments. The first "generation" of interviews, conducted in the late 1970s, stems from the efforts of student and teacher activists to capture the Jaramillista experience as a way both to learn from their history and to widen the scope of future mobilizations. After the assassination of the Jaramillo family, several Jaramillistas continued to participate in clandestine organizations that formed in collaboration with students and teachers, many of whom were survivors of 1968. Given the Jaramillista experience and Morelos's location between the capital and the state of Guerrero, where the guerrillas of Genaro Vázquez and Lucio Cabañas emerged in the 1970s, the land of Zapata was again a site of strong-willed resistance. For the new generation of participants, this moment involved not only political and military training, but also recovering histories of past struggles. Renato Ravelo's 1978 book *Los Jaramillistas* is a product of this endeavor. Ravelo recalls, "I was trying to understand the reason behind the intense and sometimes inexplicable struggles occurring in Mexico, especially after '68 when we were enveloped by this huge movement [and] the intensity of the state's reaction.... It was a time in which there was constant discussion about theories of guerrilla warfare. In those days Debray was popular, so were Che's revolutionary theories, and Mao's, the Vietnam War was waging full scale."[44] With the help of Félix Serdán, a Jaramillista combatant, Ravelo collected about forty testimonies throughout the state of Morelos and shaped the material in such a way that no single story would lead authorities to identify participants. After numerous discussions with those involved, Ravelo decided to censor instances when Jaramillistas took justice into their own hands against particularly brutal police agents or hired gunmen. Upon completion of the book, Ravelo complied with another security measure he promised the Jaramillistas, destroying all his original notes and recordings.[45] That the Jaramillistas again risked their lives by recording their stories during the decade of the dirty war reflected both a political commitment and a struggle against the forces of official history that continued to label Jaramillo a bandit.

Emilio Plutarco García, a schoolteacher from Guerrero, was of Ravelo's generation and also participated with Jaramillista militants beginning in 1965. His involvement intensified after the 1968 student movement. Recalling his reasons for joining Jaramillista veterans, he stated, "It was very important back then for us young people to learn about the Jaramillistas' experience, the discipline they had in their work and their profound sense of class consciousness. That was our motivation as militants of the left."[46] García's desire to rescue the Jaramillista experience for historical purposes came later, and in the 1980s he began to collect many more testimonies and preserve the movement's documents. García has published some of these interviews though the Coordinadora Nacional Plan de Ayala (CNPA), an independent nationwide campesino organization formed in 1979 to fight for the agrarian rights that the Confederación Nacional Campesina (CNC), as a PRI-dominated organization, continuously sacrificed. The CNPA became not only a venue of struggle but an important site for the production of Jaramillista history.

The process of investigating the history of the Jaramillistas revealed the movement's living legacy. My own work recording the words of Jaramillista veterans took place in 1999, five years after the EZLN launched its rebellion in Chiapas. This event had a visible mark on the way the Jaramillistas recounted their experiences, especially since it created a more open climate to discuss the history of Mexico's armed Left. Gaining the trust of the Jaramillista veterans was, of course, indispensable, but the same security measures taken by those who recorded their histories in the previous two decades were no longer necessary. The words of former Jaramillista combatants carried with them a sense of hope, responsibility, and determination. Telling their history in the hope of some day seeing it written stood as one of their duties. Veterans ranged in age from sixty to one woman who had lived for almost a century. They made comparisons between previous and subsequent struggles for land and reform in Mexico and treated their experience in a guerrilla group as one in a series of lifetime struggles. Zapata, Jaramillo, and *Subcomandante* Marcos often figured in the same sentence, because, as Pedro García stated, "Zapata's ideals have not died, Jaramillo fought for them, and they continue to germinate."[47]

Jaramillista Voices: Class, Race, and Gender

Two primary frameworks surround Jaramillista narratives: their condition as poor rural dwellers and the sense of empowerment witnessed through the legacies of Zapata and Cárdenas.[48] Given the prevalence of the male revolutionary figure in the construction of Mexican nationalism, it is not surprising that accounts of their struggle closely follow the life and actions of Jaramillo, itself a sign of the movement's dependence on the leader. But important notions of justice are embedded behind this loyalty to the male revolutionary figure. The words of José Allende, a campesino from Jantetelco, Morelos, capture this sentiment: "Around here almost the majority of the towns were Jaramillista, because he carried the same ideas of Zapata and like Zapata, well, he fought for land and water for the poor, and he [Jaramillo] almost said the same thing, well that's why we esteemed him. And those who have money, well, they don't approve."[49]

Women likewise articulated their commitment through this rich-poor dichotomy. Recalled Reyna Ortiz, "Everything that I heard [from Jaramillo] was for the good of the whole population because there are so many of us who are poor . . . who are exploited. . . . [Jaramillo told us] not to remain passive, to open our eyes. I don't think that's a bad thing."[50] But women faced a dual obstacle as they not only joined a movement whose leader was labeled a bandit by the dominant culture, but also confronted patriarchal norms that held politics as a man's world. Women's initial incorporation into the Jaramillista movement adhered to socially assigned roles; they mostly provided food and shelter for participants. However, through the course of the movement, these roles expanded, and women even formed their own organization. As did the male Jaramillistas, women articulated their political commitment through the figure of the male revolutionary hero, a tendency in part reinforced by Mexican nationalism's heavy emphasis on hero cults.[51] This tendency, however, is also a reflection of the extent to which poor people's movements depend on a leader. Many Jaramillistas articulated their political commitments through this allegiance. Women's accounts, especially, intertwine a sense of devotion with an attitude that their actions were simple and logical: they were poor, Jaramillo spoke in defense of the poor, and for this the government persecuted him.

The Jaramillistas' strong identification with both the Zapatista and Cardenista legacy often masked an indigenous identity. Since the myth of *mestizaje* (the racial mixing of the Spanish and indigenous population), especially after the revolution, has been a dominant paradigm indigenous voices were further veiled.[52] The legacy of the Zapatista movement as a campesino struggle, and the state's appropriation of the figure of Zapata as the emblem of Mexico's agrarismo, has obscured the indigenous component of the Zapatista forces.[53] Moreover, in Morelos there was a high degree of acculturation resulting from the region's proximity to the capital and its early integration into the international capitalist market. But despite the disappearance of the outward markers of "Indianess" such as language and dress, an indigenous identity was not foreign to Jaramillistas. Pedro Herminio, a Nahuatl-speaking Jaramillista from Xoxocotla, for example, stated, "All of us indigenous people were with him, and he spoke against the discrimination by those who called us 'indios.'"[54] Despite the glorification of various Indian civilizations as national heritage, racism against living indigenous peoples has remained a pervasive aspect of Mexican society. Among its many manifestations is the use of the term *indio* to designate someone as dirty, poor, uncultured, ignorant, or stupid. As with Zapata's struggle, indigenous people constituted a fundamental part of the movement, their claim to land based on ownership since time immemorial. The identification of individuals with an indigenous past emerges most clearly in the oral histories. However, there are also a few glimpses of this suppressed consciousness in the written documentation. For example, in what appears to be Jaramillo's draft of his will, he states,

"I declare the Indians of Morelos and in other parts of the country who still live a miserable life in the barbarous lands inherited by the Spanish conquerors to be my only and universal heirs."[55] Another declaration promulgated by Jaramillista supporters during the second armed uprising stated, "It is easy to see that this Indian's rebellion is Just and highly Patriotic."[56] In each instance, the term *indio* is used to denote the poorest and most marginalized sectors of society.

In contrast, indigenous voices and identities surface as a source of pride in some oral histories, especially those recorded in the mid- to late 1990s. As indigenous movements emerged with strength throughout Latin America—particularly with the 1992 mobilizations commemorating five hundred years of resistance—increasing numbers of people began to explore and openly discuss these roots. This was the case with some Jaramillistas. Félix Serdán, for example, recalled how, prompted by an elder indigenous leader, he began to examine his family history and discovered that his grandmother spoke Nahuatl and practiced traditional medicine. "This is how I found out that I am Indian," he stated.[57] In 1994, indigenous rebels in Chiapas, who called themselves Zapatistas, staged a rebellion against the Mexican government. This event has also influenced Jaramillista views of their past, connecting agrarian and indigenous rights. The Jaramillistas who bore witness to this latest rural rebellion were quick to identify in these new Zapatistas the legacy of their own struggle. Shortly after the Chiapas revolt, the first Zapatistas and Jaramillistas gathered in a forum to declare their support for the indigenous uprising. Here they composed a letter to the Zapatista leadership in Chiapas. One of its points reads, "Both Emiliano Zapata in his Plan de Ayala and Rubén Jaramillo in the Plan de Cerro Prieto agree with you in the restitution of land, mountains, and water to their original and legitimate owners, the indigenous groups of this country. Politically they agree as well in the struggle to overthrow the current government and establish a transitional one that will guarantee free and democratic elections."[58]

Structure and Organization

The present study largely follows the movement's chronology. Chapter 1 first sets the stage by providing a brief overview of Morelos's history, with special attention to the revolution and the Zapatistas. It then examines the state's changing political economy during the decades spanned by the Jaramillista movement. This chapter also traces some of Jaramillo's early experiences and his emergence as a leader. The episode at Zacatepec is the subject of chapter 2. The Emiliano Zapata mill was a microcosm of Cardenista policies, in both their popular and official manifestations. It is in this mill where the Jaramillista movement first emerged and the place where it developed some of its defining characteristics, such as the melding of communalist ideology with a modernizing industrial vision. The Jaramillistas, rather than resist political and economic modernization, wanted to partake in its fruits. They were not, as is often attributed to peasants, seeking to recapture some lost or imagined stability. But when their integration into this modernizing Mexico was violently blocked, following the tradition of Zapatismo, they took up arms and fled to the mountains. Chapter 3 explores this legacy. Incensed by the government's World War II military draft, campesinos flooded the Jaramillista ranks. This chapter describes the Jaramillistas' first armed uprising, their ideology as presented in their Plan de Cerro Prieto, and their confrontations with the army. The Jaramillistas at once drew on Zapata's movement but also adapted their goals to the new political realities they faced.

Jaramillo's bid for the governorship of Morelos in 1946 and in 1952 demonstrates how ordinary people mobilized within an authoritarian one-party state. The Jaramillistas organized the Agrarian-Worker's Party of Morelos (Partido Agrario-Obrero Morelense or PAOM), and their political mobilizations, the subject of chapter 4, hearken back to the tradition of Cardenismo, the moment at which a president possessing the will and ability to implement the social reforms of the revolution came to power. Profoundly marked by this episode, campesinos again sought to access the governing structure as a way to preserve and further such reforms. The 1952 campaign was especially significant, as the Jaramillistas allied with presidential candidate General Miguel Henríquez Guzmán against the PRI. The Mexican People's Party Federation (Federación de Partidos del Pueblo Mexicano or FPPM), Henríquez Guzmán's party, grouped older, revolutionary generals that split from the PRI when the latter became controlled by younger, university-trained party technocrats. But playing by the state's rules again proved impossible, and the Jaramillistas took up arms as the only means to survive and continue their struggle, a battle they now articulated in more radicalized terms. Chapter 5 traces this radicalization and the accompanying armed movements that followed both the 1946 and 1952 elections.

By examining these second and third armed uprisings and the accompanying declarations, as well as the Jaramillistas' call for a "new revolution," this chapter analyzes the profound and increasing disillusionment that accompanied the institutionalization of the Mexican Revolution in local social fabrics such as Morelos.

It is not possible to explain how the movement developed and how its legacy endured without looking closely at the role of women within it. While women appear throughout this story, chapter 6 examines their participation from a gendered perspective and shows how they proved central to the social networks that sustained the party and the guerrilla group. Focusing on the demands made by Jaramillista women, this chapter showcases their actions and mobilizations and assesses the contradictions they faced in a male-dominated movement and society. Gender roles at first determined participants' expectations, but these expanded and changed as the struggle continued. The active role of women in the PAOM structure can be seen in its attention to the needs and rights of women. It is also an indication of the way in which the Jaramillista men and women fought for participation in a modernizing political system and pushed the government towards a wider incorporation of the nation's traditionally excluded sectors.

The best example of this vision was the Jaramillista attempt to establish a type popular *colonia* in the vacant lands of Michapa and Guarín in western Morelos. Chapter 7 traces the origins and development of this project and the way in which the Jaramillista movement unfolded after 1958, when Jaramillo and several other leaders once again received amnesty from the federal government. The Jaramillistas' proposal for the colonia interwove both Zapatista ideals of campesino subsistence farming and Cardenista projects of modern agroindustrial cooperatives. But here too the government responded with overwhelming force, and both the Jaramillistas' vision and the state's treatment of militant popular groups were altered in the international political climate that accompanied the triumphant Cuban Revolution in 1959. Ultimately, the government's assassination of Jaramillo in 1962 came to symbolize the risks of placing trust in the government's words.

The Conclusion reflects on the importance of the Jaramillistas and their legacy in recent Mexican history. Subsequent campesino movements—legal and clandestine—bear the imprint of Jaramillismo, and the struggle has become a consistent reference for twentieth-century rural resistance in

Mexico. As a movement which mobilized during what is considered to be the ruling party's golden age, the Jaramillistas set a precedent for subsequent armed and legal confrontations with the Mexican state. They stand as an important and powerful example of challenges to the PRI's rule, and it is time to tell their story.

CHAPTER ONE

The Ghost of Zapata

In 1979 President José López Portillo (1976–82) attempted to move Zapata's remains from Cuautla, Morelos, to the mausoleum of the revolution in Mexico City. There Zapata's body was to lie alongside that of Venustiano Carranza, the general who ordered him killed. Morelenses, especially campesinos, insulted by the very idea, organized protests in which they stood guard day and night at Zapata's tomb. Zapatista and Jaramillista veterans were among the most visible participants. Longino Rojas, for example, declared, "Not now, not ever will they take [his] remains to Mexico City. They want to take away our only treasure, the symbol of the countryside, and forever bury agrarian reform." It was enough that the state had appropriated his image and staged official ceremonies to a hero whose ideals it consistently betrayed, but, continued Rojas, "To take him to Mexico City? Carranza defended the millionaires, the hacendados, that's why he fought against Zapata."[1] The public outcry ultimately prevented the president from carrying out his plans.

Such challenges are an important manifestation of Zapata's living legacy. Fifty years after the government initiated the appropriation of the agrarian leader's image, campesinos throughout Mexico still operated with the historical memory of the significance of Zapata's battle and were not willing to let the government take *their* patrimony.[2] Across Mexico, campesinos would challenge the government in Zapata's name, an example of the limits in the government's mystification of the revolution.[3] This legacy was especially significant in the case of the Jaramillistas, given the number of Zapatistas who participated in the movement and the fact that the struggle unfolded in Zapata's homeland. In fact, one of the most significant elements of the Jaramillista movement was the way in which the Zapatista legacy shaped the modalities of the later struggle. When Jaramillistas relate the history of their movement, Zapata appears time and again as a legitimizing framework. Also present, however, is a continuous appeal to Mexican law, a link Jaramillistas made based on their understanding that the Zapatista struggle had bequeathed to them certain constitutional rights. In this sense, the battle waged by the Jaramillistas was a continuing strand of the tensions and contradictions set forth by the revolutionary compromise. This compromise, Alan Knight notes, "was ambivalent and unstable; yet it was at least grounded on the broad shared assumption that a revolutionary regime was in power committed to a variety of reforms."[4] Popular sectors still had to mobilize to achieve these reforms, and in the countryside they would do so in Zapata's name. As Jaramillo and his followers hearkened back to the Zapatistas, they both drew legitimacy from that struggle and nourished its legacy.

Jaramillo's early life, ideals, and leadership qualities took shape in a state alive with the memory of the Zapatista struggle. The territory that today comprises Morelos had long been a political hotbed. Its population played a significant role in the major insurgencies of the nineteenth century, including the independence movement (1810–21), the War of the Reform (1858–60), and the national fight to oust the French emperor Maximilian that finally succeeded in 1867. But it was during the revolution that Morelenses waged the most remarkable and strong-willed battle, one centered around agrarian reform and local self-governance. The Zapatistas held these two interrelated ideals to be sacred and fought for their implementation—first against the Díaz regime, then against Francisco Madero, who only sought limited reform in his fight against the dictatorship, and eventually against the Constitutionalists—the northern hacendados who led the triumphant faction of the revolution. As the Zapatistas waged a war against better-equipped outside armies, redistributed land, and ousted the local elite, their forces and support base acquired a regional cohesion unequaled in other

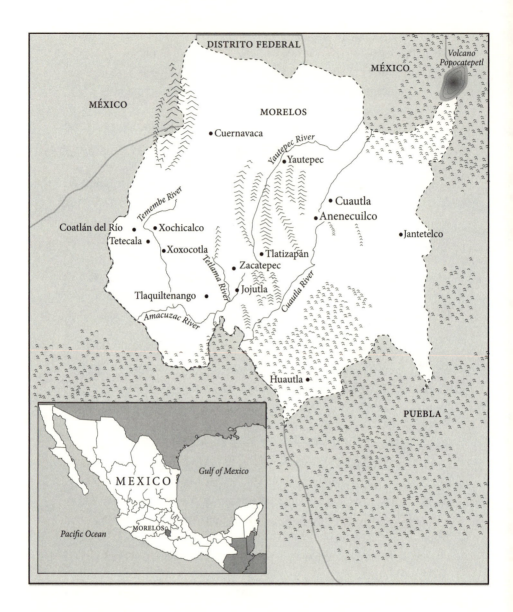

Map 1. Map of Morelos.

parts of the nation. Even though the Zapatistas were defeated, this experience had a long-lasting effect on regional identity, and campesino ideals of community, later reinforced through memory, ritual, and myths, were passed on to future generations.[5] The spirit of Zapata was kept alive in religious festivals, community rituals, and in the many legends that described how he had not actually been killed at Chinameca, but instead continued to ride through the countryside watching over campesinos. To do away with these myths, acknowledged news accounts of the time, would require the elimination of the injustices that had produced Zapata.[6] Indeed, the power of Zapata's enduring legacy is best understood through an exploration of Morelos's history and the rebellion he led.

Morelos: A History of Resistance

Located just south of Mexico City, the state of Morelos was constituted in 1869, taking its name from independence leader José Maria Morelos y Pavón. Although it is a small state, Morelos is geographically diverse. To the north, the forested Sierra del Ajusco provides a natural border between Morelos and the Valley of Mexico. Towering at 17,883 feet, the Popocatéptl volcano exerts an imposing presence throughout the northeastern part of the state, the region known as *tierra fria* (cold land). The cool and heavy moisture keeps this area lush and green year round, and the pines, cypress, and cedar are more reminiscent of Mexico's colder regions than they are of the warm terrain for which Morelos is so well known. The mountainous northwest and northeast contours of the state descend quickly to the warm Cuernavaca and Yautepec valleys, where vineyards, vibrant bougainvilleas, and orchards begin to replace the forest. This is the most fertile area of the state, and aside from maize and fruit trees, tomatoes, onions, chile, squash, walnuts, and avocadoes also grow well here. The climate becomes increasingly arid as one travels south, towards the state's border with Guerrero, the region known as *tierra caliente* (hot land). The vegetation in this terrain is sparser, characterized mostly by shrubs and thorny scrub. The area's high temperatures cause rainwater to evaporate quickly, but the irrigated sugarcane, maize, and rice fields provide extensive green patches. This geography influenced hacienda-village settlement patterns, as large estates imposed a solid control over lowland population, incorporating them in the sugar production process as dependent laborers and residents. Highland communities, on the other hand, were able to maintain a certain degree of autonomy, since even when they worked as hacienda laborers, they could still maintain small plots of land to cultivate products for subsistence or for sale in local markets.[7]

Since the colonial period, Morelos had been one of the most important centers of sugar production in Mexico. The favorable climate, access to indigenous labor, and proximity to the Mexico City market all contributed to its formation and growth. Under the mandate of Hernán Cortés, the first refineries in Morelos were established in the sixteenth century, and their numbers expanded during the seventeenth and eighteenth centuries. Sugar haciendas relied on seasonal indigenous labor and managed to coexist in relative peace with village communities until the eighteenth century, when these estates exerted increasing pressure on campesino land, water, and autonomy. As Morelos's hacendados diversified production and cultivated maize, indigo, and vegetables, they competed with villagers for both land and water. Hacendados argued that the social order was best served by having villagers reside as laborers on estates, a position that would be echoed after independence by Morelos's Liberals, who justified their economic privilege in social Darwinist terms.[8]

In dispute with the local population, hacendados had a strong advantage in court, since the judges deciding their claims often owned large estates themselves. When silenced in court, communities frequently turned to acts of sabotage: for example, damaging hacienda water sources and thus placing a dent on profits. And while large landholders tried their best to pit communities against one another, the battles waged by these pueblos often fortified them internally.[9] Still, while conflict marked the relationship between village and haciendas, the possibility of employment at these estates, as well as Morelos's climate (which did not produce the same droughts as in other parts of New Spain) mitigated the extent of popular discontent. Morelenses did join the independence movement, but their support was more tempered than that of regions such as the Bajío, whose population had been hard hit by famine.[10]

Mexico's independence from Spain in 1821 did not fundamentally alter the social landscape of Morelos. However, a national merchant bourgeoisie soon replaced the old Spanish landholders in sugar production and solidified their political control of the region. Sugar production became increasingly lucrative, as growing urban centers such as nearby Mexico City continually fueled demand.[11] With the help of new legislation that overturned political autonomies dating back to the colonial period, large-scale production quickly overtook peasant cultivation. Communities became increasingly surrounded by private property, and federal authorities restricted the political identities these villages could lay claim to, thus limiting their ability to defend themselves as collective entities. Indian communities would suffer an additional blow during the mid–nineteenth century, as the government granted political recognition more readily to ethnically mixed villages and bypassed the century-old claims of Indian ones.[12]

But elite greed did not proceed unchecked. Seeking to recover what had been theirs, campesinos waged battles through other means, including invading land and destroying hacienda property. Testament to this resistance were the measures the hacendados took to combat peasant protest, including the creation of mercenary forces, groups later fortified by the national government.[13] In their efforts to secure vast landholdings, hacendados frequently betrayed their national loyalties in favor of class allegiances. For example, during the series of foreign invasions that Mexico suffered in the first half of the nineteenth century, hacendados often called on these foreign armies to help "liberate" their properties from peasants who took advantage of a weakened national authority to recover their land.[14] While hacendados may have been able to protect some of their holdings by siding with foreign armies, their country would lose half its territory to the invasion by the United States in 1846. Mexico had little time to recover, for in 1862 the French would arrive and occupy Mexico for a period of five years. Although Emperor Maximilian initially allied with Mexico's Conservative Party, during this time he also attempted to mitigate resistance to his rule by making some concessions to rural dwellers, who continued to push for recognition of their land rights. Ultimately, however, any nod to villagers' rights undermined the power structures of the emperor's allies, and thus even the limited progressive legislation he approved remained unimplemented.[15] But as peasants continued petitioning, they expanded their repertoire of struggle, creating a solid foundation for the "forms of local emancipatory discourse" which would be such a mainstay of Zapatismo.[16]

Amidst the foreign invasions, Mexico also suffered a civil war, as Liberals and Conservatives battled over what national project to undertake. Conservatives looked longingly to Mexico's colonial past and sought to retain clearly demarcated privileges for the upper class and a strong role for the Catholic Church. Liberals, on the other hand, embraced, at least in rhetoric, the principles of individual rights and the sanctity of private property. They sought a strong separation of church and state, believing that colonial institutions such as the Catholic Church and corporate landholdings were preventing Mexico's emergence as a modern nation. Both groups viewed the poor, especially the indigenous population, as an obstacle to modernity and sought to institutionalize their exclusion from political life. But the poor, "often illiterate, but not inarticulate," Paul Hart writes, "effectively adapted elite-inspired ideas and language to meet their own needs and defend their interests, and they changed the debate in ways that neither the Conservative nor Liberal leadership anticipated."[17] Despite elite efforts to graft onto the poor a national project that had at its core their exclusion, popular sectors proved adept at grasping at the moral fibers extant in these conceptions of nationhood.

This process was keenly evident in Morelos, where campesinos took Liberals at their word and began implementing liberalism's egalitarian principles in a fashion that one scholar characterized as eerily similar to the Zapatistas' land distribution during the revolution.[18] When combatants in Morelos supported the Liberal cause during the War of the Reform, as the civil war between Liberals and Conservatives became known, they did so under the conviction that such a leadership would help bring them justice. But for Liberals some were more equal than others, and when villagers in conjunction with hacienda peons insisted on their rights and in 1856 began to cultivate disputed land, the liberal government called in the National Guard. To its dismay the government encountered the soldiers' equally progressive interpretation of justice. Soldiers refused to take action against mobilizations that protested useless laws and unresponsive authorities, arguing that they would effectively be acting against their own rights, since "we all belong to the popular class."[19] It is because of this popular conception of liberalism that the Zapatistas' Plan de Ayala would appeal to the principles of the Liberal Reform Laws, which many Morelenses understood as unjustly applied, rather than unjust in principle.

Indeed, as national projects were drafted from above, villagers, hacienda laborers, and campesinos adopted and adapted state rhetoric to local conditions. They appealed to the Liberals' proclaimed doctrine of equality and individual rights and in so doing actually revealed a greater adherence to enlightened principles than much of the elite. For example, although hacienda owners usurped village land based on the argument that they would make more-modern and efficient uses of it, the labor relations that characterized such private estates displayed a seigniorial mentality that included the desire to wield "correctional powers over their dependents" in order to "moralize" their workers.[20] Laborers were not blind to such contradictions and protested against the revival of "the days of feudalism."[21] When the state ruled time and again in favor of hacendados, villagers extended their appeals, originally based on Liberal laws, to broader moral principles of citizens' rights, in the process questioning the social stratification that undergirded rural society.[22]

But the situation continued to worsen as the nature and degree of land dispossession intensified during the *Porfiriato* (Porfirio Díaz's reign, 1876–1910). In Morelos, prior to 1880 the hacienda expansion affected mainly campesinos living in lowland areas. However, in the decades thereafter, the worldwide growth of the sugar market and Díaz's push for privatization threatened community lands even in the mountains.[23] Technological improvements in sugar production, access to railway transportation, and hacendados' increasing propensity for systematic violence changed the Morelos landscape in dramatic ways, as *ranchos* (hamlets) and pueblos (villages) began to disappear in the wake of expanding private sugar estates. From 1876 to 1887, for example, the number of ranchos in Morelos dropped from 53 to 36, and the number of villages fell from 118 to 105; by 1909 there were only 100 villages in the state. Thanks to new laws from the Ministry of Public Works, planters bought "almost all the public land left in the state" and acquired the rest through nebulous means, their suspect titles rubber-stamped by friendly judges.[24] The complicity of state and federal authorities let the process of land concentration continue unchecked. The extent to which haciendas dominated crop production in Morelos was evident in the state's land-tenure pattern. On the eve of the revolution, sugar haciendas possessed 63.7 percent of Morelos's land, while nonsugar haciendas and small properties constituted 7.4 percent, and communities held 28.9 percent. The domination of sugar haciendas was even greater in the more valuable irrigated lands, with large private estates occupying 90 percent of this acreage, compared to 62 percent of the state's rain-fed lands.[25]

As sugar plantations expanded throughout Morelos, campesinos were expected to deliver themselves, heart and soul, to an enterprise that offered them little, if any, benefit. Villagers, however, brought with them memories of community life that preserved a degree of cohesion sufficiently evident for estate owners to perceive as threatening. As they settled on the haciendas, their grievances began to merge with the more traditional labor demands of hacienda workers such as higher wages. In the process, earlier social and ethnic distinctions began to dissipate, and "a more inclusive rural working culture began to emerge."[26] Combined with the memory of village autonomy and the moral outrage of lost agrarian struggles, the seeds of Zapatismo were sown.

Zapatismo and the Mexican Revolution

Nowhere was this sense of moral outrage so clearly expressed as it was in Anenecuilco, the birthplace of Emiliano Zapata. Like other villagers in Morelos, Anenecuilco residents suffered repeated hacendado assaults which ate away at their farmland. In 1910, on the eve of the revolution, Anenecuilcans desperately petitioned the state governor for a permit to cultivate fields recently enclosed by a hacienda. The rainy season was fast approaching, and if villagers did not begin cultivation a year's worth of crops would be lost. Campesinos faced the threat not only of hunger but also a loss of land that threatened the integrity of a community that could trace its history back seven centuries.[27] When Morelos's governor, Pablo Escandón, received the appeal, he turned the decision to the estate owner himself. The hacendado replied, "If that bunch from Anenecuilco wants to farm, let them farm in a flowerpot, because they're not getting any land, even up the side of the hills."[28] Such was the legal system the Morelenses encountered during the Porfiriato.

This situation was not unique to Morelos. Nationwide, Díaz's economic model based on foreign investment and the sanctity of private property had produced a desperate situation in the countryside. Díaz provided generous concessions to foreign railway and land surveying companies. The latter were entitled to receive one-third of the land they surveyed and could purchase the remaining two-thirds at a discounted price. These territories were hardly the *terrenos baldios* (vacant lands) the regime claimed to be regularizing. Any lands for which villagers could not prove ownership were subject to privatization. And even when campesinos managed to produce paperwork, their documentation was little match for Mexico City lawyers or *Porfirista* judges who invariably found some flaw that rendered their claims invalid. The percentage of communal villages that lost land throughout Mexico reached an alarming 95 percent in the three decades of Díaz's rule.[29] The dispossessed flooded the haciendas, where the wages they received decreased consistently between 1876 and 1910, even as prices for basic foodstuffs rose rapidly. The result was that by 1910, the real cost of staples such as corn, chile, and beans was higher than it had been before independence from Spain.[30] Although rural dwellers sometimes fought this process, Díaz quickly moved to repress any opposition. For example, in northern Mexico, where the Yaqui and Mayo indigenous people had managed to preserve some degree of autonomy since the colonial period, Díaz took special pains to break their resistance and shipped thousands of Indians to labor in the southern henequen plantations of Yucatán. Shackled and working in conditions virtually indistinguishable from slavery, most of the Yaqui laborers perished on these plantations.[31]

Díaz was equally ruthless with worker mobilizations. Two strikes in particular—one in the mining town of Cananea, Sonora, in 1906 and another a year later in a textile factory in Río Blanco, Veracruz—would be emblematic. In both cases the state intervened on the side of management, leaving numerous workers dead. Cananea would become especially notorious because Arizona Rangers joined Díaz's mounted *rurales* in protecting foreign interests on Mexican soil. The episode appeared symbolic of Díaz's generosity towards foreign investors, his disregard for the lives of Mexican workers, and his increasing reliance on brute force. Despite the heavy control over the press, underground publications such as the anarchist newspaper *Regeneración* began to spread, contributing to a growing political awareness among various sectors of the working class. Moreover, the economic growth Díaz was so credited with bringing to Mexico began to falter, as international market fluctuations affected key sectors of the economy, especially mining. Díaz's strong-handed tactics eventually succeeded in alienating even the class that benefited from his economic policies. Unwilling to share political power, the dictator inadvertently nourished an opposition anxious to break open a system based on patronage, loyalty, and the punishment of dissenters. This opportunity seemed immanent when, in a 1908 interview, Díaz declared he would not seek an additional term. But when in 1910 the dictator refused to leave the presidency, Francisco I. Madero, the son of a wealthy family from the northern state of Coahuila, launched a presidential campaign under the motto "effective suffrage and no reelection." When Díaz reacted by jailing him, Madero called for a national uprising on November 20. The discontent brewing throughout Mexico erupted into a violent civil war that would last ten years.

Unwittingly, Morelenses would become one of the centerpieces of this struggle. Led by Zapata, campesinos there joined Madero's revolt and proclaimed their adherence to his Plan de San Luis, which called for moderate political reforms and promised land redistribution. But when the dictator was ousted, Madero hesitated on the matter of land reform and instead demanded patience from the Morelenses. In the meantime, he staffed his new, purportedly revolutionary, government with Porfirista officials. Congressmen, state legislators, judges, and local officials who had served under the dictator now returned to their posts. This might have been tolerable in Morelos if Madero had not reneged on the land reform provisions made in the Plan de San Luis, attempting instead to appease Zapata with side deals. When Madero suggested on one occasion that "Zapata deserved 'a good ranch' for his services," the agrarian leader from Morelos shot back that he "had not . . . entered the revolution to become a hacendado."[32] The radical differences between the grievances that had initially united the northern hacendados such as Madero with the Morelense campesinos who supported Zapata were now beginning to emerge. The Zapatistas soon saw Madero as a traitor and an opportunist. Against his hacendado revolt, the Morelenses formed a popular revolution demanding genuine land redistribution and local autonomy.

"Revolutions will come and revolutions will go," Zapata would later declare, "but I will continue with mine."[33] But "his" revolution would indeed profoundly alter the course of the decade-long war. Although he was not interested in taking power, Zapata's goals entailed a major clash with the state that ultimately contributed to its dissolution.[34] The Zapatistas formalized their rebellion against Madero by proclaiming the Plan de Ayala in November 1911. In it they articulated their grievances and enumerated their demands. The document acquired an almost sacred aura and stood as the movement's banner against the continued assaults of factions who attempted to violently crush or appease them by offering narrow reforms. Written by Zapata and Otilio Montaño, an Ayalan schoolteacher, this new document laid out clearly the Zapatistas' expectations for land reform. Actually quite moderate in nature, this plan hearkened back to the 1857 Liberal Reform Laws, an ironic point given that these very laws, which prohibited corporate landholdings, had provided the legal basis for the hacendados' assault on the ejido during the Porfiriato. But as previous generations of Morelenses had done, the plan's adherents applied notions of justice inherent in Liberal doctrine: despots could not be tolerated. The Plan de Ayala's political clauses included a call for Madero's deposal and the formation of a junta to declare a provisional president once the revolution had triumphed.

But the plan's most significant provisions concerned agrarian distribution. It decreed the restitution of all illegally usurped land, the nationalization of sugar mills, and, to confront the extensive poverty of Mexico's pueblos, the expropriation of one-third of large estates. Full expropriation would only apply to those "landlords, *científicos,* or bosses" who directly opposed the plan, from whom two-thirds of their goods would be expropriated and earmarked for the victims of war.[35] Zapatista demands would later grow to encompass broader social legislation, such as education and labor rights.[36] Thus, while the Zapatistas began as local rebels allied to Madero's national revolt, over the course of the revolution—as they were joined by urban intellectuals, established control of Mexico City, and forged links with Francisco Villa's northern army—their project came to present a genuine proposal for the transformation of society, one that began not from the top but from the base.[37] It was this ideological project which leaders like Madero, and later Carranza, would combat.

Madero would soon fall—not to Zapata's hands, but to the counterrevolutionary forces of Victoriano Huerta. Originally part of Madero's revolt, Huerta exhibited his ruthless character early on. During Madero's short tenure in office it was Huerta who, at the behest of the state's hacendados, traveled to Morelos in an effort to control the Zapatistas who had already began to reclaim their land. Huerta proclaimed he would pacify Morelos by depopulating the state, a pledge that his emissary, Juvencio Robles, attempted to implement after Huerta assumed the presidency in 1913.[38] Indeed, Robles articulated this strategy with equal candor when he declared to a Cuernavaca resident, "What a nice place it will be once we get rid of the Morelenses! If they resist me, I shall hang them like earrings to the trees."[39] In an effort to isolate the Zapatista forces, Robles applied principles of modern counterinsurgency warfare and relocated the civilian population. As if to fulfill Huerta's promise to depopulate the state, Robles instituted a military draft that sent thousands of Morelenses to fight in distant corners of the country.[40] But such ruthlessness only succeeded in swelling Zapatista ranks. As previously neutral civilians witnessed their villages burned and their relatives carried off or shot, they increasingly turned to Zapata. Either way they faced the enemy's wrath; at least by joining the Zapatistas, they had a chance at defending themselves. And so the Zapatistas continued to wage their revolution, this time against Huerta, who, as their revised Plan de Ayala now declared, was worse than Madero. As their fighting continued, so did their resolve; their earlier moderate goals were radicalized, and their defensive position became one of moral indignation about the betrayal of the revolution. From its heart in Anenecuilco, Zapatismo quickly spread throughout Morelos, and Zapatista forces would even come to control the bordering region in the states of Puebla, Guerrero, Mexico State, Oaxaca, and Tlaxcala.

The Zapatistas were not the only group objecting to the Huerta government. In the north, powerful forces led by Carranza and Pancho Villa also rebelled against Huerta, who was finally defeated in 1914. But the new revolutionary coalition quickly fell apart, with Carranza (a hacendado from the northern state of Coahuila) leading what came to be known as the Constitutionalist faction, which called for moderate political reform in the tradition of Madero. Against them Zapata and Villa formed a powerful, though often unstable, alliance. The social composition of the Zapatistas and Villistas differed, but their revolutionary projects had much in common. For the southern revolutionaries, the community was of primordial importance, and from this stemmed their demands for land and local autonomy. On the other hand, the *serrano* northerners, as Knight termed the Villistas, "displayed a more self-interested concern for goods, land and power" and aimed their grievances against the power of caciques.[41] Despite the regional differences that sprung from their distinct socioeconomic contexts, Villa and Zapata both possessed a commitment to a bottom-up reform—measures the Constitutionalists viewed with hostility.

Nowhere was this grassroots revolution more evident than in 1914, when the Zapatistas gained control of Morelos. Their actions provide a glimpse of what a society structured under their notions of justice might look like. The Zapatistas carried out their land distribution program in accordance with the "customs and usages of each pueblo."[42] Village autonomy became part and parcel of the distribution process, as communities decided on the type and extent of land reform. While the concluding motto of the Plan de Ayala was "Reform, Liberty, Justice, and the Law," it is remembered to this day as "Tierra y libertad" (Land and Liberty). Their will and ability to implement the Plan de Ayala while waging military battles created a particular cohesion between Zapatista forces and the communities that sustained them. In their fighting they turned for "leadership . . . more readily to their village chiefs than to their revolutionary army officers" and soon constituted forces that were "simply an armed league of the state's municipalities." It was the strength of this bond that allowed the Zapatistas to sustain their position against powerful outside armies. During 1914, under the structures set forth by the Plan the Ayala, campesinos were able to cultivate their land and actually had more to eat than in 1910—this at a time when those in Mexico City were going hungry.[43]

But the Constitutionalists would soon gain the upper hand. By 1915, the Carrancista general Álvaro Obregón led a series of decisive battles against the Villistas, while another trusted general, Pablo González, set out to pacify Morelos. This task he carried out by presiding over mass executions such as that of Jiutepec, where 225 people were shot after a summary trial, or Tlaltizapán, where 132 men, 112 women, and 42 children were murdered by Constitutionalist forces.[44] As the Constitutionalists secured other parts of the country, Carranza concentrated on Morelos, where increasing numbers of Zapatista forces were defecting in exchange for amnesty, exacerbating internal rivalries and putting a strain on Zapata's army.[45] Carranza dealt his final blow in 1919, when his men invited Zapata to a meeting in Chinameca and there assassinated him.

But if Carranza succeeded in getting rid of Zapata, eliminating the legacy of his struggle would prove a lot harder. In 1916, when the northern leader called for a convention that would draft a constitution and, he assumed, declare him president, agrarista demands proved their resilience. As in the 1914 Convention where delegates voted to accept "in principle" the Plan de Ayala's land reform provisions, there was an increasing recognition that the government had a responsibility to the poor. While not a triumph of the Zapatista project, this did stand in sharp contrast to the científicos' social Darwinist principles—"marked where and how far the revolution had advanced in the public's sense of justice. And the driving force of the change had been the Morelos revolutionaries."[46] Indeed, neither Carranza, nor subsequent leaders, could continue to ignore the campesinos' demands. The constitution drafted by the convention in 1917 contained key social measures, among them Article 27, the provision recognizing campesinos' right to land.

If the Plan de Ayala had reached almost a sacred status in Morelos during the revolution, Article 27 would become, for Mexico's campesinos in the twentieth century, its national counterpart. This article asserted the state's responsibility towards the rural poor and made campesinos' access to land the government's obligation. The 1917 constitution thus imbued campesinos with more than just abstract rights as citizens.[47] Article 27 provided the framework for campesino mobilizations in which they demanded the land they were now legally entitled to. Nowhere was this process more vivid than in Morelos, where the rural poor shared the legacy of Zapatismo. And even though the agrarian leader had been assassinated by the triumphant Constitutionalists, the postrevolutionary state would soon pay him homage, conferring further legitimacy upon his followers. Nevertheless, agrarian reform still had to be spearheaded from below. Not surprisingly, Morelos had a higher volume of land petitions than other regions in the years immediately after the revolutionary fighting.[48] In this way, the Zapatistas successfully transformed the agrarian structure of Morelos, eliminated the old hacienda economy, and expelled most of its landlords.[49] This strong grassroots pressure ensured that land redistribution took place, even if it occurred in a framework of state concessions, rather than restitutions, as decreed by the Zapatistas in 1914. And while most of the sugar refineries remained under the control of their prerevolutionary owners, the ejidatarios now possessed the surrounding lands.

Álvaro Obregón, who became president in 1920 after rebelling against his former ally Carranza, used the land distribution process of the triumphant revolutionaries to both pacify and control the rural population, especially those who had shown the greatest militancy. Obregón ignored the land reform implemented by the Zapatistas and proceeded anew, fashioning an elaborate top-down *agrarismo* that assured campesino dependence on the state. Plutarco Elías Calles, his successor, formally solidified this system. His government chose a few Zapatista veterans, many with spurious credentials, to carry out the land distribution. Unlike the land reform undertaken by the Zapatistas during the years of war—where repartition of lands was carried out in conformity with the "customs and usages of each pueblo"—the postrevolutionary government decreed all land and resources to be the property of the nation, to which campesinos could be granted access.[50] Rural dwellers had to apply to the federal government to receive land, credit, or irrigation projects. The process of land redistribution reinforced the power of the state. Campesinos became dependent on the government and corrupt public officials to administer agrarian credit, while price gougers operated unhindered.[51] In essence, campesinos were clients of the state and, by extension, of the newly emerging official party. The rural poor may have received *tierra*, but they did not secure *libertad*. In 1929, when the process of land distribution was decreed complete for Morelos, only 1 percent of the approximately two hundred thousand hectares of distributed land had been restored to their original campesino owners.[52] The government granted the rest as ejidos and transferred the authority previously vested in village leaders to an ejidal commissariat, who was directly dependent on the Ministry of Agriculture.[53] Nevertheless, the Morelense rebels had managed not only to eliminate the hacienda structure but also to secure a place in the postrevolutionary order, one that would not be easily ignored in decades to come.

The Zapatista Legacy

The culture surrounding the legacy of Zapata is palpable in Morelos. His agrarian struggle remained alive in the collective memory of campesinos whose parents or grandparents lived through and fought in the revolution. Stubbornly, Zapata's spirit refused to die and soon appeared intertwined in the state's cultural fibers. From ballads that sung of his heroic acts, to religious festivals that incorporated him on an almost equal level with saints, to the legends that surround both his life and death, almost a century later Zapatismo continues to define Morelense culture. Robert Redfield's anthropological study of Tepoztlán, an indigenous community in northern Morelos, noted the extent to which the memory of Zapata encompassed "an aura of the miraculous." Stories recounting the revolutionary battles imbued both Zapata and his horse with qualities that were otherworldly. Moreover, villagers often attributed the Zapatistas' successful ventures to the interference of patron saints, such as those who in Tepoztlán had thwarted Carrancista attacks by flattening their bullets as they hit the chapel doors. In this vein, noted Redfield, the status accorded to Zapatista veterans was the secular complement of local patron saints, as they were "both symbols of the ideals, the wishes, of the group."[54]

In Xoxocotla, another indigenous town in southern Morelos, descriptions of Zapata imbue his birth with a certain amount of predestination. Moreover, the stories told here appear infused with strong pre-Columbian overtones. In one account, there appears in the village outskirts a beautiful but untamable white horse. When a villager asserts that he will tame and make the horse his own, he is informed by an old man (who appears and disappears with equal mystery) that the horse has an owner who has not yet been born. The villager insists. And so the old man counsels him to seek the advice of "the elders" he will find in a nearby cave. The man's journey possesses many of the elements of the pre-Columbian conceptions of the underworld, such as his encounters with both the devil and the Virgin—invoking a duality of good and evil and of male and female deities. Caves, as passages into the underworld, represented sacred places for pre-Hispanic civilizations.[55] Ultimately, the villager's journey is fruitless, for upon return he is informed that the horse's true owner, Emiliano Zapata, had just been born.

Redfield found in the legends and myths that surround the figure of Zapata a moral barometer by which the conduct of other leaders would be judged. "Zapata as a symbol," he stated, "embodies the group consciousness of the Indians of Morelos which developed during the revolution." While this fame would grow throughout Mexico, "it is only in Morelos, in Tepoztlán and scores of Indian villages like it, that Zapata becomes truly legendary, and even mythical."[56] Even in the 1990s, as the neo-Zapatista movement emerged in the heavily indigenous state of Chiapas, similar legends appeared, and the agrarian leader became reincarnated in a mythical Mayan figure known as Votán Zapata. Possessing distinct features of a Mayan deity, Votán Zapata is invoked in Chiapas, especially in commemorations of Zapata's assassination, in ways that offer a culturally distinct, local counterpoint to the government's claim over the agrarian leader's image.[57]

Early on, the government was wary of Zapata's legacy and such popular incarnations and thus sought to appropriate his image. The first official commemoration of Zapata's death came in 1924, only five years after his assassination. Plutarco Elías Calles used the celebration as a political platform during his presidential campaign, and various speakers proclaimed the candidate would follow Zapata's agrarian program.[58] As part of their state consolidation project, the victorious Callistas sought to establish Zapata as one of Mexico's founding fathers.[59] But this was no easy feat; campesinos would honor Zapata, but not always in the way the government wanted.

In fact, in the decades to come, ongoing battles ensued surrounding public celebrations of this agrarian martyr. Campesinos throughout the country would use their hero's birthday, as well as the commemoration of his death, to remind the regime that it had not fulfilled its revolutionary obligations.

As the culture surrounding Zapatismo spread both through popular means and official celebrations, so too did the legitimacy of the battle waged in Morelos. To many campesinos, the significance and power of taking up arms was not lost. The idea of *"tomar las armas"* [to take up arms], affirmed one Mexican historian, can be seen as a constituting element in the collective rural *imaginaire*.[60] A comment by a Zapatista veteran illustrates this sentiment: "We had power back then because we had the arms. That's why now we're not worth anything, because they took them away from us, and because we're old."[61] Campesinos had not fought a revolution in vain, and the collective memory of that struggle emerged in new ways.[62] Not only had they experienced meaningful reform; most still had recent memories of their own, or their parents', participation in the struggle for land.

As Jaramillistas mobilized, they repeatedly hearkened back to the memory of Zapata to gain adherents to their cause. Lino Manzanares, a campesino from Los Hornos, Morelos, recounts an example of one such instance: "My father asked the two Jaramillistas who came to see him, 'What plans do you have?' and one of them answered, 'We fight for liberty, that's what interests us. Not to be beholden to anybody, to have freedom, like Zapata who fought for land, to have that freedom to own land. We don't want the government to control us, to dominate us. That's why we fight.'"[63] Such encounters not only invoked the memory of the struggle waged by the Zapatistas; they reinforced it, making it a crucial element for gaining adherents. Moreover, new leaders would emerge to continue Zapata's legacy and adapt and refashion previous forms of resistance to the changing national context. Rubén Jaramillo was one such figure.

Rubén Jaramillo: The Making of a Leader

The events of the revolution punctuated Jaramillo's early life. Born in 1900, he spent his first few years in the State of Mexico, where his father, Atanasio Jaramillo, worked in the mines of Zacualpan, and Morelos, where his mother, Romana Ménez, moved in 1904 after the death of her husband.[64]

Ménez, a campesina, was left to care for six children and would herself die ten years later from a scorpion bite. By the time Jaramillo was 15, the revolution had been raging for five years; for him, as it was for many youths in Morelos, joining the Zapatista struggle—either out of conviction, defense from federal troops, or because the whole community had done so—was probably inevitable. In his autobiography Jaramillo is brief in his reasoning, stating simply that, "convinced by the revolutionary ideas of 'Tierra y Libertad,'" he joined Zapata's forces and quickly ascended to the rank of captain in the First Cavalry, in command of seventy-five men. By 1918, things did not look good for the Zapatistas, and Jaramillo is likewise brief in explaining why, that year, he disbanded his cavalry and withdrew from the army. From the distance of time, Jaramillo wrote that he was disillusioned by the many military leaders who "neglected the authoritative voice of Emiliano Zapata and devoted themselves more to looting than to fighting against the enemy."[65] He soon went to make a living in Tlaquiltenango, Morelos, as a rice cultivator.

In the mid-1920s, Jaramillo became pastor of the Methodist Church in Tlaquiltenango. This episode, however, has left scant historical documentation. Jaramillo, who towards the end of his life began to record his memoirs, does not mention his role as a religious leader. This omission most likely resulted from his self-conscious position as an agrarian leader. Given the state's longstanding anticlerical tradition, a religious past was not a credential that furthered political legitimacy. Instead, his autobiography traces his lineage to participants in Benito Juárez's army as a means of establishing himself in a long line of anticlerical social reformers.[66] Yet, while Jaramillo does not mention his role as a pastor, in several moments his text conveys a religious tone. The autobiography is written in the third person, which, according to the work's editor, stemmed from his "religious principles that prevented overt self-praise."[67] This third-person voice gives his rustic and unfinished text a peculiar feel that is accentuated by an almost biblical quality in some of the passages. The following is a perfect example: "Jaramillo held meetings with the people to explain his situation and the issues that led him to take defensive measures. Of this the people were convinced and satisfied." Early in the text he described himself as "always . . . seen surrounded by people," whom he, with his "modest and pleasant character, always tended to."[68] Many of the passages, especially those in which he offered instructions, conclude with the phrase "and so it was done."

1. Rice was an important crop in southern Morelos.
Archivo Fotográfico, Rodrigo Moya.

Although the Methodist Church severed ties with Jaramillo after he took up arms in 1943, he did rely on religious networks for the movement's sustenance. Many of those who had attended his church would provide food, shelter, and refuge for the Jaramillistas. Still, his appeal was hardly restricted to Protestants, and most of his followers were Catholics. Overall, Jaramillo's religious training served to imbue him with the qualities of a motivating speaker who could elicit trust and loyalty. The few comments on his Methodism that can be found appear mostly in the testimonies of women. Hermelinda Serdán, for example, recalls, "When Jaramillo preached he would say, 'we have to defend ourselves, our Lord Jesus Christ died, but he had already done his part for the world. Why are we going to turn the other cheek? Only to be slapped again? We still haven't given our part to this world.' That was my compadre's message when he fled to the mountains."[69] Women's open reflection on Jaramillo's religious past is not surprising, given that their participation in the Jaramillista movement tended to follow socially assigned gender roles. Patriarchal norms confined them to the domestic sphere or other socially appropriate spaces, such as the marketplace or the church. These contributions are reflected in women's stories, accounts which are often framed within their roles as caregivers whose commitment is on par with a religious faith.

Jaramillo's Methodism is best contextualized with a discussion of his membership in the Masonic lodges. While there did not necessarily exist a direct relationship between Freemasonry and Methodism, these two practices were often associated in the minds of outside observers, with liberalism a third component in the mix.[70] In the nineteenth century, Protestant groups—as minorities in a predominantly Catholic society—and secret associations such as Masonic lodges constituted information networks through which new ideas could be transmitted and debated. The nature of these groups' discussions counterposed the view of the individual as a political and social actor against previous notions of humanity as an organic entity, thus helping to develop "a renewed vision of an egalitarian society, founded on the autonomy of the individual subject as a democratic actor."[71] While Protestantism was quite compatible with the ideals espoused by nineteenth-century Liberals, the contradiction between the Protestant ethic of economic self-improvement and the deteriorating socioeconomic conditions suffered by the vast majority of Mexico's population during the Porfiriato led significant numbers of Protestants to side with the revolutionaries. In general, Methodists tended to side with the Maderistas and Carrancistas, the winning factions in the revolution. Moreover, since Methodists constituted a small minority, they were less affected by the state's anticlerical regulations than were Catholics. Rather, in the face of the new legislation, Methodists opted to obey the law and, in contrast to Catholics, were not directly involved in the battle between church and state or confronted by religious persecution. Unlike the *Cristeros,* the group of Catholics who in 1926 declared war on the government, Methodists looked upon this conflict as an opportunity to gain new converts.[72] Finally, given the highly nationalist character of the Mexican Revolution—a nationalism that framed itself in opposition to the United States—Mexican Methodists were distanced from their American sponsors and thus staved off some of the reactionary elements that would mark Protestantism in Central America.[73]

In the nineteenth century, Masonic lodges, like the Protestant churches, provided an atmosphere conducive to the formation of an oppositional consciousness, and this politically republican role continued into the twentieth century. As were many other Mexican reformers, Jaramillo was drawn to the enlightenment principles of Freemasonry.[74] In his autobiography, he stated that he joined the Masons' Cuautla chapter in 1931. From that date, "he became a defender and father of the poor, for whom he possess[ed] a pure and profound respect." In recalling how he came to meet Cárdenas, Jaramillo stated that when he found out the presidential candidate was also a Mason, he immediately decided to support his bid for the presidency.[75] Since Jaramillo makes no mention of his Freemasonry elsewhere, it is curious that he tied his decision to defend the poor to this specific experience. More likely, he sought to present his membership in the Masonic lodges as a credential indicating that he could be a skilled political leader, despite his lack of a formal education. After all, many great historical figures had been members of these secret societies, and in Mexico the Masons actively promoted the notion that they had made central contributions to democracy.[76] Moreover, the Masons did provide some lifesaving connections. For example, a soldier spared the life of one Jaramillista when he found out they were both members of the secret society.[77]

Jaramillo's early trajectory provides a glimpse into the variety of political strategies he would employ in the following decades. Moreover, the whirlwind changes he experienced within his first thirty years of life—his orphan years during the Porfiriato, his participation in the Zapatista forces as a teenager, and the land reform in Morelos he witnessed as a young adult—presented a particularly rapid series of dramatic social transformations. Aware of such waves, he continuously searched for productive means to participate in the new political structures. He carefully studied the government's propositions, learned the rights to which campesinos were entitled, and did not hesitate to speak up before authorities. His popularity increased, yet he did all this while living a humble existence—despite numerous government attempts to buy him off. In this way he never lost touch with the life, customs, and sentiments of the campesinos in whose name he spoke. Jaramillistas recount numerous stories in which their leader was offered suitcases of money, elegant houses, or a comfortable bureaucratic position. And yet, they recall, when he died, he had ninety cents in his pocket.

Early on Jaramillo became conscious of his leadership position and assumed it wholeheartedly. When he moved back to Tlaquiltenango after the revolution, he became involved with the League of Agrarian Communities, an organization dedicated to the protection of small-scale cultivators. As a rice farmer, Jaramillo used this organization to fight for better prices for rice producers in the region. In 1938 he ran for state representative from the Jojutla district but claimed to have been denied the position through fraud that favored an opponent who toed the official party line.[78] Jaramillo, though, would soon become widely known outside Tlaquiltenango through his involvement in the mobilization at the Emiliano Zapata sugar cooperative. His status as a veteran of the revolution gave him further legitimacy. Also, Jaramillo had qualities that made him a natural leader. Those who heard him speak say he had a way with words: that he articulated the *sentir* (the feeling) of the people and did so in simple language. This command of public speaking was likely cultivated during his years as a pastor. He was also a disciplined man who did not drink. Finally, Jaramillo's physical qualities played a part as well, for he had a strong build and appeared taller than the average campesino. He had a dark complexion, large forehead, a determined look, and a serious demeanor. In conjunction with his resolute personality, these characteristics made for an imposing presence.

Ironically, although the Jaramillista movement centered so heavily on its leader, it is difficult to draw a clear picture of Jaramillo the man. Between official sources that portray him as a ruthless bandit and the words of his followers that hail him as a paternal figure who protected and inspired them, his personal traits become quite obscured. Jaramillo's own autobiography is even less helpful. Not only did he leave it unfinished, but Jaramillo's narrative appears to be more a construction of how he wanted his movement to be perceived than an explanation or rationale for his actions. He recounts events in his autobiography matter-of-factly and without much descriptive color. Moreover, his use of the third person to refer to himself in this public testimony further distances the reader from his private persona. Amid these sources only Jaramillo's demeanor comes through clearly: a calm exterior that disguised an internal process constantly searching for ways to achieve his goals. He was serious and abhorred indolent behavior, especially if it involved drinking. On numerous occasions he spoke about the necessity of prohibiting alcohol. He was accessible to his followers but in political or military battles acted with the coldness of a war strategist. And still, his followers say, in personal interactions he was warm and simple, an image that many convey by relating how, when he would arrive at their homes, even their dogs took to him.

As Jaramillo was exposed to Marxist, anarchist, and, later, Maoist ideas, a dynamic ideological cross-fertilization took place. This accounts for the language of many of the Jaramillista proclamations, especially those issued during the armed uprisings, all of which were written with other organic intellectuals. These "village revolutionaries," to use Boyer's term, translated campesino grievances into a "radical, class-based discourse."[79] While less-political campesinos may not have expressed their plight in terms such as *capitalist exploitation, bourgeoisie, proletarians,* or *imperialism,* their own condition as poor rural dwellers contributed to a sense of indignation that the Jaramillista leadership could channel into familiar dichotomies: rich, poor; *político,* campesino; gringo, *mexicano.* Moreover, Jaramillistas spoke a language discernable to all in Morelos: that of Zapatismo.

Unlike the Zapatistas, the Jaramillista movement was not a community-based rebellion triggered by a violation of a village's moral economy. But the Jaramillista mobilizations did initially reflect immediate, local concerns. These might include work to oust a corrupt public official or cacique, a campaign against the sale of alcohol, restitution of certain lands, or a demand for farming credit and price guarantees on agricultural products. Renato

Ravelo, who in the 1970s compiled testimonies from Jaramillistas, characterized their struggle in the following way: "The Jaramillista movement was the sum of all those in Morelos who turned to Rubén Jaramillo to solve a specific grievance or make a demand. . . . Jaramillo almost came to incarnate a revolutionary party in the sense that he could take any demand at the level at which the people presented it to him and mount a struggle. . . . The unifying thread of the people who appealed to him was that they called themselves Jaramillistas."[80]

In this sense, the term *Jaramillista* reveals both the strengths and limitations of the movement. Jaramillo's followers grew dependent on him, and when he was killed in 1962 they found it extremely difficult to regroup. Jaramillo gave direction to the discontent of the people around him and channeled that energy into programmatic action. In this way he gained the unwavering support of so many of Morelos's poor campesinos. Jaramillo understood both local popular concerns and the national political system. But since these points of struggle—corruption, clientelism, electoral fraud, selective repression—were the very nodes that held together the PRI's political web, Jaramillista demands, originally local in nature, reverberated nationally.

Like Zapata's, Jaramillo's movement had originally been local in nature. Like Zapata, Jaramillo established alliances with outsiders of different ideological stripes. And like Zapata, Jaramillo was firmly committed to his principles, intent on not betraying his base. In both movements the leader was of fundamental importance not only because of this commitment, but because each was an expression of a popular agrarianism so fundamental to the survival of Mexico's campesinos in the twentieth century. The particular ways in which the Jaramillistas drew on Zapatista tenets are important for understanding the legacy created by popular upheavals. If the Jaramillistas inherited the culture of resistance bequeathed by Zapatismo in Morelos, they also operated in a national political context that had been shaped by the Zapatistas' participation in the revolution. And from this derived some of the differences in the each movement. The longevity of Jaramillismo, when compared to Zapatismo, and Jaramillo's willingness to assume the reins of power through elected office reflected the fact that Jaramillo both built on Zapatismo and adapted his movement to the postrevolutionary politics. That both were martyred served to enhance their legacy for those who carried on their memory.

Morelos: A Changing Landscape

The social composition of the Jaramillistas reflected the changing nature of Morelos's political economy after the revolution. The state's landscape transformed dramatically beginning in the 1940s, at a pace that quickened with every decade thereafter. These changes were strongly determined by the state's shared border with Mexico City. Politically, Morelos's proximity to the nation's capital contributed to a relatively weak local elite, one whose power often derived from the federal government. While the practice of naming outsiders as state governors—one of the catalysts of the Zapatista rebellion—waned in the early postrevolutionary decades, by the 1950s Mexican presidents were again appointing non-Morelenses (who tended to leave once their term ended) to govern the state. Economic power, too, lay in the hands of the elites in Mexico City and abroad who controlled the capital of industry, housing developments, and tourist ventures.[81]

The nation's capital also conditioned much of Morelos's political economy. In the 1940s, the state government increasingly sought to attract industry by granting tax exemptions for periods of ten or fifteen years.[82] The time period covered by these tax breaks expanded in 1965, when the state legislature approved further laws to attract industry. These included state and municipal tax relief measures for the tourist, construction, and industrial sectors for periods of five, ten, and twenty years, respectively.[83] In 1963, construction for the industrial city of CIVAC (Ciudad Industrial del Valle de Cuernavaca) began in the municipality of Jiutepec, outside Cuernavaca. Soon after, the government expropriated the communal lands of Tejalpa for CIVAC's further expansion.[84] This city paved the way for a series of industrial corridors in three principal areas: Cuernavaca in the north, Cuautla to the east, and Jojutla in the south. That such projects and legislation were enacted in the wake of the elimination of the Jaramillistas and their proposal for Michapa and Guarín vividly reveals the type of development the state and federal governments would commit to.

Morelos's pleasantly warm climate and numerous naturally occurring springs were additional factors in the state's transformation during this period. The lightly tropical vegetation and medicinal springs had lured elites as far back as pre-Columbian times, when Aztec lords had lavish gardens built in places such as Oaxtepec. Hernán Cortés also made note of Morelos's beautiful landscape. During the colonial period the region not only became an important site of sugar production but also functioned as a location for elites to enjoy natural beauty, as well as leisure and recreational activities.[85] These activities continued throughout the nineteenth century; although they were disrupted by the revolution and its aftermath, in the 1950s Mexico's tourism industry began to boom, and entrepreneurs immediately set their sights on Morelos. Its proximity to the nation's capital rendered it easily accessible to Mexico City's population. In the coming decades, water parks sprung up across the state's entire landscape. Already in the 1940s developers began soliciting land and water concessions—most often held by ejidatarios—and their projects became increasingly ambitious in the 1950s and 1960s. In addition to swimming facilities and other recreational areas (golf courses, tennis courts, walking trails), many of these projects included luxury hotels and weekend homes.[86] Housing developments soon became big business, as land speculators flocked to satisfy the upper classes' desires for vacation homes in the "city of eternal spring," as Cuernavaca became known.

The violent process that accompanied the development of Cuernavaca as the tourist haven for Mexico City's upper and middle class is vividly illustrated by the case of the community of Ahuatepec, which lay in the outskirts of the state's capital. There, *comuneros* (communal landholders) had been in possession of their land since "time immemorial," and in 1944, President Ávila Camacho (1940–46) officially issued them these lands as ejidos. In 1958, however, the American businessman Donald Stoner and the Mexican banker Agustín Legorreta sought to build the housing project "Jardines Ensueño" on these ejido lands. Stoner and Legorreta grounded their claims by citing the clause in Ávila Camacho's 1944 presidential decree which stated that, if there existed within the Ahuatepec lands *pequeñas propiedades* (small properties), these needed to be respected as such and were eligible for sale.[87] But the comuneros of Ahuatepec refused to sell their lands and faced constant intimidation by state police, who on one occasion invaded Ahuatepec and set several houses on fire. Thanks to his allies in the state government and to the loopholes in Ávila Camacho's decree, Stoner appropriated 1.1 million square meters of this land. Some ejidatarios reported that the police tortured them until they agreed to sell their plots.[88] Jaramillo joined the Ahuatepec comuneros in defense of their lands and spoke at some of their rallies. In 1965, Enedino Montiel, one of the leaders of the Ahuatepec struggle, was murdered, together with his wife. Ahuatepec residents attributed the grisly assassination, in which Montiel and his wife were hacked to death with machetes, to orders from Stoner and Legorreta.[89]

Finally, national infrastructure projects further accelerated the transformation of Morelos. The increase in the price of land and the number of visitors resulted from each additional kilometer of highway that traversed the state. The Mexico City–Acapulco highway, constructed in 1952, had significant implications for the state. Morelos became the connecting zone between the nation's capital and the Pacific coast resort which, in addition to its historic significance as a port city, soon grew to become Mexico's most popular tourist destination. The rate of highway construction picked up pace in the 1960s, as roads were built to connect major cities within Morelos. Cuautla and Cuernavaca were joined by a new highway, which also branched out into other popular destinations such as Tepoztlán and Yautepec. The Cuautla motorway—which, noted one scholar, seemed to conveniently avoid private estates—partially or completely destroyed many irrigated ejido plots.[90] Roads brought with them increased commerce, encouraged the cultivation of cash crops, and introduced new consumer goods. Moreover, Morelos's economic growth would act as major population pull, placing an additional strain on the state's resources. Heavy migration had already begun by the 1940s, at which point one-fifth of the population had been born elsewhere. This figure increased to one-fourth by 1960 and to 27 percent by 1970.[91]

The composition of the Jaramillistas reflected this situation of social and economic flux. While much of the countryside's population increasingly underwent a process of proletarianization in the second half of the twentieth century, campesino culture persisted, often sustained by a multiplicity of social relations still possessing ties to the land. Despite their diverse social makeup, the Jaramillistas consistently defined themselves as a campesino movement even as their demands expanded, as in Michapa and Guarín, to include large cooperatives, infrastructure, and social services. As their demands for land acquired these broader political and economic dimensions, they increasingly posed new threats to regional and national elites. In this way, Jaramillista grievances and forms of struggle foreshadowed the type of rural mobilizations Mexico increasingly witnessed in the 1970s, which revolved around "issues of production, self-management, autonomy and democracy."[92]

This dynamic acquired particular poignancy as Morelos slowly became engulfed by demographic and market changes resulting from the needs of

Mexico City, an urban leviathan that would grow to become one of the largest cities in the world. While the Jaramillistas at first glance appeared as the remnants of the Zapatista movement, their program, strategy, and goals consistently emphasized participation in a modernizing Mexico. As their movement emerged in the early 1940s, it did so in the context of a lived experience of the revolution in which they or their parents had fought. There is, in the Jaramillista story, a real sense of possibilities for a different political order, one they imagined could still incorporate and expand the legacies of Zapatismo and Cardenismo. Instead, Jaramillistas encountered a state intent on abandoning both these elements. But the government's path was continuously haunted by the ghost of Zapata, because, as one campesino put it, "If the government is not with the campesinos, I tell you, there will be another Zapata. Yes, there has to be another Zapata."[93]

CHAPTER TWO

Jaramillo, Cárdenas, and the Emiliano Zapata Cooperative

Located in the southern municipality of Zacatepec, the Emiliano Zapata mill exerts a striking presence. Even amid the urban sprawl that today characterizes Morelos's cities, the mill's smokestack, spewing a constant black stream, towers over all other construction and is visible from miles away. As harvest time approaches, a light layer of ash from the burning cane fields covers much of the city. Trucks loaded with sugarcane line Zacatepec's main road, which leads directly to the mill's entrance. Over the mill's gates giant letters read "EMILIANO ZAPATA," and just before this entrance there is a roundabout with a statue of Lázaro Cárdenas. The mill's architecture is in itself a monument to postrevolutionary Mexico, and its history follows an uncanny resemblance to the way the revolution came to unfold in the twentieth century. Built under the administration of Cárdenas and christened with the name of Mexico's most revered popular revolutionary hero, it was sold five decades later by President Carlos Salinas de Gortari (1988–1994), in the name of efficiency, to an economic consortium that at the time owned the largest Mexican Pepsi-Cola bottling franchise.[1] As with some other state enterprises that Salinas de Gortari privatized, the new mill's owners later declared bankruptcy and were bailed out by Mexican taxpayers.

The dynamics behind the creation, development, and outcome of the Emiliano Zapata refinery represent a microcosm of larger national political and economic policies. In many respects, Jaramillo's experience at the Zacatepec sugar complex brings together the mosaic of ideological tendencies that comprise Jaramillismo. In what one author termed the "unexpected result of an encounter between two projects," the situation at the Zacatepec refinery illustrates the contradictions in Cardenista policy and the limitations of reforms whose power structure reside at the top.[2] While Jaramillo and other campesinos may have originally conceived of their participation in the Emiliano Zapata sugar mill as an alliance with the state, the difference in power between the two parties soon overrode ejidatario needs. Administrative greed, official party interests, and structural constraints imposed by Mexico's sugar industry became the driving forces at Zacatepec.

Built between 1935 and 1938, the Emiliano Zapata mill began operation with four hundred workers and received crops produced by nineteen thousand campesinos from thirty-two ejidos covering thirteen thousand hectares.[3] As a quintessentially Cardenista project, the mill also provides an important glimpse into how Cardenismo unfolded in Morelos. As in other regions of Mexico, the policies of President Cárdenas were shaped by the particularities of local history, as well as by its actors.[4] Because the power of Morelos's elite had been so undermined by the revolution—most fled during the fighting and upon return saw their wealth shrunk by the state's early and extensive land reform—Cárdenismo did not face the same obstacles there as it did in states such as Yucatán, where regional power holders sought at every step to sabotage his policies.[5] And viewed from below, the Zapatista legacy lent a distinct local flavor. For example, popular memory holds Jaramillo responsible for originating the idea of the mill and presenting it to Cárdenas during the general's presidential campaign. This story of origins reveals a vision of reform that privileges grassroots initiative over top-down largesse.[6]

By 1938 Jaramillo had become an outspoken campesino leader in the district of Jojutla, in southern Morelos. In the late 1920s and early 1930s he was a representative of the National Campesino Confederation (CNC) and fought for credit and higher prices for rice producers of the region.

Just before the mill was to begin operation, an assembly of ejidatarios in Cuernavaca met to discuss their participation in the new enterprise. They elected Jaramillo as president of the council in charge of the mill's affairs. The Zacatepec refinery had been designed as a cooperative that would be jointly owned by campesinos and mill workers. In theory, their governing council oversaw the actions of the mill's management. However, because the manager was directly appointed by Mexico's president, this position was subject to the changing political winds of each administration. Unlike President Cárdenas, who during the first two years of the mill's operation intervened in conflicts on the side of campesinos, presidential administrations increasingly sided with management against popular demands. Because the mill had been contemplated as part of a national economic strategy to reinvigorate the sugar industry, while simultaneously incorporating workers and campesinos into the official party structure, there existed no mechanism by which ejidatarios could secure a position of strength vis-à-vis the state. The worker-campesino council notwithstanding, the authority lay with the president whose will was articulated through the manager, a position that acquired enough power to neutralize the council.

Rather than improve the situation of sugar cultivators, the Emiliano Zapata mill came to reproduce many structures of rural exploitation.[7] If ejidatarios wanted credit, water, and transportation for their cane milled at Zacatepec, they needed to support the PRI. As a state party, the PRM (which later became the PRI) used government industries to strengthen its political control. The Zacatepec mill, like other government-owned industries, was beholden to this logic. The workers and, above all, the campesinos' economic ties to Zacatepec translated into political ones. The federal government invested heavily in the mill, which was needed to ensure a steady supply of sugar to the country's urban centers. And yet, as an enterprise, the mill continuously lost money while ejidatarios received meager compensation for their cane.[8] Rather, campesino labor created wealth for the Zacatepec management and ensured low prices of sugar for urban centers. Despite the cooperative structure at Emiliano Zapata, government-appointed managers appropriated much of the profits. The PRI's agrarian rhetoric not withstanding, after 1940, it was the cities, not the countryside, that preoccupied Mexican presidents.

Jaramillo thus came face to face with the limitations of Cárdenas's populism. The needs of the rural population may have been met by a president committed to courting campesinos to solidify his political project, but once Cárdenas had established the basis for Mexico's official party, subsequent administrations felt little need to make such grand concessions. This situation, however, generated its own contradictions. Jaramillo, initially a proponent of the Zacatepec refinery, an active supporter of both Cárdenas and Avila Camacho's presidential campaigns, and the first president of the refinery's board of directors, ultimately took up arms against the state. As the government disavowed its responsibility to the countryside, it generated intense opposition. The Jaramillistas are a prime example: Zacatepec began as a popular project which corrupt overseers appropriated, with the tacit support of post-Cardenista presidents. When workers and campesinos challenged such actions, they encountered an unsympathetic legal system, party bureaucrats attempting to buy them off, or the manager's hired thugs.

The trajectory of the cooperative involved the intersection of populist politics, sugar production policy, administrative corruption, and mobilization from below. As such, it provides a clear picture of how the state party's ruling mechanisms and its economic policy unfolded at the local level. For Jaramillo, the Zacatepec experience was the first in a series of truncated efforts to work within the Mexican legal framework to defend campesino interests. In a situation that would repeat itself on two other occasions, their frustrated attempts led Jaramillistas to radicalize both their demand and tactics.

The Emiliano Zapata Sugar Mill and the Cardenista Project

Inaugurated in February 1938, the goals of the Emiliano Zapata sugar complex were twofold: to revive the state's sugar production and to provide a viable economic option for a portion of the Morelense population who had not yet benefited from the agrarian reforms of the 1920s. As the refinery's name indicates, the Cárdenas administration presented this giant and modern mill as a vindication of the sacrifices made by the Zapatistas during the revolution. The Zacatepec factory was meant to fuse the Zapatista ideal of communal ownership with the capitalist vision of progress propelled by the Cárdenas government. As such, it was subject to the same contradictions as other Cardenista projects that attempted to create "'islands of socialism' floating in a sea of capitalism."[9]

As a way of abolishing old privileges, the postrevolutionary state took the country's natural resources out of the hands of foreigners. Its development project, especially as conceived under Cárdenas, relied on mass popular mobilization under state direction. Viewing the masses as the motor which propelled social change, Cárdenas sought to harness this force as a means to imbue the state with sufficient strength to carry out the economic transformation Mexico needed. This he sought to achieve by unifying and organizing the general populace under the leadership of the revolutionary state, with the executive institution as the most powerful entity.[10] As Cárdenas himself expressed it, "Only one political force should stand out in the government: the president of the Republic, who should be the only representative of the democratic sentiments of the people."[11] By strengthening the executive office to such an extent, Cárdenas established Mexican *presidencialismo,* the seemingly unlimited power enjoyed by presidents during their terms in office.

But there were numerous contradictions in this project; one of the most significant lay in Cárdenas's commitment to a capitalist development plan. His central concern for Mexico was to alleviate, but not necessarily eliminate, class exploitation. The difficulty in establishing a system of harmonious social relations stood, as one analyst put it, in the fact that "these social classes were divided into exploiters and exploited and that, to preserve these classes implied preserving an exploitative relationship, in which, the exploited would eventually end up losing."[12] While Cárdenas conceived of the state as the entity that would mediate these social relations and protect those at the bottom, this conception failed to take into consideration the extent to which the government itself was beholden to the bourgeoisie. The Cardenista project was made possible because of the particular historical juncture created by national and international circumstances. The Great Depression, an imminent world war, and a weak national bourgeoisie permitted certain policies that in later years became impossible to sustain, due to, as Nora Hamilton characterized it, "the limits of state autonomy."[13]

In Mexico, these contradictions became complicated by the existence of a state party, which, in Zacatepec as elsewhere, resulted in a heavier dependence on the state. During Cárdenas's presidency the cooperative functioned as intended. But because subsequent administrations intervened on the side of management, workers and, above all, campesinos, lost control. Sugar production required centralization and direction over an extensive region. Growers were tied to the central administration through their need for credit and irrigation water. And because sugar was ultimately more profitable than other crops such as maize or beans, growers had little choice but to put up with the abuses of the centralized management. Finally, the Zacatepec mill became marred by corruption and state party needs. The wealth it generated, coupled with the extensive network of cultivation, milling, and maintenance, provided ample opportunity for solidifying party ties over a significant portion of the population.[14]

Jaramillo and the Emiliano Zapata Cooperative

Jaramillo emerged as a popular leader in the Emiliano Zapata sugar complex. By attributing the idea of the cooperative to him, campesinos cast the origins of the mill as a negotiated process and not a gift from the state. According to this version, Jaramillo agreed to mobilize and support Cárdenas's bid for the presidency in exchange for his promise to build a sugar mill in the southern region of Morelos to benefit the state's campesinos. Félix Serdán, a sugar farmer who later joined Jaramillo's armed struggle, recounts, "He found out that there was going to be a convention in Querétaro to elect a candidate for president of the republic. He was not then a member of an organization so he went on his own. At one point he asked to speak and put forth the need to establish a sugar industry in Morelos. And the candidate, who was Lázaro Cárdenas, sent someone to tell him not to leave, that he wanted to talk to him personally. When the meeting was over, they talked, and Cárdenas told him, 'I like your proposal, and if I become president I guarantee you that it will be met.'"[15] In some ways, this account is an allegory for Cardenismo in Morelos: a former Zapatista combatant approaches the figure who would become Mexico's most revered reformer with a concrete proposal for improving the lot of the state's rural poor. Cárdenas's policies thus appear solidly anchored in the Zapatista legacy, and the Jaramillistas are central actors in their implementation. It is no coincidence that most narratives on Jaramillo begin with this moment.

But this was not the only petition for such a project. In a letter sent to President Cárdenas in September 1935, the ejidal commissariats from Cuautla, Casasano, Cuautlixco, Ixcatepec, and Anenecuilco requested that Cárdenas build the promised refineries as worker and ejidatario cooperatives to "prevent reactionary capitalists willing to relegate the revolutionary gains to mere illusions."[16] Proposals came from government officials as well. One state senator, for example, urged the construction of two or three centers of sugar production as a solution to private capital's monopoly over the industry. In this way the government could take charge of the sugar industry, assure better distribution, and reduce the cost of the product.[17]

But given the exploitative history of sugar cultivation in Morelos, many campesinos were less than enthusiastic about the project, and their reluctance foreshadowed one of the many challenges Jaramillo would face as he engaged in reforms spearheaded by the state. While the cooperative nature of the Emiliano Zapata mill gave campesinos an opportunity to change the structure and share ownership of an industry that had historically exploited them, ejidatarios did not easily overlook the legacy of the sugar production system, and these memories made them reluctant to participate in the enterprise. Some campesinos expressed doubt about reinvigorating an industry notorious for its labor abuses. Said Gorgonio Alonso, "Here, we were against cultivating sugarcane. We still had it in our heads that the hacendados had enriched themselves from our work in the production of sugar. People felt strongly about it; they thought this was the first step in taking away our lands."[18] Another ejidatario expressed a similar sentiment: "When the refinery was established, I told Rubén [Jaramillo] this plant will do us in."[19] Benigno Coronel, a cooperative member, reflected on the involvement of Antonio Solórzano, the brother-in-law of President Cárdenas, who served as manager during the refinery's first year: "Solórzano warned us: 'You have to be strong, right now the refinery is yours; who knows if you will still be in charge tomorrow.' You see, he foresaw what would happen."[20] These memories carry in them the painful history of sugar cultivation, a crop with a particularly brutalizing labor process, and the reflection that once Cárdenas left office campesinos were at the mercy of an unsympathetic government. Future Jaramillista proposals would place a greater emphasis on campesino autonomy, but at that moment, the mill's cooperative structure convinced Jaramillo that it would benefit the region's rural poor. He tried to assuage ejidatario fears and assured them that they would be justly remunerated for their sugarcane. According to Jaramillo, it was precisely the transformation in the system of ownership—from hacienda to cooperative—that would provide campesinos the opportunity to break free from previous bonds of exploitation. They would no longer be subject to the will of a hacendado;

instead, they would be represented by a rotating board made up of campesinos and workers. This council would have power over the mill's administrator.

Much fanfare accompanied the cooperative's inauguration. Government officials made loquacious speeches about the fulfillment of revolutionary objectives, portraying Cardenismo as the maximum expression of the revolution's ideals. The following declaration is a perfect example: "Zapatismo and Cardenismo are but two elements in a common ideal, but their tactic of struggle and action are different. Zapatismo focuses and fights bravely for the agrarian ideal, struggling to make it a reality. Cardenismo realizes, enhances, complements, and perfects that ideal in the present. But it is one ideal, unique in its evolution."[21] National newspapers ran stories lauding the project. One magazine article stated, "Proletarians of Morelos should see in [the mill] an act of vindication that the revolution makes to end popular suffering, the fulfillment of a promise made in the days of armed struggle, and the realization of economic improvement for the working class." The article continued, "Precisely at the scene of the most arduous social battles the government constructs the factories necessary for Mexico's progress. In this way it erects the strongest pillars of the wealth and prosperity of the fatherland."[22] While such rhetoric is an expression of government attempts to co-opt or institutionalize Zapatismo, it was also a tacit recognition that the postrevolutionary state had to comply with certain reforms, especially in areas such as Morelos, where the population had fought with such militancy.

As a social project, the Zacatepec mill was to extend beyond factory walls, and the institutions accompanying it would correspond with the most modern urban engineering standards. Zacatepec would constitute the "center of a proletarian metropolis" and include a municipal hall, post office, market, hospital, school, children's parks, sports facilities, pools, a theater for both plays and movies, an assembly hall, a casino, a bank, and various plazas.[23] This model city revolved around the economic activity of the Emiliano Zapata refinery. Telling of the mill's importance, the federal government declared Zacatepec a municipality the same year the refinery began to function.[24] The bloodshed of the revolution now gave way to the promise of progress. With its cooperative structure, the Emiliano Zapata mill provided an opportunity for campesinos to participate and benefit from the nation's economic process on their own terms. Or so it seemed.

Jaramillo's involvement with the mill gives an important glimpse into his vision and ideological formation. While he often portrayed himself as a disciple of Zapata's agrarianism, Jaramillo was more interested in the creation of modern industrial projects that would improve the condition of the rural population than he was in land restitution. This difference in views is not surprising. Jaramillo's world differed vastly from Zapata's. Thanks to the Zapatista struggle, Morelos's landscape had been transformed: in 1923, 115 of the state's 150 villages received ejido grants; by 1927, 80 percent of the state's farming families held 75 percent of the arable land as individual fields.[25] Jaramillo experienced the outcome of Zapata's struggle and championed a project he thought would improve the lot of campesinos. Unlike Díaz's full-fledged liberal economic policy, Cárdenas's populist project had a specific niche for workers and campesinos. Indeed, Cárdenas presented his political structure as a means to protect the interests of the masses. Jaramillo's own experience in the Zacatepec refinery, however, revealed the limited extent to which such institutions were actually in the hands of the people.

In 1938 Jaramillo was elected head of the board of directors made up of worker and campesino representatives. Since the workers and ejidatarios shared ownership of the cooperative and, the government argued, there existed no employer-employee relationship, the presence of a union was deemed superfluous. But the government did use the national sugar workers' union to recruit skilled workers for the mill when qualified employees could not be found in Morelos.[26] These workers, who usually came from other sugar-producing areas such as Veracruz, expected union representation in Zacatepec and relied on union structures to make demands or file complaints. The process of labor recruitment was problematic on another front: a portion of the Morelos population was both landless and unemployed, and local jobseekers resented the union's policy of recruiting outside workers for the mill.

When he learned about the practice of recruiting outside workers, Jaramillo reacted immediately on behalf of Morelos's campesinos. His decision to side with the rural poor against union workers from other states led to even further controversy. As a local leader, he would not sacrifice the needs of his community for more abstract goals of union solidarity. While Jaramillo would later come to recognize the common cause shared by workers and campesinos, at this time his interests were local, and so was his vision. But in speaking out against workers from other states, Jaramillo elicited union reprisals. Representatives from the National Sugar Workers' Union (Sindicato de Trabajadores de la Industria Azucarea y Similares) filed complaints to the president, charging that Jaramillo, as head of the governing council, had prevented 91 workers from assuming their positions in the Zacatepec refinery.[27] Pedro Castillo, a laborer recruited from Veracruz to work on the factory's central water pumps, recounted one occasion when Jaramillo, together with several campesinos, arrived at Castillo's workstation and attempted to remove some workers who were not from Morelos. "Jaramillo said that the refinery had been made for the people of Morelos, and those running the machines were people from Veracruz, Oaxaca, Puebla, and all over the country. 'The people of Morelos,' said Jaramillo, 'were left empty handed.'" According to Castillo, the manager had no choice but to admit that Jaramillo was right: the refinery was not meeting its goal of giving work to the people of Morelos. However, the manager insisted, the refinery could not hire unqualified workers. Jaramillo, "who was very sharp," pointed out Castillo, proposed that if jobseeking campesinos were not qualified to work in the factory, then at least their sons should be hired and trained to run the machinery. "On that occasion fifty young men began to work there. They were spread throughout the factory, and we were all in charge of training them."[28] These trainees would later occupy some of the technical positions.

This experience marked the beginning of a tense relationship between mill workers and ejidatarios. Even though they would form common cause in some mobilizations against the mill's administrator, a social and economic gulf—accentuated by the fact that refinery workers had far better working conditions—separated them. Workers received relatively good wages, had vacation time, and were provided with decent living quarters.[29] The dramatically distinct circumstances under which each group labored further divided them: one group planted, grew, harvested, and delivered the crop, the other processed and packaged it. While mill workers did face workplace abuses and violations of their labor contracts, their overall better conditions drove a considerable wedge between the two groups and limited the extent to which workers would risk their well-being to engage in a struggle with ejidatarios. Zacatepec soon became notorious for its exploitation of campesinos. The comment of one man whose family originally farmed sugarcane for the Emiliano Zapata mill is particularly illustrative: "Lots of times we preferred to sweep the floors of the refinery than to produce cane for it, because sugarcane producers were left with nothing."[30]

The conflict between the mill laborers and the ejidatarios reached a climax in 1940, when workers attempted to stage a labor stoppage demanding higher wages. Faced with this situation, ejidatarios could not deliver their sugarcane, and Jaramillo encouraged them to run the machines themselves so the harvest would not be lost. Jaramillo's actions instantly earned him notoriety among the workers and deepened hostility between the two groups. In this and other conflicts, campesinos complained that they were excluded from the cooperative's decisionmaking process. For example, on one occasion, when ejidatarios tried to attend a meeting regarding the running of the cooperative, they found union representatives were holding the discussion behind closed doors.[31] Board members, including Jaramillo, met with President Cárdenas to discuss this conflict. In response, Cárdenas issued a declaration emphasizing worker-campesino ownership of the cooperative but asserting that authority lay with the federal government, "which would secure the interests of all workers."[32] In this way he fixed the executive as the institution with the power to oversee the refinery, and he effectively undermined the power and influence of all cooperative members.

Indeed, in the years to come, management slowly wrestled control away from cooperative members. Official party mechanisms of control began to take root in Zacatepec through changes in the decision-making process that drastically altered the balance of power. Pablo Ortiz, an ejidario associated with Zacatepec, recalled, "Originally, the planning structure was presented through general assembly. We would all meet in the big soccer field. And people would get up there and ask for clarifications, and there would be a discussion. But then these meetings began to be reserved only for the delegates of each ejido. . . . They'd be called just to sign the program. Then, after signing, transportation would be waiting at the office doors. They'd take them all in two or three buses to Tehuixtla or San José, and there they could have everything they wanted to eat and drink."[33] The manager, using official institutions such as the League of Agrarian Communities or the Secretariat of Industry and Commerce, increasingly appointed the council delegates. When ejidatarios protested such designations and elected their own delegates instead, their choices were not accredited or were denied access to the meetings.[34] The administrator could count on state resources which included the money to bribe and the guards to repress. Workers and campesinos repeatedly confronted the power of the state when protesting against irregularities or demanding reforms. Most campesinos recall that all the managers after Antonio Solórzano were corrupt officials who enriched themselves from the profits that were due to associates. The course followed by the cooperative sowed disillusionment throughout the Morelos country-side. One campesino bitterly recounted, "We see that the poor campesinos are not being helped; instead these other parasites are helping themselves. They become capitalists and millionaires with the products that belong to us, the campesinos. What manager has entered the hacienda and not come out a millionaire? And this wealth comes at the cost of our own well-being. The refinery was not made to favor the campesino; it was made to hurt him."[35]

By using the term "hacienda" to refer to the cooperative, this campesino further reveals the continuities in exploitation suffered by those who culti-vated sugar. Others emphasized the government's role in creating and over-seeing the unjust practices. Pedro Herminio, an indigenous campesino from Xoxocotla, recalled, "Rubén solicited the Zacatepec mill for the campesinos, but then the government took it over for its own political ends, to steal. The government's practice was to steal from the campesinos. That's what the system was all about, because the campesinos wanted it to be run cleanly."[36] Clear to ejidatarios was the extent to which their own labor generated the wealth enjoyed by others. The mill had created high expectations and, for a brief period, given hope of economic prosperity to ejidatarios. Their disap-pointment foreshadowed the difficult times ahead.

Cardenismo: The Gap between Theory and Practice

In theory, the benefits of the industrial cooperative stemmed from members' ability to join forces, work for a common goal, and redistribute the fruits of their labor. Based on the principles of self-sufficiency, administrative respon-sibility, and equality, such projects should promote the common interests of their members. In Zacatepec, however, these principles confronted serious obstacles. Sugar, as a capital-intensive product, required institutional or eco-nomic support from the state, an involvement that translated into control. Moreover, campesinos, by participating in the sugar industry, were drawn into international relations of production and instantly subject to a myriad other conditions determined by the vicissitudes of the market. Furthermore, the state intervened to keep sugar prices low for urban consumers rather than support higher commodity prices that would have benefited those who cultivated it. Finally, an important contradiction emerged between the communal principles of a cooperative and the market relations imposed by the nature of a cash crop such as sugar. Although government intervention was intended to mediate this contradiction by providing the necessary capital and credit while maintaining a stable price for sugar, in Mexico, the presence of a state party complicated matters.

The inextricable link between the ruling party and the state became not only a means of political control but also a tool for political mobility. As a consequence, the administrator ran the mill to satisfy political criteria determined at the federal level. The priorities became the maintenance—through money, votes, or popular presence—of the sociopolitical order.[37] The refinery served the ruling party as an institution for political campaigning. Administrators would call meetings purportedly to discuss issues such as the price of sugar and then turn these sessions into campaigns for official candidates.[38] Management continually threatened to (and often did) cut off irrigation, suspend credit, or expel members who protested. Campesinos mounted numerous protests, many aimed specifically at the managers' abuses. Often spearheaded by Jaramillo, the nature of these complaints revealed a system increasingly based on force and coercion.[39]

The manager further derived his power from the fact that the Emiliano Zapata mill was an economic force to be reckoned with. It generated so much wealth that many people of the region believed the manager had more power than the state governor himself. Mexico's president appointed the manager on the basis of his willingness to toe the party line. The Emiliano Zapata mill became one of the most important industries in Morelos, and its annual budget was twice that of the state government. These funds the administrator used with little or no accountability.[40] Already in 1941, representatives from ten different ejidos affiliated with the Zacatepec refinery complained that they had not received their share of the profits.[41] While the general council of workers and ejidatarios was the "the supreme authority" responsible for "resolving all business agreements and problems of importance," the very process by which these council members were chosen effectively silenced the voice of the affiliates.[42] Council representatives were not selected by ejidatarios; most, rather, were field inspectors or ejidal commissariats who had ingratiated themselves with the administrator.[43] One member recalled, "Sometimes they tell us to take our own representative to the board, but it's useless. The manager only accepts the weak ones, and when a stronger guy comes around they soften him up with money."[44]

Roberto Orihuela, son of a council member close to the manager, recalled quite candidly how he obtained his position as zone inspector: "My father was a council member, and one day some of them came and told me, 'You have to prepare yourself, because on such and such a day there will be a meeting, and you will be sworn in as *consejero* [council representative].' 'And with what authorization?' I asked. 'With mine,' responded my father; 'I nominated you.' After this I had to go get my paycheck every two weeks. For about three months I didn't even know what my job was, but I got my paycheck. I even felt embarrassed when people asked me what I did, because I didn't know."[45] This practice was not uncommon; such workers were known as *aviadores* (aviators) and were often drawn from the ranks of official campesino organizations. There were several additional mechanisms by which the administrator controlled the council representatives, including the oversight of their salaries, funds, and resources. One public functionary recalled that the consejeros were paid "mainly to shut their mouths."[46] The refinery generated a whole series of corrupt relations, as ejidal commissariats and field inspectors engaged in their own share of corruption: stealing from group funds, appropriating ejido credit, and renting out communal lands.[47]

A corrupt management team also siphoned off money at various levels. Administrators skimmed funds owed to cultivators by inflating transportation costs and subtracting these from the amount the growers were paid, by billing for services that campesinos should have received for free, and by cheating ejidatarios who did not know how to read or write. The weighing system was one of the primary means through which ejidatarios were robbed. Sugar producers complained that management fixed the scales and witnessed in disbelief as the weights recorded for the same truckload of cane shrank as years passed. Campesinos observed that in the first harvest season a truckload of sugarcane weighed between nine and eleven tons, but by the 1941–42 harvest season this same load weighed six or seven tons.[48] Truck drivers, too, reported that the weight on the scales did not correspond to the weight they "felt" in their trucks.[49] Pablo Ortiz, a sugar cultivator from El Higuerón, recalled, "They wouldn't accurately weigh our cane, and we protested . . . ; the scale was always the main way the refinery's administration stole from us."[50] This weighing system would be one of the principal issues discussed at the 1948 national convention of sugarcane growers held in Mexico City, where representatives demanded that they be allowed to control the scales themselves.[51]

Taming the worker-campesino council and those who protested against such tactics was also a violent process. Benigno Coronel, a worker in the Zacatepec mill, recalls how Teófilo Cervantes, who became head of the council shortly after Jaramillo, was killed by the manager's gunmen: "Teófilo was also a campesino, and he opposed the manager, saying that if campesinos did not want to farm sugarcane they shouldn't have to. . . . Teófilo was very popular among the people of the countryside, and he disagreed with the administration. . . . He wasn't the only one they killed; there were many dead."[52] Another case, cited time and again by cooperative members, was the death of one young *basculero* (the person in charge of weighing the cane). Carlos Ocampo Carreño, a young man remembered affectionately by his nickname *"El Maisito"* (the little corn), publicly declared that the scales were fixed. Soon after, a soldier stationed at Zacatepec shot him.[53] Management dismissed his death, accepting the soldier's explanation that his rifle had accidentally discharged while he was cleaning it, killing El Maisito. Had this been an isolated incident, cooperative members might have been more inclined to accept Ocampo's death as accidental. However, the numerous cases of management's violence led workers and campesinos alike to insist that his death was retaliation for exposing administrative corruption. The general impunity at Zacatepec led one member to comment, "The law around here has two standards, just like those scales."[54]

Worker and campesino reports of corruption and repression at Zacatepec emerged consistently after 1940. Management's use of force was part of a larger structure of political control in Mexico, one that combined cooption and repression. Cooperative members constantly complained about unlawful arrests, violent attacks on meetings, and assassinations or disappearances.[55] The administrator's bodyguards doubled as hit men, and the refinery's management also had access to the state police force and the soldiers stationed at Zacatepec. This force was often used to curtail worker mobilization. Union representatives pointed out that if workers stood up for their rights, they would not only lose their jobs, but their lives.[56] Others were threatened by military officers stationed at Zacatepec. On one occasion, Captain José Martínez declared that he had federal military orders to dissolve any public meeting held by campesinos.[57]

What began as a populist project to propel worker and campesino management and self-sufficiency instead provided opportunities for corruption that generated unseen levels of exploitation, leading one study to conclude

2. Cane workers load truck. *Archivo Fotográfico, Rodrigo Moya.*

that in Zacatepec, "mechanisms of domination appeared in new, 'modernized' forms adapted to postrevolutionary populist needs."[58] Ejidatarios simply observed that their situation at the cooperative revealed the "fallacy of campesino independence."[59] The corruption at Zacatepec was so widely known that in 1998, one of the state government's own publications remarked, "Don Lázaro never would have imagined that the modern sugar factory, which had been a source of such pride, would turn into a frightening haven of corruption where dozens of administrators competed with one another to see who could steal the most."[60]

That a cooperative could so quickly fall prey to such practices stemmed, in part, from the contradictions in the Cardenista project. While Cárdenas established political and economic mechanisms to integrate campesinos into the national sphere, greater structural forces or official party needs conditioned the market process and the organizations. Campesinos could not alter the goals of the national sugar industry, which in Mexico kept prices low for domestic, and primarily urban, consumption. Herein lay the key limitation of fusing communal principles with a market-oriented, capital-intensive industry. Thus the price paid to cane producers became a constant source of conflict. Ejidatarios who sold their cane to the Zacatepec refinery repeatedly wrote to the president requesting a price increase. To make their case stronger, petitions often included a detailed list of production costs that showed how little their earnings from sugar cultivation left for their living expenses. They bitterly complained that planting sugar placed them in the same state of hardship as that of their ancestors during colonial times.[61]

The cooperative structure notwithstanding, the mill was the property of the nation, and the president had the final word in all matters. Besides not having control of the cooperative, workers and campesinos had no autonomous organizations through which to assert their rights. While Cárdenas saw himself as a defender of the popular classes, he could not assure that those who followed him—even those he personally picked—would show the same commitment. As subsequent presidents became more and more allied with private capital, both foreign and domestic, they would find increasingly less reason to intervene on behalf of popular sectors. On the contrary, to the extent that the burden of peripheral capitalist development fell on the poor and working class, the state would increasingly have to intervene to keep these groups in check.[62]

The presidencies of Ávila Camacho and Alemán brought an abrupt move away from Cárdenas's policies. These two leaders affirmed close ties to the United States, promoted business interests, cemented personal loyalties, and showed little tolerance for leftist ideologies. Ávila Camacho, for example, reformed the agrarian law by expanding the amount of land for export crops exempted from expropriation, eliminated socialist education, and replaced an earlier government rhetoric of class struggle with calls for "unity at all cost" to confront the fascists in the war effort. His successor, President Alemán, solidified this process by demanding peace in the countryside, limiting the workers' right to strike, and declaring that development was best left to private enterprise. He refined the doctrine of natural concordance between the PRI, the constitution, the nation, and the government, using the power of his office to undo many of the reforms instituted by Cárdenas. Ironically, Alemán was able to follow this path thanks to the mechanisms put in place by Cárdenas, who "had bequeathed the political principle that the official party was a political instrument at the president's disposal."[63]

In Zacatepec, these economic and political transitions meant that Ávila Camacho privileged the needs of the sugar industry over those of ejidatarios, who found themselves beholden to new policies regulating what they could cultivate. For example, a presidential decree in 1942 established certain supply zones for each of the country's sugar refineries. The ejidos in these zones were ordered to dedicate 50 percent of their land to farming sugarcane, 25 percent to rice, and the remaining 25 percent for rotation purposes. Citing the ejidatarios' lack of efficiency in farming rice and managing water, the decree promised to improve and systematize both the production of sugarcane and rice. To enforce the new law, the refinery's administration was given the power to deny loans through the National Bank of Agrarian Credit. The law also gave the administrator of each refinery the right to oversee and control the zone's water supply.[64] Where these methods failed, the mill's administration sought federal forces to destroy the crops of those who refused to cultivate sugar.[65]

Campesinos deeply resented this ordinance and the administration's mechanisms of enforcement. While some ejidatarios chose to cultivate sugarcane because of its higher market value compared to corn, others explained that the crop cycle of sugarcane was so long that in the equivalent amount of time they could farm three plantings of subsistence crops. Clearly, Ávila Camacho's decree stifled campesino autonomy by imposing a development model that made ejidatarios even more dependent. Campesinos now had to cultivate sugar in parts of their land they previously devoted to subsistence crops, or other commercial products such as rice and cantaloupes. The tone of their complaints reveals the bitterness with which they received this new mandate. One appeal sent from the ejido "Eusebio Jaúrigui" read, "The piece of land that we till with the sweat of our brow, is the heritage of our elders and we will one day pass it on to our children for them to secure a living. Furthermore, with all due respect, if it is not our wish to farm sugarcane it is an abuse of our rights to force us to do so. It is unjust that if local authorities want to produce cane, they make everyone do it."[66] These complaints were ignored by Ávila Camacho, who in 1943 expanded his earlier decree by allowing the Ministry of Agriculture and Development to designate the supply zones necessary to produce sugarcane. Less than a year later, the president extended the decree for the state of Morelos, mandating that 75 percent of the ejido lands in sugar-producing zones be dedicated to sugarcane and the other 25 percent held for rotation purposes.[67] While originally justified as wartime emergencies, these decrees remained in effect until the 1970s.

Jaramillo's Emergence as a Campesino Leader

On the eve of the 1942 worker-campesino strike at Zacatepec, Morelos governor Epildio Perdomo detained Jaramillo and demanded he call off the mobilization. After threatening to have him killed, the governor reminded Jaramillo that it was Ávila Camacho, and not Cárdenas, who was now the president of Mexico.[68] Perdomo's warning was indicative of the changes taking place in Mexico as Cárdenas left office. During the last two years of his presidency, national and international structural constraints had already slowed the pace and limited the extent of social reforms. When Cárdenas picked the conservative Ávila Camacho as the official party candidate for the 1940 presidential election, he provided a clear indication about the course state policy would now follow.

"I am a partisan of just ideas and of the people, not of men," Jaramillo responded to Perdomo's warning that Cárdenas could no longer intervene on the campesinos' behalf.[69] These ideas were greatly influenced by his experience at Zacatepec, where he emerged as a voice for campesinos and where his political formation really began to take shape. While he would continue to espouse Cardenista ideals at other points in his life, the contradictions he encountered at the refinery made him increasingly skeptical about subsequent regimes. As president of the mill's administrative council, Jaramillo witnessed numerous injustices and attempted to correct them. One ejidatario recalled, "He was aware of how much one ton of sugarcane was supposed to produce, and saw how campesinos were paid. He fought for the campesinos, and he began his struggle with a lot of experience because he knew how the mill was managed, and he knew how the administration worked."[70] Said another sugar farmer, "The ploys began when Jaramillo was no longer head of the council. The new council was loyal to the administrator's orders, and then the council obeyed the will of the administrator, rather than the administrator following the will of the council. The administration named the council members through delegates it already had under its wing."[71] Jaramillo also began to understand the importance of linking the struggle of workers and campesinos. Central to this development was Jaramillo's friendship with Mónico Rodríguez.

Rodríguez had arrived in Zacatepec in 1936 to work as a mechanic in the construction of the refinery. Born in 1919, Rodríguez spent his childhood and early teens in the oil fields of Veracruz, where his father worked as a pipe fitter for an oil company. "My father was an anarchist," recalled Rodríguez, "and also, I think, a member of the Communist Party, because he would receive several copies of *El Machete* and then have me distribute them. He'd take me everywhere so I'd always hear what they talked about."[72] Rodríguez devoted his entire life to revolutionary struggle. When he died in December 1998, he had participated or was linked to the mobilizations at Atencingo and Zacatepec, movements of railroad workers, students, and teachers, Lucio Cabañas's struggle in the state of Guerrero, and the urban guerrillas who, after the Tlatelolco massacre of 1968, formed clandestine cells in the hope of generating widespread revolutionary change. He was also a sometime member of the Mexican Communist Party, although he was expelled on several occasions for defying the party's leadership. In 1994, when the EZLN rebelled against the Mexican government, only Rodríguez's age and physical debilitation resulting from a series of strokes kept him out of Chiapas, where he wanted to join the Zapatistas.

Rodríguez first encountered Jaramillo in 1935, when he came to Zacatepec as a delegate from the National Sugar Workers' Union. Rodríguez recalled that one afternoon, when he and his friend were drinking in a cantina, Jaramillo entered the establishment and began to address the people there. "He gave a beautiful speech; he said 'Gentlemen, forgive me for interrupting your moment of happiness, but your happiness should not be one achieved through the consumption of alcohol. Rather, you should be filled with joy by doing good unto others.' The next day, before leaving, I went to see him to say goodbye; he had made quite an impression on me."[73] When Rodríguez came to work in Zacatepec a year later, he sought out Jaramillo and invited him to meetings he held with the barber Francisco Ruiz (better known as "*Gorra Prieta*"—black hat). Their conversations must have opened up another world for Jaramillo. Rodríguez recalled, "We'd talk about everything here, the Soviet Union, socialism, China, the events unfolding in Spain. Rubén would come to those meetings; he had incredible discipline. He was there every Sunday, from nine in the morning to eight or ten at night. . . .

We would talk to him; he had such patience for me. He provoked you and he made you talk, and at the same time he inspired trust and he gave you confidence and all with such patience. He listened and said 'I see, I see,' with the patience of a religious devotee."[74]

The group's discussions emphasized the importance of international-ism, the unity between workers and campesinos, and the impending fascist threat. According to Rodríguez, Jaramillo's religious beliefs were a constant source of tension between him and his communist friends, "who would of-ten attack his religion, telling him that it was the opium of the masses." [75] It is unclear to what extent this criticism affected Jaramillo, but his Methodist background did not lead him to reject the analysis offered by his Marxist *compañeros*; however, as a public figure, he seemed to have made few reli-gious allusions.[76]

The impact of Rodríguez's and Ruiz's discussions on Jaramillo appeared most clearly in the Plan of Cerro Prieto, first drafted by the Jaramillistas during their armed uprising in 1943.[77] While it is difficult to reconstruct precisely what elements influenced the vision presented in this plan, its lan-guage resembled Rodríguez's style. This document criticized the adverse situation faced by campesinos in Morelos and the Mexican capitalist sys-tem in the context of unequal systems of economic exchange and pressure from the United States to fall behind its political objectives of hemispheric hegemony. The Plan de Cerro Prieto clearly demonstrated an understanding of the poverty of workers and campesinos in an international context, and these were precisely the types of conversations Rodríguez recalled having with Jaramillo. These discussions influenced Jaramillo as he began to change his attitudes about the Zacatepec workers, whom he now started to see as compañeros in the struggle rather than as the usurpers of campesino jobs. Under Jaramillo's leadership, ejidatarios would join mill employees in a 1942 strike. His position towards the workers had clearly changed from the one he had espoused earlier as president of the cooperative's council.

The Atencingo Connection

Not far from Zacatepec, a similar struggle occurred at the sugar refinery in Atencingo, Puebla. Direct ideological links existed between both move-ments, as key players moved to and from each mill.[78] A brief history of the

Atencingo mill is worth exploring for the parallels it offers with the situation in Zacatepec. The links created between the two sugar complexes are in themselves an important testament to organizational webs the Mexican Communist Party sought to establish in the region. The organizers of the PCM were workers who primarily mobilized their fellow proletarians, though inevitably they came into contact with campesinos and did not hesitate to offer an analysis of their situation. In this way, Zacatepec and Atencingo came to share a group of central actors, including Rubén Jaramillo's brother Porfirio.[79]

Porfirio Jaramillo arrived at Zacatepec in 1936, fleeing repression at the Atencingo mill, whose owner, the American-born entrepreneur William Jenkins, had amassed the greatest concentration of land in the history of Puebla. Faced with Jenkins's control of the region, former Zapatistas in Puebla mobilized landless peasants in the area and by the mid-1930s had managed to strip him of more than 90 percent of his total holdings. Still, Jenkins retained an enormous amount of wealth, power, and property, including irrigated fields, nine haciendas, and the Atencingo refinery. Altogether these constituted the "single most important agricultural and industrial unit in the state of Puebla, and the most productive sugar enterprise in Mexico." When these remaining holdings also came under attack, Jenkins, with the help of Puebla governor Maximino Ávila Camacho, brother of president Manuel Ávila Camacho, managed to manipulate the agrarian law so that only his peons and workers—and not the surrounding villages—gained access to the property. But this group gained ownership in name only and had little say in the production or distribution process. Jenkins, with the help of his administrator Manuel Pérez, fashioned his power through the control of elected and appointed positions, through influence on the state's governing structure, and, when needed, through force.[80] An ejidatario from Atencingo said of the situation under Jenkins, "In the days of Pérez, terrorism and hired guns were clearly there. Anyone they did not want around disappeared overnight. Those who took their turn at defending the rights of the rest of the peasants were chased away or killed. Nobody could say anything about the boss, or raise his voice to protest the wages or ask for more work, because there was no freedom."[81]

Porfirio Jaramillo had been one of the main campesino leaders at Atencingo and as a result was the target of repression. Other organizers fled as well: "Some were fired, others were chased out with guns," recalled Rodríguez.

The group who went to Zacatepec included Jaramillo, Adalberto García, Prisco Sánchez, and Agapito Vargas, all of whom had participated in the founding of the short-lived "Karl Marx Union" at Atencingo. In Zacatepec they continued their organizing efforts and gathered enough funds to begin mobilizing the workers at Emiliano Zapata. "We set up a barbershop, as a strategic move. Francisco Ruiz was a barber and a committed revolutionary. So anyone who went there to have their hair cut had to hear about the Spanish Civil War or about the Soviet Union." Francisco Ruiz also attended the sugar workers' union meetings, where he spoke to the workers about the importance of class solidarity. According to Rodríguez, the sugar workers' union in Zacatepec donated the money to sponsor this small group from Atencingo to return to Puebla and continue their organizing efforts in Jenkins's sugar mill.[82]

The Atencingo and Zacatepec refineries differed in an important way. Jenkins's mill began as a private enterprise, a capitalist venture aided by state officials with whom he maintained close connections. After the expropriation of the complex, Jenkins used these ties to ensure a continued profit. The Emiliano Zapata mill, on the other hand, was directly controlled by the government, and it was state officials who profited. Nonetheless, the dynamic that developed among workers and campesinos at each refinery revealed how the mechanisms created by Cárdenas to protect the popular classes broke down almost immediately under elite pressure. In fact, Jaramillo himself, upon visiting Atencingo in 1939, wrote a distressed letter to President Cárdenas. It read, "I must tell you, Mr. President, with all due respect, that in Atencingo your noble wishes have not been fulfilled, since the land is monopolized by a single individual who has submerged our compañeros in economic misery. . . . I implore you, Mr. President, to intervene in the affair of our Atencingo compañeros, so that some day not far off they may enjoy the fruits of the Revolution, as other areas of the republic have done."[83]

After Cárdenas's expropriation in 1939, campesinos at Atencingo were entitled to the lands around the mill. But Jenkins still maintained control of the mill and used his power to prevent a fundamental structural transformation. Moreover, the government's policy towards the countryside implicitly or explicitly sanctioned Jenkins's actions. The dynamic at Atencingo, like Zacatepec, exposed the continued vulnerability of Mexico's rural poor. The ejidatarios wanted to diversify their crops and cultivate a combination of subsistence and market products. The state, however, pushed for increased sugar production, as the industry was critical to the nation's economy and a mainstay of powerful political and economic elites.[84] The difference in power between the state—or private enterprises increasingly allied to the state—and campesinos determined the policy that won out. Institutions designed to protect popular interests were neutralized on several fronts.

The fate of Porfirio Jaramillo is a case in point. In 1947 he was elected head of the ejidatarios' cooperative linked to Jenkins's enterprise at Atencingo, but the administration and local government continually obstructed his efforts by sowing division among the ejidatarios. Ultimately, they caused so many conflicts that the federal government, now in the hands of Miguel Alemán, formed a special commission to take charge of the cooperative and exert renewed control over ejidatarios.[85] Cultivators like Porfirio Jaramillo, who resisted, suffered repression. Jenkins's gunmen, in collusion with state police, repeatedly attempted to kill Porfirio, and in 1955 finally succeeded, kidnapping him and a fellow leader, Fortunato Calixto, from the Mexico City hotel where they were staying on a trip to consult with the Agrarian Department.[86] His funeral ceremony was surrounded by soldiers hoping to capture his brother Rubén, who had taken up arms as a result of the repression that followed his 1952 campaign for governor of Morelos.[87]

As it was at Atencingo, reform at Zacatepec was only possible with government support, and this presidential backing came only when it served the state's interests.[88] The fourth clause of the cooperative's governing statutes established the refinery as the property of the federal government and gave the president final say in its affairs.[89] Seeing the profits generated at Zacatepec, the mill's manager and other local power groups moved to gain control over the refinery. This shift in power became possible under Ávila Camacho, whose consistent actions on the side of management placed ejidatarios under greater control of the Zacatepec administration. As with all Cardenista projects, ultimate power lay in the executive. As head of an administration that sought to establish Mexico's campesinos as a pillar of the state, Cárdenas supported their demands and extended them benefits. However, when the production of a major staple such as sugar was at stake, Ávila Camacho and later presidents reacted by forcing them to cultivate the crop. Finding the cooperative's built-in mechanisms insufficient to protect their interests, workers and campesinos in Zacatepec resorted to strikes.

Mobilizations at the Zacatepec Refinery

The 1942 strike was the first in a series of mobilizations at Zacatepec seeking to defend the principle of worker-campesino ownership and compel the state to honor its laws. The outcome reflected the limited control that workers and ejidatarios actually held over the cooperative. This strike erupted when a group of twenty-six workers demanded compliance with a presidential decree to increase their salaries by 15 percent. Severino Carrera Peña, the manager, responded by firing them. His actions triggered a strike of three hundred workers and two thousand campesinos, calling not only for the restitution of the fired employees but for a series of other demands. The petition drawn up by the strikers concentrated on worker grievances—an odd fact, given how many more campesinos participated in the strike. The first two points called for an increase in workers' salaries, in accordance with the General Contract Law for sugar industries, as well as an adjustment to bring salaries in line with the higher wages paid to workers at other sugar mills. The petition also included a demand for worker compensation in accordance with federal labor laws and paid vacation. Refinery workers also made an appeal for the establishment of clean housing and a guarantee of sugar provisions for their families. To ensure the recognition of their union, the petition called for the designation of office space for the sugar syndicate. Only two of the demands focused on the cultivation of cane: one calling for an increase in the amount paid to the cane cutters and the other demanding an increase in the price paid to ejidatarios for their crops.[90]

The strike committee issued this petition in early April and set the twenty-first of that month as the date to launch a strike if their demands were not met. But the administration did not take them seriously and threatened to use force to disperse any meetings. The governor of Morelos, Epildio Perdomo, called Jaramillo into his office and threatened to have him killed if he did not call off the general assembly where the cooperative members would discuss the strike.[91] When the strike erupted, the administration refused to negotiate and instead ordered striking committee members arrested and immediately halted all credit and transportation facilities to participating ejidatarios. Management acted with the support of the federal government, as is evident in the minister of the economy's order to dismiss the 2,300 people involved in the mobilization.[92] When the strike erupted, Félix Serdán recalled, "people in the factory and in the fields responded really well. But the military arrived and took over the refinery, the manager hired inexperienced people to work and spilled over 10,000 liters of syrup. The manager ordered the detention of strike organizers. On that day, six of us were arrested, four workers and two campesinos."[93] Also—in flagrant violation of the general agreement with the health department—the refinery terminated the health coverage of all participants and their families.[94]

The local and federal governments' reaction to the strike demonstrated the state's priorities. The minister of the economy stated that, as a cooperative, neither federal labor law nor laws governing the sugar industry applied to Zacatepec. Instead, the cooperative had to comply with agreements issued by the mill's governing assembly and approved by all other members. In theory, this was a reasonable argument, except that by 1942, all council members who opposed the manager had been removed. In his statement, the minister of the economy declared that the administration had not fired any workers but had merely suspended their rights as cooperative members. President Ávila Camacho declared that union activity had no place at Zacatepec, since all workers and campesinos, as partners, were equal members. Ávila Camacho did acknowledge the workers' entitlement to the 15 percent raise, but stated that it be applied not in absolute terms but in proportion to the rank of each member.[95]

Authorities also used repression. Indeed, the strike was defeated in great part through the management's use of force. Carrera Peña, the manager, employed the military forces stationed at Zacatepec to intimidate participants and to harass the strike leaders. One newspaper article commented that Zacatepec appeared more like a military fortress than "a center of production that was once said to belong to the working class." The manager dispatched soldiers to the striking ejidos and forced campesinos to farm the sugarcane. Six participants in the strike, including the ejidal commissariat of the nearby town of Tehuixtla, were incarcerated.[96] One campesino recalled, "When our depositions were being taken, the judge or agent, I don't know what he was, asked all these questions, [and] when I answered energetically and a bit strong he accused me of being a leader. 'I don't know what that is; I just defend my rights and those of my compañeros.' At this point the person representing us intervened: 'Don't forget that the revolution has created men that can defend themselves without being leaders.'"[97] Félix Serdán recalled how the manager specifically ordered the arrest of the strike organizers: "We were in the fields supervising the strike activity when *El Polilla*

[Teodomiro Ortiz], the gunman at Zacatepec, came and got us. We were only in jail a short time because the workers and campesinos from other refineries began to protest."[98] While most striking workers held out for a month and a half, many returned to work after the end of the second month, and the rest were fired.[99]

But the issues that brought together workers and campesinos in the 1942 strike would not go away. And while the manager expelled Jaramillo from the cooperative, this would not be the last time he participated in labor struggles at Zacatepec. In 1948 ejidatarios solicited his help in a mobilization of workers and campesinos to oust Rodrigo Ampudia del Valle, a particularly ruthless manager. Ejidatarios recall Ampudia's unabashed corruption, his conspicuous use of Zacatepec funds for his ostentatious houses, cars, and mistresses, and his penchant for the use of force. One ejidatario described him by saying, "I don't think there was a vice that that man did not have."[100] Mill worker Pedro Castillo recalled, "It got to the point where a group of four or five people could not risk talking together outside because, right away, we'd be accused of conspiring something."[101] Other cooperative members continuously complained about the repressive acts carried out by Ampudia's bodyguards and the military outpost at Zacatepec.[102] On one occasion, for example, Major Tirado Salido and eight of his soldiers went to the home of union leader Mateo Torres Ortiz to detain him. Since he was not at home, they beat his wife and kidnapped two other of his relatives, Ramón Orbe and Francisco Baeza, whose whereabouts could not be established for several days.[103] The climate of intimidation was augmented by the fact that Ampudia distributed guns to loyal ejidatarios.[104] Federal authorities themselves were quite aware of his use of force, noting that he was "always surrounded by armed men, some of whom had shady backgrounds."[105]

Ampudia triggered the 1948 strike when he fired workers as a way of cutting production costs.[106] Jaramillo again played a prominent role in the strike, drafting petitions and organizing campesino defense groups.[107] His support for the 1948 strike was characteristic of Jaramillo's struggles in Morelos. People sought him out, and he assumed the leadership of groups attempting to address particular grievances. With the aid of Jaramillo, an armed contingent of workers and campesinos even managed to briefly take over the factory.[108] One participant in this action recalled, "We took the factory, we got in and thought, 'Now we're really done for!' We went in with weapons and everything; the situation got really tense. . . . When the soldiers surrounded the factory, they started off easy: 'Bring the leaders to the front.' But they were hidden behind some domes. Just with twenty of us we could have held them off, but a lot of soldiers would have died, and the machinery would have been totally destroyed."[109] The standoff did result in management's compliance with some of the demands, as Ampudia, the manager, was increasingly worried about the loss of money caused by the continued work stoppages.[110]

In years to come, Jaramillo continued to provide support for ejidatarios seeking to assert their rights as cooperative members. Abuses increased in the 1950s, and members again complained bitterly about the new manager, Eugenio Prado. Prado used *guardias blancas*—private paramilitary "white guards" whose salaries, campesinos pointed out, came out of money made on their cane—as well as threats to eliminate water and credit rights to ensure ejidatarios' compliance.[111] Cooperative members pointed out that the manager and administrative members close to him lived in luxurious country estates thanks to the money they made off campesino labor and through illicit business ventures such as alcohol production.[112] The following public letter seeking the removal of Prado states eloquently, "The Emiliano Zapata refinery is not, as you have taken it, an inheritance for you and yours; it is a legacy bequeathed by the revolution to us, the campesinos and the workers of the sugarcane region. . . . We will continue to fight against you, Mr. Prado, until this refinery becomes a workplace and not a political center, as you run it now."[113] The government's own assessment of the Emiliano Zapata mill in 1958 reveals the severity of the situation. An official report candidly concluded, "Zacatepec operates under a capitalist system: a cooperative order that would protect small producers is missing. . . . Zacatepec is a good business for the state, [but] ejidatarios are poorer than before they were members. . . . The Revolution is thus still in debt to the campesinos of Zacatepec."[114]

The Lessons of Zacatepec

The early history of the Emiliano Zapata cooperative provides a glimpse not only into Jaramillo's formative years as a campesino leader, but also into the fate of many Cardenista projects and the actors they involved. In Morelos, ejidatarios came to Zacatepec with the memory of Zapatismo. The state, in turn, validated this experience by presenting the cooperative as an accomplishment of the Zapatista struggle. Jaramillo, in essence, personified much of this process, which would continue to develop in the Jaramillista movement itself. The Zacatepec cooperative represented a fusion of Zapatista and Cardenista ideals. Jaramillo came to participate in the complex as a representative of Zapata's agrarismo. But, as someone who lived in Mexico's postrevolutionary world, Jaramillo conceived of Cardenismo as a means of realizing Zapata's ideals and integrating them into the national economic and political project.

However, the fusion of these two projects brought about a series of contradictions. The refinery's proper functioning as a cooperative was immediately hampered by a number of structural constraints. Within these parameters, it was impossible for workers and campesinos to protect their interests as cooperative members or effectively prevent administrative abuses without risking their lives or losing their jobs. After the first two years of operation, the manager wrested control away from the representative council and exerted his will. As presidential appointees, the managers possessed considerable power. Since the general law on cooperatives dictated that the chief executive had ultimate ownership and control over the refinery, workers and ejidatarios were at the mercy of the president's goodwill. Moreover, the nature of the PRI, as the official party of the state, guaranteed that any of the government's projects would be subsumed to party needs. As such, the cooperative did not operate for the benefit of its members. Instead, it served local politicians and caciques as a stepping stone from which to launch their political careers. Therefore, while at the mill, aspiring candidates showed their worthiness by fattening official party ranks.

In addition, the production of a cash crop such as sugar brought with it another layer of constraints. The government had to assure an affordable price for this staple in the urban population's diet, as well as guard the industry from international competition. But in maintaining prices at a low level, the state could not guarantee a living wage to the ejidatarios selling their cane to the refinery. In this way, administrations after Cárdenas revealed their commitment to the urban sectors at the cost of the rural population. Finally, the high levels of corruption characteristic of the Mexican political and economic system further prevented workers and ejidatarios from receiving their fair share of profits and contributed to the enrichment of government bureaucrats, even in a cooperative setting.

The refinery administration's way of handling worker and campesino protest paralleled the Mexican government's strategy for dealing with dissidents elsewhere. With its high profits and considerable budget allocation, management could buy off many people. When these mechanisms of control did not suffice, the administration relied on state authorities, the army, and hired gunmen. When Jaramillo spoke out against the abuses and responded to the appeal of cooperative members, he suffered persecution. He was not the only ejidatario to elicit repression, and this explains why, after numerous attempts on his life, he decided, in 1943, to arm himself and go underground. "I am convinced," he wrote, "that to speak in favor of campesinos, as is dignified, is a crime in the eyes of the government."[115] One hundred other campesinos followed him.

Campesinos throughout Morelos and in parts of Puebla provided the armed Jaramillistas with food, shelter, and cover from the authorities, frustrating the army's efforts to eliminate the group. During this period of clandestine activity, Jaramillo reconsidered the viability of the Cardenista project; although he never completely lost hope in Cárdenas's model, he realized the limitations of a populist state. Ultimately, his decision to take up arms alongside other campesinos indicated the exhaustion of, and their frustration with, legal channels. In the Plan de Cerro Prieto, a document composed by Jaramillistas during their first armed uprising, they expressed a vision in which workers and campesinos owned and controlled the nation's sources of wealth. This clause affirmed that popular groups could not simply hand over control to the executive and trust the government to guard their interests. The Plan de Cerro Prieto also fused other elements of the Jaramillista experience at Zacatepec. The friendship and struggle alongside rank-and-file members of the Mexican Communist Party had a profound influence on the political formation of campesino leaders. Calling on Jaramillo for counsel and leadership, campesinos made common cause with workers and began to view local structures of exploitation as intrinsically linked to national and international ones.

CHAPTER THREE

The Agrarista Tradition

In his autobiography, Rubén Jaramillo wrote that in 1918, when he withdrew from Zapata's army, he advised his men, "The people, and even more so our future generations, will not allow themselves to live enslaved. We will once again continue our struggle. And even if we are far from each other we will not lose sight of one another, and when the moment comes we will once again reunite. Put your rifles away where you can easily find them again."[1] Whether he actually made this declaration at the time or constructed it years later in composing his autobiography, it offers an important example of the ways in which he sought to frame the Jaramillista struggle as a continuation of Zapata's. When faced with a political system designed to co-opt popular leaders, tone down their demands, and channel them into the government bureaucracy, Jaramillo resisted, taking up arms to confront state repression.

In Zacatepec this process played itself out as management proceeded unchecked and wrested control away from the worker-campesino council. When cooperative members protested, the administration resorted to selective repression. Jaramillo became a principal target, and, to protect himself, he took up arms and fled to the mountains in 1943. Zacatepec ejidatarios, suffering repression, and other aggrieved campesinos joined him and went underground. Like Jaramillo, many of them were former Zapatistas. This episode marked the first of three Jaramillista armed uprisings. In 1944 and in 1951, when the Jaramillistas put down their arms and mounted a political campaign running Jaramillo for governor of Morelos, the state responded again with repression, and the Jaramillistas again turned to armed resistance.

The Jaramillistas' use of both armed and legal mobilizations, a hallmark of their movement, can best be understood as part of the "ambivalent and unstable" compromise reached as a result of the revolution.[2] The various factions that characterized the revolutionary conflict continued to surface in subsequent decades, as local actors either rejected or sought to push further for long-overdue reforms. The process often produced violent outbursts, as the state attempted to replace the "'folk' variant of the revolution with the official version of the revolutionary order."[3] In Morelos this folk variant inevitably referenced Zapata, whose spirit continued to inform and validate campesino actions. Jaramillo thus framed his turn to armed struggle as a simple continuation of the Zapatista battle.

But given the dramatically different world of the 1940s, the Jaramillistas adjusted their appeals and critiques to Mexico's postrevolutionary context. Thus, while Zapata had fought for the restitution of campesino lands, Jaramillo pressured the government to implement the necessary mechanisms— credit, water, and fair prices on agricultural products—so that campesinos could make a living off this land. As Jaramillo confronted the limitations of a system increasingly designed to suit the needs of an export economy, corrupt public officials, and a new group of *latifundistas* (large landholders), he put forth a plan that envisioned a complete economic restructuring. Named after one of their hiding places, the Jaramillistas originally composed the Plan de Cerro Prieto to counter the charge that they were mere armed bandits. Although it was modeled after Zapata's Plan de Ayala, this document responded not only to Mexico's changing socioeconomic context but also reflected the expansion of agrarian ideology triggered by an alliance with Marxist teachers and workers. It set out a vision for a socialist society in which land and industry were in the hands of campesinos and workers. Such goals revealed an understanding of the state that had betrayed the ideals of the revolution and blocked the possibility of change from within the system. The force of their critique was a measure of this betrayal.

The first Jaramillista armed uprising must be understood within the context of the institutionalization of the Mexican Revolution. While Cárdenas's policies had consolidated the relationship between the state and its official party, subsequent administrations reversed his social reforms and invited a measure of popular discontent. In this sense, not only did President Ávila Camacho revisit old problems; in the countryside he contributed to a return to more militant forms of resistance. Triggered by unpopular legislation such as the military draft, remnants of the previously suppressed Cristero Rebellion emerged in a few states, including Morelos, where participants' grievances at times merged with those of the Jaramillistas. Despite this overlap the Jaramillistas were of a different ideological bent, one clearly evident in their Plan de Cerro Prieto, the first expression of a radicalization that would reemerge in decades to come. Their clandestine activity deepened previous relationships and fomented social webs that later undergirded broader social mobilizations. This overlap between legal and clandestine activity helps explain why armed struggle continued to remain a possibility and, in turn, accounts for the decades-long history of the Jaramillista movement.

Pacifying the Countryside

In the years after the revolutionary fighting ended, the government confronted a series of militant challenges, most notably the Cristero Rebellion that erupted in the states of Puebla, Oaxaca, Jalisco, and Michoacán in the 1920s and 1930s. The Calles government triggered the religious rebellion by enforcing the anticlerical legislation of the 1917 constitution. This legislation went beyond nineteenth-century Liberal laws and sought to curtail the power of the Catholic Church by closing religious schools, convents, and seminaries, as well as requiring priests to register with civil authorities. Religious processions, too, were outlawed. The militancy of the reaction revealed not only the continuing power of the church but also the importance of Catholicism to Mexico's rural population. Between 1926 and 1929, campesinos, in defense of their faith, waged a powerful battle against the government. The Cristeros, as the rebels became known, attacked civic symbols, burning down numerous schools and chasing out or killing their teachers. This rural, Catholic revolt did not present agrarian demands but instead sought to reinstate a social and religious order that looked to the past. The ranks of the Cristero army were extremely diverse and included hacienda laborers, sharecroppers, small-scale cultivators, and independent farmers. Ironically, their social positions were often quite similar to those of agraristas, the beneficiaries of the government's land reform and tended to support the postrevolutionary state. An important question for scholars of this rebellion has thus been to address why campesinos would fight so passionately against a government presumably working to fulfill their need for land.[4] Interpretations vary: some see the campesinos as pawns of a conservative clergy, some view the movement as deeply imbedded in peasant religiosity, and still others place the causes in a combination of local culture and a rejection of government interference.[5] What does seem clear is the extent to which the Cristeros challenged the actions by which the new government attempted to consolidate its hegemonic rule. Although they were branded reactionary for their religious slant, the specific label of counterrevolutionary was applied by a government who had appropriated the revolution for its own agenda.[6] Ultimately, the Cristeros represented one of the varied responses to the institutionalization of the revolution.

While President Calles defeated the Cristero uprising in 1929, the conflict would once again emerge in 1934, leading Cárdenas to mount a major military operation that by 1938 succeeded in finally putting an end to the *Cristiada*. But the forces that produced the religious uprising found new, albeit somewhat more measured, expression in the Unión Nacional Sinarquista (UNS), established in 1937 by right-wing Catholic activists in opposition to the policies of Cardenismo. *Sinarquismo*, in part, represented the church's attempt to maintain a strong presence in Mexico without directly confronting the state, which had made it clear that the church was to stay out of politics. The *Sinarquistas* were hardly a unified group and were characterized by three broad tendencies. The first, represented by much of the Catholic hierarchy, followed closely the directives from the Vatican that redefined the church's position in a world in which its power was increasingly constrained by the modern state. The second contained many of the hard-line Cristeros who opposed any reconciliation with the Mexican state and continued to exert a combative stance. The third wing, which would come to dominate the UNS, advocated civic forms of participation and attempted to contain the more militant challenges to the state articulated by the Catholic hierarchy and its armed base.[7]

Anxious to avoid any military confrontations with the government but intent on capitalizing on the resentment still extant in the countryside, the UNS designed a platform based on a mixture of Catholicism and radical nationalism that advocated a Christian social order in opposition to both capitalism and communism. Moreover, the Sinarquistas held a stance solidly opposed to the United States, counterposing Hispanic values to what they saw as an encroaching and corrupt "*Yanqui*" order. Sinarquismo's vision of a society based on campesino small property owners resonated in the countryside in part because of its "mystic faith in the spiritual values of rural life, in the beauty of family, in the virtues paternalism can illicit: frugality, piety, work, resignation, a sense of duty."[8] The UNS provided a forum and structure to channel campesino frustration with the postrevolutionary order. Like the Cristero Rebellion, the Sinarquista movement revealed both the importance of Catholicism in rural Mexico and the extent to which religion served to channel particular grievances.[9]

To a certain extent, the increasingly right-wing nature of the Mexican government allowed a reconciliation between church and state.[10] President Ávila Camacho not only tempered many of the revolution's social reforms but also eliminated the state's previous revolutionary language of class struggle, replacing it with a doctrine of order and unity. Such rhetoric could not help but resonate with some middle- and upper-level Sinarquistas. This was not the case, however, with much of the Sinarquista base, who, devoid of a voice in this reconciliation, willingly took up arms to be heard. In fact, some of the same grievances that drove campesinos to join the Jaramillistas pushed others into the ranks of the Sinarquistas. Like the Jaramillistas, the Sinarquistas opposed the military draft instituted in 1942 as Mexico entered World War II. Moreover, just as the Jaramillistas would protest the electoral fraud of the 1946 and 1952 elections, the UNS objected to the 1940 presidential election results, viewing Ávila Camacho as an official imposition against the right-wing candidate Juan Andreu Almazán. Finally, both the UNS and the Jaramillistas spoke out against the draconian policy that the government implemented in the late 1940s, at the behest of the United States, to combat hoof-and-mouth disease afflicting Mexican cattle. These parallels reflect the shared rural base of each movement, however, rather than any ideological congruence. And while in Morelos this overlap caused the leadership to briefly consider joining forces, ideological difference soon prevailed. Jaramillo's Methodist background notwithstanding, the solidly secular Jaramillistas recognized in the Sinarquista project a hierarchical order ultimately detrimental to the rural poor.

As they did elsewhere in Mexico, in the decades following the revolution Morelos's campesinos in various ways attempted to preserve their autonomy from a modernizing state that sought what were often costly allegiances. The Jaramillistas used the knowledge gained from the revolutionary struggle and the elements of social justice mandated by the 1917 constitution and by Cardenista reforms to formulate a vision of a new society. The Sinarquistas, on the other hand, completely rejected the new order and looked to re-create a past—mythic or real—in which campesinos lived out their lives unencumbered by outside forces. While the Cristero or Sinarquista movements were not strong in Morelos, the postrevolutionary government nevertheless generated enough discontent that the UNS did find some willing adherents, many of whom formed small armed bands. Thus, when Jaramillo went underground in 1943, his group was not the only one in open rebellion. In the early 1940s, it was Ávila Camacho's forced military conscription that enraged campesinos enough to lead them into a local insurgent group before they would consider training to fight a war on a distant continent.

In Zacualpan, a town in eastern Morelos where the entire community organized against the draft, this resistance acquired particular militancy. When Mexico entered World War II in 1942, Ávila Camacho ordered all young able-bodied men to report for military training in nearby—and often not so nearby—urban centers in order to have reserves ready to fight in Europe when needed. Campesinos referred to these weekly training exercises as "*las marchas*" (the marches) and found them a huge imposition. For many, the government's nationalist justification rang hollow, and they saw no logic in the call to participate in a war to which they felt no connection. If the government had acquired an obligation to fight the fascists in Europe, the prevailing logic held, it should fulfill it without placing the burden on campesinos. When the people of Zacualpan were given no say in the matter, their resistance to the draft turned into a resistance against the federal government. Taking up arms often became the only logical option. As one of the families who sent their young boy to the mountains stated, "If the government is going to take him anyway, he might as well join you in armed struggle." And so emerged the *bola chiquita* ("little group" as opposed to Zapata's *bola grande*, or "big group"). For the Zacualpan community, armed struggle was the surest way to preserve their autonomy. Many combatants would explain, "In that way we could defend ourselves."[11] The men who had participated in the revolution emerged with their .30–30 rifles, and those former revolutionaries too old to join the armed group donated their weapons to the younger men.

In other communities in Morelos, many seeking to avoid the military draft joined Jaramillo. Lino Manzanares, a campesino from Los Hornos, presented the same logic as the people of Zacualpan when describing the collaboration with the Jaramillistas: "People preferred to take to the nearby mountains rather than to go march in Mexico City. That's why many here joined Jaramillo; they didn't want to march with the soldiers."[12] Other bands of armed campesinos formed throughout the state. In January 1943, the Barreto brothers, Cecilio and José, organized groups of about seventy-five men in Jonacatepec, Jantetelco, and Zacualpan. In Chinameca, another band led by Zapatista veteran Concepción Pérez also took up arms. This latter group had a confrontation with federal forces, which left fifteen of Pérez's men dead. In the nearby municipality of Temoac, federal forces killed five men belonging to another rebel group that was also resisting the draft.[13] That same year, more armed groups joined local movements opposed to military conscription. In Tlanepantla, one hundred people took up arms under the leadership of José Inclán. On the outskirts of Mexico City, one group of 100 men and a smaller group of 18 also took action. Significantly, according to a government memo, these last two groups took refuge in old Zapatista camps. Nearby, in the State of Mexico, another group of 150 men was also up in arms. Rafael Castilla, who once was a Zapatista and was now an "old man with completely gray hair," had had confrontations with alcohol inspectors in both Morelos and the Federal District.[14] After a skirmish, the group fled to the base of the Popocatépetl volcano, leaving two inspectors dead and the rest stripped of their weapons. The report pointed out, "The reason for their uprising is due to their disagreement with the obligatory military service. They were trying in this way to protect the young men . . . who would have to provide their services in the current year." According to this account, it was primarily the areas in the east and north of Morelos—"the isolated and remote regions with little access to communication"—that reacted in this way to the draft.[15] Due to their distant location, these communities had likely preserved some degree of autonomy, and they were now resisting the new wave of state control.

While these movements were small and lacked coordination among one another, they were an example of the more generalized discontent that produced violent outbursts against the logic of top-down state consolidation. They provide a context for understanding how Jaramillista armed uprisings found willing participants. Their logic functioned alongside the recent experience of revolutionary armed struggle. Many, and in some cases most, of those who took up arms against the draft were aging revolutionaries and not the eighteen-year-old draftees.[16] This pattern suggests that these older men, many of them Zapatista veterans, were drawing on armed resistance as the surest way of defending their autonomy. They acted to protect their community, whose harvest would have suffered if the bulk of its workforce was lost to military conscription.

The Jaramillistas came out in fierce opposition to the government's levy. Among the various armed resistance movements, theirs stands out in the way Jaramillo channeled this discontent into both legal and armed mobilizations and constructed a program that contextualized such grievances within larger national and even international frameworks. For example, of the government's forced military conscription, the Jaramillistas declared in the Plan de Cerro Prieto, "The current European war is neither democratic nor much less liberating; this war is a capitalist, bourgeois, and imperialist war to divide the world's weaker [nations] among themselves. For this they are dragging the poor, who have nothing to do with this war, to the slaughter because it is not a war of the people, since neither Germany, nor the United States, nor England . . . are democratic countries friendly to workers with whom democracy and the true desire for liberty lie."[17]

Despite the Marxist language that marks much of the Plan de Cerro Prieto, this position on World War II appears distinct from that of much of Mexico's Left, including the Mexican Communist Party. On one level, the Jaramillista position reflects resentment concerning the state's imposed levy. But it also reflects a critique of bourgeois democracy that is consistent with the Jaramillista vision of true democracy, which stems only from the rule of workers and campesinos and which refuses to place individual privileges above collective rights.[18] Indeed, the government's position during the war would have important implications for social groups in Mexico. Aside from the levy imposed on campesinos throughout the countryside, in 1942 President Ávila Camacho decreed the doctrine of "national unity" to confront the fascist threat. But this policy signaled more than a strategy against Nazism;

it was also an official declaration toning down the language of class struggle previously popularized by the revolutionary state, especially the Cárdenas administration. Rather than see their interests as antagonistic to those of the elite, campesinos and workers were to put aside economic grievances for the sake of national harmony. But this doctrine quickly began to fray at the seams, not only because it placed a disproportionate burden on the poor but because supposedly wartime measures such as these not only survived the war's end but actually intensified in subsequent decades.

While Jaramillo, Inclán, and the Barreto brothers all led actions against the government's military draft, Jaramillo's ideological formation stemmed from leftist principles, while the other leaders allied themselves with rightist elements such as the Sinarquistas. Still, both movements represented objective expressions of a widespread rural discontent, and the government would react in much the same way to them all.[19] José Barreto and his partner Abraham Sánchez were gunned down in November 1944. An intelligence document provides detail on the strategy to eliminate them: "They could only be captured by bribing one or two individuals who could tell us at what time they would arrive at their house. There, soldiers dressed in civilian clothing ambushed the home."[20] Attached to the memo are two chilling photographs of the bloody corpses.

The state did not want to have another Cristero Rebellion on its hands, and the ranks of the Sinarquistas were growing. From 1939 to 1940, UNS membership grew from 90,000 to 360,000, and by 1941 it had increased to 460,000. By 1943, the party had over half a million members, with committees organized in six hundred municipalities. Moreover, UNS adherents showed an incredible discipline and organizing capacity, holding rallies of between 10,000 and 40,000 people.[21] Employing a nationalist, religious, anticommunist rhetoric, the UNS gained support because it criticized unpopular government policies such as the military draft. Even in a heavily agrarista state like Morelos, campesinos joined Sinarquista ranks. In November 1943, campesinos from the Colonia Emiliano Zapata took up arms after the harvest, "following a well-known Sinarquista leader."[22] In Cuautla, the Sinarquista party was growing at an alarming rate.[23] The UNS also gained support among sugarcane workers in Morelos.[24] The government kept a close eye on the Sinarquistas and even conducted an investigation of the postal services to gain access to the list of all people throughout the country who received the party's newspaper.[25] While the UNS leadership consistently denied any plans for armed actions, the government felt threatened by the movement's ability to channel the discontent of many rank-and-file campesinos who had arms and might not hesitate to use them. In addition to the threat posed internationally by fascism's strength in Europe, the presence of small armed groups, or the rumors of them, in Mexico undermined the extent to which the state controlled the countryside. Finally, while no single rebel group in and of itself posed a serious threat to the government, there was always the possibility that they could make common cause.

And indeed, these groups did attempt to establish alliances. In his autobiography, Jaramillo wrote of an invitation made by José Barreto to hold a meeting in the rancho of Zacopoalco. Jaramillo was reluctant to meet with this group, because they fought for a "purely religious order that would return Mexico to the colonial era."[26] The meeting failed to take place on this occasion because, moments before the scheduled encounter, the Jaramillistas received word that the *federales* (soldiers) were moving in on them. Pedro García, a Jaramillista from Jojutla, described how Barreto and Inclán were anxious to have Jaramillo join them. According to García, these campesino leaders spoke of receiving support from Germany and Japan and stated that these countries would provide airplanes, arms, and technical assistance to carry out a revolution in Mexico. In interviews, some Jaramillistas mention a German emissary sent to offer support to Jaramillo in exchange for his allegiance to the Axis powers. Jaramillo, however, did not want anything to do with the Sinarquistas, "because they weren't consistent with his own ideals. The Germans would have wanted to derail Rubén's social struggle—its essence and popular base."[27] Moreover, explained another Jaramillista, the Germans would support Jaramillo in exchange for access to Mexico's natural resources, which merely meant turning over the reins of exploitation to another imperial power.[28]

Their stance against Mexico's involvement in World War II reflected the Jaramillistas' commitment to the principles of economic nationalism. Whether or not there was a German agent seeking an alliance with Jaramillo, and whether or not a meeting actually took place, such accounts reveal the ideological foundations of Jaramillismo and the extent to which the Jaramillista leadership understood itself within an international framework. Likewise, if the meeting did take place, it points to the way in which these groups were recognized by international powers as potential avenues through which to exert influence in Mexico. The Jaramillistas' brief flirtation with Sinarquista factions and, specifically, the decision not to form an alliance appear as important moments of ideological definition to a movement otherwise characterized by its tactical heterodoxy.

The Plan de Cerro Prieto

The Plan de Cerro Prieto represented a maturing of the Jaramillista movement. Emerging as a clandestine group after the 1942 Zacatepec strike, the campesinos following Jaramillo were only now becoming known as the Jaramillistas. Against a government who quickly labeled them bandits, the Jaramillistas drafted a political program that linked local grievances to larger national and international structures. The language of the document provides a taste of some of the Jaramillistas' ultimate aspirations. Its significance lies not so much in its concrete demands—which would have necessitated another revolution—but in the analysis it presented and the vision it contained. Reading the document, one gets the sense that the writers—pushed into operating outside the law and aware of government intransigence regarding even limited reforms—opted to lay out their own contrasting vision of justice. Their condition as an armed group provided them the space to do so. Much of the plan's importance thus lies in its understanding of local injustices in a national and international context.

Moreover, the plan reveals another layer of Jaramillista ideology, or at least that of its leadership, whose analysis of class exploitation and understanding of imperialism is enunciated in no uncertain terms. This tendency was a concrete manifestation of the influence of communist workers on Jaramillo and an example of how these ideas could circulate in the Mexican countryside. A close collaborator of Jaramillo and one of the contributors to the Plan de Cerro Prieto recalled that Jaramillo began to read Marxist-Leninist works that "came to shape much of his ideological position, even though he was quite reserved and never declared himself a Marxist-Leninist." Jaramillo, he said, "simply chose from those works what could be useful to our regional struggle in the state and the conditions in Mexico at the time. He did this especially given the permanent [official] hostility with which he and the party had to operate in."[29] As the government rendered hollow much of its revolutionary rhetoric by blocking legal channels of participation, it pushed those searching for reform into alternative tactical and more-radical analytical frameworks. These frameworks provided additional elements from which to critique the Mexican state.

Indeed, the Plan de Cerro Prieto launched into a full-on condemnation of government officials for "collaborating with capitalist, bourgeois, or pseudo-democratic forms of government."[30] Under the new order envisioned by the Jaramillistas, politicians—from the president down to municipal authorities—were not to receive a salary above their basic needs. This would ensure that officials were performing their job out of duty to the country and not for economic gain. Likewise, the plan called for the retraining of soldiers so that they understood their weapons to be for the protection of the entire Mexican population and not just to serve the interests of a small group of exploiters.[31] The Jaramillistas also made a call in a general sense for the elimination or reform of any law detrimental to the people. The plan proclaimed the need to create new legislation that was more protective of workers' rights.

The plan also called for an industrialization process that ended Mexico's dependence on manufacturers from other countries. Its writers criticized Mexico's disadvantaged position as a producer of raw materials poorly remunerated on the world market. "Mexico," they stated, "should go from a purely agrarian nation, to an industrial one that gives life to a working population, especially since it possesses the primary materials indispensable for producing what the Mexican people need."[32] This industrialization process was not to replace small-scale farming, but rather to provide the agricultural sector with the appropriate technical support so campesinos could live off the land. The Jaramillistas proposed to expropriate wealth from those who had enriched themselves at the cost of the poor and called for a tax system that did not place an undue burden on those with the least resources. These points in particular captured the feeling, expressed time and again in the Mexican countryside, that the labor of rural workers had generated wealth that had gone to benefit everyone but themselves. Elsewhere, Jaramillo captures the sentiment: "The little our crops leave us is snatched from us at ludicrous prices, prices that mean hunger. Hoarders, *criollos*, foreigners, enrich themselves and impoverish us."[33]

Jaramillo's use of the term "criollo," a reference to Spaniards born in Mexico, is noteworthy, for it is an implicit criticism of a class structure that in Mexico is heavily correlated with race. In Morelos, as in other parts of Mexico, the racial hierarchy established after the conquest placed those of lighter skin at the top, and this social order did not fundamentally change after independence. During the revolution the cry against "gachupines" (a pejorative term for Spaniards) could still be heard across Mexico and, especially in the countryside, it continued to be part of the rural lexicon in subsequent decades. But as the presence of the United States in Mexico grew in the twentieth century, *gringos* increasingly replaced gachupines as the objects of nationalist critiques. This sentiment is expressed in the Plan de Cerro Prieto in its call for an end to Washington's intervention in Mexico's affairs.[34]

The social reforms the Jaramillistas envisioned emphasized the development of human creativity. While they hailed the importance of work (the statement "Work is our motto" was written into this point in capital letters), they expressed the conviction that once the national wealth was in the hands of the people, workers were to enjoy all the comforts it engendered. The plan called for a six-hour work day (limited to five hours for night shifts) so that workers could spend more time "reading, thinking, writing," and engaging in other creative and educational activities.[35] At the same time, the Mexican people were to have access to all the resources necessary to facilitate travel throughout the Mexican territory so that they could get to know their entire country. Education was to be neither "capitalist nor officialist, nor religious."[36] Instead, schools should emphasize practical knowledge that could be applied to improve people's daily lives. Point 15 of the plan called for the relocation of tiny villages that, due to their isolation, did not have access to the infrastructure necessary for the well-being of their inhabitants. Housing was to be made available to everyone, and the concept of rent eliminated. In addition, families were entitled to have the necessary resources to maintain their cohesion and well-being, thus doing away with "the current situation in which many heads of household have children without food or nutrients, without clothes or shoes, and with no education. Instead, their home is a small shack, a nest of parasites and bugs that frequently kills the children of poor families."[37]

With these social changes, the Jaramillista plan argued that women would not have to resort to prostitution and seek work when their children were too young to be left alone. Every community—even the smallest village— would have child-care centers where children would receive the attention necessary for their full development. Such a demand shifted the burden of child rearing from the mother to the community aided by the state. The sense of collective responsibility is further evident in the plan to tend to elders, whose specialized needs would be met through the establishment of adequate, integral facilities that would do away with the situation in which "our progenitors, after giving children and more to the fatherland, now exhausted, remain completely abandoned. . . . The fatherland is ostensibly rich and well able to provide its people who worked and work to make it great."[38]

While much of the language of the Plan de Cerro Prieto has a marked anarcho-syndicalist tone, demands such as the one above revealed more traditional campesino notions of community, such as respect for elders. In this way, the document reflected the social composition of its authors who, besides campesinos, also included a few workers and rural schoolteachers. The anarchist or communist ideology of the somewhat more urban rebels provided the framework to an otherwise rustic document with a genuine campesino feel to it. One of the authors of the document explains, "The Plan de Cerro Prieto is a summary of the goals made during the uprisings. The Plan de Cerro Prieto was inspired by the 1910 movement and the agrarian actions of 1914 here in Morelos."[39] While the Plan de Cerro Prieto is quite distinct from the Plan de Ayala—each a reflection of its time and the nature of the movement—there are some parallels in the way the authors made provisions to care for the more vulnerable members of society and in their tendency to embrace rather than reject notions of progress.[40]

Like the Plan de Ayala, the Jaramillista plan looked to notions of progress that benefited Mexico's rural poor—especially through their call for industrialization and an increase in the technical assistance for agricultural production. Point 5, for example, called for "the intensification of agricultural production, but in a way that the producers benefit from [the profits] of these goods." Here it put forth a strong critique of intermediaries, who, it charged, were responsible for the high cost of living.[41] Nonetheless, in contrast to the Zapatistas, the Plan de Cerro Prieto contains socialist elements in its call for the nationalization of certain industries, redistribution of wealth, workers' ownership of factories, and a government of rural and industrial workers. This attention to workers' rights is noteworthy, for it demonstrated an expansion of Jaramillo's own political vision from his earlier focus on campesinos to embrace the common interests of agrarian and industrial workers. Even if the social basis of the Jaramillista was predominantly rural, by placing such emphasis on workers' rights, the plan established elements for an alliance with labor. Moreover, the plan presented the analysis that workers and campesinos had been defeated during the revolution because of their inability to come together and mount a common struggle.

In essence, the critique espoused in this document is actually far more radical than any proclamation the Jaramillistas made when they operated through legal channels. So long as they were clandestine, it seemed, the leadership might as well lay out their ideal for a just society. More significant, perhaps, was the fact that its assessment of the Mexican reality reflected the input of communist workers such as Mónico Rodríguez and rural schoolteachers like José Rodríguez who were trained in the socialist tradition. Such input resulted from the alliances made by the Jaramillistas, and they are an important example of how the movement was transformed as it came into contact with different social actors. As the Zapatistas did during the revolution, the Jaramillistas relied on organic intellectuals to articulate a larger vision within which to couch local demands. While the analysis that these leaders presented may have been distinct from that of the rank-and-file campesino participants, they shared an experience rooted in a similar reality of poverty. When teachers, who themselves came from poor families, arrived in remote and highly impoverished communities, they often began to identify with the plight of the campesinos.[42] Their role as facilitators of agrarian distribution placed them in a natural position as advocates of campesino rights.[43] To many, socialism may have been "more a feeling than a theory,"[44] and in the countryside teachers were able to present it "not as some abstract and alien doctrine, but rather in terms of an old, comprehensible polarity—rich and poor, exploiters and exploited."[45] In fact, when teachers were sent to instruct distant communities, they too were to become "ruralized" and were often given ejidal parcels to cultivate.[46] The words of José Faria, a rural schoolteacher close to Jaramillo, provide an example of how these socialist ideas were presented. "What is communism really?" asks Faria, "If we look for its root, it means to live in common. But the bourgeoisie took it as an enemy word because a socialist or communist system means to distribute the wealth more or less equally."[47] Such was the language of socialism in Mexico's countryside.

Existing studies on rural schoolteachers focus primarily on the period of revolutionary state consolidation ending in 1940. Some of these works assess the role of educators as agents of the expanding state, as well as the resistance of many campesinos to be molded into a particular type of citizen.[48] But the role of socialist teachers in the post-1940 period, and especially their relationship to campesino organizing, remains to be explored. Such an extensive analysis is beyond the scope of this study, but the influence of a handful of teachers in the Jaramillista movement suggests they could have a radicalizing effect on campesino organizing. Indeed, even though socialist education was officially abandoned by the Ávila Camacho administration, a certain radicalism had been imbued by the initial focus on class analysis, as well as the hostility these teachers experienced from the church and the large landowners. This consciousness was heightened as teachers labored in conditions of utter poverty. As these educators became the first to encounter the contradictions of spreading the government's doctrine of progress and modernization, they often went from agents of state consolidation to village leaders who articulated community grievances against the state itself. That a large proportion of teachers were members of the communist party added another layer of radicalism to their interaction with rural dwellers.[49] The role played by teachers in the Jaramillista movement presaged an important dynamic evident in later armed movements in Mexico, where teachers became central protagonists.

The Jaramillistas' analysis of the revolution extended to the new structures of exploitation that emerged in postrevolutionary Mexico. Campesinos were subject to the vicissitudes of the market, to the producers and their rules of exchange, and to private agricultural industries doing everything in their power to dispossess them of their land. When campesinos attempted to use government channels to solicit land or credit, not only did they encounter reluctant local and federal authorities, but they also had to navigate a bureaucratic morass so complicated, time consuming, and costly that it provided little hope.[50] It was precisely these grievances that led many campesinos to join Jaramillista ranks. In combating the local manifestation of larger structural problems such as uneven land distribution, political bossism, and price gouging, the Jaramillistas touched issues that reverberated nationally. For example, if workers and campesinos had gained control of the Zacatepec sugar mill, not only would they have affected an entire power group within the sugar industry, but their actions would have set important precedents for other cooperatives or nationalized industries.

Moreover, Jaramillo's analysis of local problems most often extended towards the national and international economic order. Thus, not only did he demand higher prices for particular crops cultivated by campesinos; he criticized the international economic system for placing little value on these products. The attention the Plan de Cerro Prieto gives to workers is especially significant, given that it was produced by what was at its core a campesino movement. The vision of a just society, in which campesinos take power in alliance with labor, belies traditional conceptions of peasant movements as ones that present narrow solutions to local demands. The far-reaching structural changes outlined by the Jaramillistas in this plan present another example of the multilayered nature of peasant consciousness, one deepened in alliance with other social groups.

The Army's Pursuit

The Jaramillistas used the Plan de Cerro Prieto to garner support and educate the rural population about their rights. In the process they created the networks that would later support their political party. Soldiers—*el gobierno* or *guachos*, as campesinos still refer to them—were hot on the Jaramillista trail. Thus, Jaramillo's original plans to "concentrate solely on protecting" himself led to several open confrontations with the army.[51] In the process, the Jaramillistas' use of armed struggle became both a measure of self-defense and a political tactic of last resort. Many of those who had taken up arms with Jaramillo in 1943 had also done so as a means of protecting themselves. Some of them had suffered attempts on their lives for speaking out against abuses in the Emiliano Zapata sugar mill. Cirilo García describes how Zacatepec gun men targeted his entire family after a dispute between his uncles and the local cacique. One of his uncles was killed, another was wounded, and much of his family fled the state. "So I had to join just to save myself from persecution."[52] Other participants in the Jaramillista armed struggle were acquaintances or *compadres* who insisted on following Jaramillo.[53] The social networks that constituted and sustained the movement were thus at once ideological, pragmatic, and familial.

Moreover, since Jaramillo had been a Methodist pastor, he had quite an extensive social organization in the municipality of Tlaquiltenango, the largest territory in Morelos. This region was lush in its vegetation, had numerous small mountains, and was dotted with little villages, or *rancherías.* Here, Jaramillistas depended on the population for their survival. Samuel Piedra, from El Higuerón, recalled how Jaramillo and his men would stay at his house and hold meetings of between ten and twenty people under the cover of darkness. "Jaramillo would stay in that little room with four or five other people. When they left, only they knew in what direction they headed. They would travel, visiting other towns, and there were many people who received them in this way." Jaramillo met Piedra's father and had baptized his children when he was Tlaquiltenango's Methodist pastor. When the Jaramillistas could not enter the town due to the presence of the authorities, Piedra recalled how his father sent him to take food to the rebels. "I was young, between eight and ten, and my father told me, 'Get on the mare; you are going to take them food.' There were lots of federales, and they would rough us up, especially if we had food or water."[54] Pedro Herminio, from Xoxocotla, also participated in this way. As a young boy he acted as the group's messenger. Aside from transporting correspondence, he let people in the villages know where and when the Jaramillistas would hold their next meeting. Herminio was also in charge of buying the supplies for the group. "You had to buy everything separately, the salt here, sugar there, cigarettes somewhere else, or people would get suspicious."[55]

Herminio's description provides an idea of the repressive climate that the government created as it pursued the Jaramillistas. And yet the group could not have operated clandestinely without the support of a substantial part of the local population. They depended on other campesinos not only for food and water but, just as importantly, for their silence. As with other guerrilla groups, the armed nucleus of Jaramillistas had hundreds of children, elderly, men, and women who were silently complicit or actively provided information, food, routes, clothes, arms, medicine, and correspondence.[56]

The Jaramillistas tapped into a vast social network throughout the state of Morelos and in parts of Puebla. Armed cadres fluctuated between 25 and 150 men, depending on the municipality. Jaramillo's contacts in each town helped sustain the web of support and communication. One area where Jaramillo had many supporters was Los Hornos. A small town in the municipality of Tlaquiltenango, located in the southern part of the Morelos, Los Hornos is surrounded by low mountains, a perfect location to hide a guerrilla group. As he had in El Higuerón, Jaramillo had gotten to know many people there through his work as a Methodist pastor. His second wife, Epifania Zúñiga, was also born and raised there. Moreover, community members in Los Hornos were staunchly opposed to the government's military draft and not only provided material support but also additional recruits to the armed group. In this town, the Jaramillistas even received help from members of the federal rural defense forces, yet another example of the incomplete consolidation of the postrevolutionary state. In Morelos, the government had incorporated into the rural defense league former Zapatistas who did not want to give up their arms. But it was not always successful in gaining their complete allegiance. Don Lino Manzanares described how his father, Lencho Manzanares, a member of this guard, provided food for the Jaramillistas and kept quiet about their presence in the area. "My father would tell me to take them food. 'Be discrete,' he ordered. No matter what my father saw, he said nothing. When the government asked him, he always replied, 'I saw nothing.'"[57] Lencho Manzanares was not the only member of the government's armed forces to help out Jaramillistas. Crescencio Castillo, a Jaramillista from San Roque, Puebla, recalled how, on his way home from distributing leaflets—and making a brief stop at a local cantina—he was followed and momentarily detained by an army officer. When the officer saw the Jaramillista literature, he gave Castillo a harsh scolding—not for his affiliation with Jaramillo, but for drinking when he had such responsibilities to the movement: "'You're lucky it was me you ran into; had it been someone else, just think how many people you would have incriminated. Next time you are doing this, stick to the task at hand.'"[58] The allegiance shown to Jaramillo in these ranks of governmental authority stemmed from a loyalty to Zapata's legacy.

These members of law enforcement were the exception, though. State and federal authorities were on the constant lookout for Jaramillistas and on numerous occasions detained participants and sympathizers. In August 1943, for example, the military captured Victoriano Reynoso Sánchez, Pedro Díaz, and Amador Ocampo in the district of Jojutla. When interrogated about their affiliation to Jaramillo, they stated that Jaramillo had taken up arms in opposition to the draft. In their deposition, however, they also mentioned that Jaramillo spoke of a rebellion at the national level. Two of them admitted having been detained—and pardoned—on a previous occasion for their association with Jaramillo. But their commitment was not easy to break, and they had rejoined Jaramillo a week after their pardon.[59] The military confiscated a modest amount of weaponry and charged them with the crime of rebellion and seditious behavior. This event also appears in Ravelo's collection of Jaramillista testimonies. But in these testimonies, the men report that the authorities tortured them to obtain information. Their accounts state how, after detaining them in Puente de Ixtla, their captors proceeded to hang and beat them until they confessed the whereabouts of Jaramillo. They were also forced to identify a list of thirty-five other people and to take the soldiers to the place where they stored their weapons.[60]

Three months later, three other individuals were captured by the military. One of them, Guadalupe Visioso, was shot and killed, supposedly while escaping. The federal troops searched the homes of the other two, and in the house of Francisco Rosales they unearthed Jaramillo's portfolio, consisting of 221 pages, six small notebooks, two Communist Party statutes, and the General Law on Cooperative Organizations. In their defense, the prisoners stated that they barely knew Jaramillo. They claimed to have no contact with him and that they had been offered money to join him or had been forced to do so. Francisco Rosales argued that he had no idea how Jaramillista literature ended up in his home. The same file with their depositions included a list of twenty-two individuals compiled by the military—all from Tlaquiltenango, El Higuerón, and Nexpa—who had been charged and later pardoned for their association with Jaramillo. Of the twenty-two, eighteen rejoined Jaramillo's ranks after being pardoned, and for two others this was their third "offense" as Jaramillistas.[61] Based on this information, and knowing that they could face harsh punishment, it is likely that the confessions, in which individuals distanced themselves from Jaramillo, were an attempt to disguise their actual relationship to the movement's leader.

With soldiers in hot pursuit, the Jaramillistas also had several confrontations with the army. Such battles contributed to the characterization of Jaramillo's group as a significant rebel force. During one of their early confrontations with the army in December 1943, Jaramillo's wife, Epifania Zúñiga, who had joined the rebel forces, saved his life by shooting a lieutenant just as he and his men were moving in on the rebels. On this occasion, the soldiers shot and wounded the Jaramillista Félix Serdán. The army took him captive, simultaneously obtaining several of the rebels' documents and a Mexican flag. The group also lost two horses in the battle, including Jaramillo's own "El Agrarista," a present from President Cárdenas.[62]

Other confrontations during the following year resulted in much higher casualties, such as when the army caught up with the Jaramillistas between San Rafael and Chinameca. Here the group of about fifty Jaramillistas had stopped at a water hole when the army began shooting. The rebels tried to escape along the riverbank, which was a few meters below the road, but the army saw them and began shooting. According to Cirilo García, one of the rebel combatants, the Jaramillistas, armed mostly with .30–30 rifles, the standard weapon during the revolution, were able to shoot quite a few soldiers. But when they began to run out of ammunition and retreat, the government forces shot and killed six of Jaramillo's men. The local authorities took the bodies and exhibited them in the municipal hall of Jojutla, where their relatives could come and claim them.[63] In contrast, the army rarely made public its own losses, thus avoiding the appearance of vulnerability.

The bodies of fallen Jaramillistas were not always returned to family members, especially when the casualties resulted from targeted persecution rather than an armed confrontation. On one occasion, two federales arrived at a house where Crescencio "Chencho" Castillo and Ambrosio Pérez had come to deliver a message. Castillo managed to escape thanks to a combination of luck and wit: when the federales entered the house he fled into a back shed where the homeowner stored cantaloupes. When the officer found him, Castillo had already sat down and sliced a piece of fruit with his knife. The officer then demanded to know, with his rifle in Castillo's ribs, what he was doing there. Castillo simply answered, "Eating cantaloupes." The officer wasted no more time with Castillo. He continued to search for Jaramillistas and managed to capture Ambrosio Pérez. "They disappeared him; we never heard from him again. They killed him," recalled Castillo.[64] Support for or collaboration with the Jaramillistas was thus punishable by death.

Jaramillo's Amnesty

When the Jaramillistas first took up arms in 1943, they entered a terrain where the folk version of the revolution persisted and was kept alive by popular ballads, memories, and the meaning people attributed to their participation in this major national upheaval. Moreover, by appropriating the image of Zapata, the state had also disseminated his message, including the legitimacy of armed struggle. The presence of an armed group of campesinos in Zapata's homeland dramatized the inherent contradiction of a ruling party who claimed Zapata as a founding father but who paid increasingly little attention to the principles of his struggle. The army's inability to eliminate the Jaramillista rebels without a major counterinsurgency operation led the government to opt for a different strategy and, in 1944, President Ávila Camacho offered Jaramillo amnesty. Jaramillo enjoyed a degree of legitimacy in Morelos that the government could not afford to ignore. At a time when much of Mexico's high-ranking Left had heeded calls for national unity to join the war effort in Europe, the state attempted to also bring into its fold the more recalcitrant popular elements. Much of the government's energies had been dedicated to combating movements from the Right, such as the Cristeros and Sinarquistas; reducing hostilities with a group that spoke the same language of revolution could only further its legitimacy.

This would not be the only time Jaramillo received an official pardon, a dynamic that revealed the particularities of Mexico's twentieth-century state. The various strands that loosely held together the postrevolutionary consensus at times unraveled, laying bare some of the profound divisions that had fueled the decade-long civil war. In their rebellion, the Jaramillistas evoked the very process from which the state claimed to derive legitimacy. Even their turn to armed struggle had a basis in the Mexican Constitution. Article 39, consistently invoked by Jaramillo and many other groups, including today's Zapatistas, states, "National sovereignty resides essentially and originally in the people. All public power originates in the people and is for the benefit of the people. The people have at all times the inalienable right to alter or modify the form of government."[65] This legislative principle has served to situate popular protest within the constitutional framework, even when, as with the Jaramillistas, they were operating outside the law.

The counterpart to this dynamic was the government's propensity to offer amnesty to the very individuals it declared subversives. Pardoning the leadership, often the first step in the process of co-option, would come to be a classic PRI tactic, one that contributed to an image of political flexibility. With leaders that could not be co-opted, repression often ensued. Years later, when Jaramillo wrote about the meeting in which President Ávila Camacho granted him amnesty, he described it skeptically. In reply to the president's offer, he said, "Look, Mr. President, to the politicians in my state these safe-conducts do not command any value or respect, for the day that these men wish to hurt us, they [will], justifying themselves with any pretext, true or untrue. . . . I will continue to consider myself as a man without any guarantees before these men, and if I encounter an aggression, I will defend myself."[66]

The amnesty was accompanied by an offer of some land in the San Quintín Valley, in the northern state of Baja California. But Jaramillo viewed this proposal as a thinly veiled exile.[67] Instead, he would use this opportunity to continue organizing in Morelos, this time through a political campaign for state governor. That a rebel, soon after receiving amnesty, could run for state governor reveals the degree to which the government continued to seek legitimacy in Zapata's homeland. Whether it would adhere to its own rules was a different matter.

CHAPTER FOUR

"Like Juárez, with
Our Offices on the Run"

The Jaramillistas achieved some of their most massive mobilizations during the 1946 and 1952 elections, when Jaramillo ran for governor of Morelos. The decision to create the Agrarian-Workers' Party of Morelos (PAOM) and participate in Mexico's electoral system is one of the clearest examples of how elements of Cardenismo continued to coexist in the Jaramillista movement alongside other traditions such as Zapatismo. Cárdenas's policies empowered the rural population by legitimizing their demands and making these a priority during his administration. For the Jaramillistas, Cardenismo was the model of how, in the right hands, power could be used to benefit the poor. Taking this idea one step further, they would now promote a "genuine campesino" for governor of Morelos.[1]

The decision to form a political party in a country whose government came to be controlled by a single party provides an important glimpse into the resistance that accompanied the consolidation of this ruling structure. It is a measure of the possibilities the Jaramillistas still saw of influencing the course of the revolution. In the 1940s and 1950s, many popular groups still envisioned an alternative political future that could be realized within the system. The north of Mexico was host to similar electoral contentions. In the state of Sonora, for example, the Popular Party (Partido Popular or PP) challenged the PRI in the 1949 gubernatorial race, one that, like the PAOM's, would be strongly marked by state repression.[2] In Sonora's southern city of Ciudad Obregón, the popular campesino leader Rafael Contreras lost the mayoral race, "despite overwhelming popular support."[3] These local and regional electoral challenges coalesced at the national level in 1952, when the Henriquistas—disaffected members of the PRI who sought a return to Cardenismo—mounted a powerful campaign against the official party. By joining them, the Jaramillistas had, for the first time, the opportunity to establish alliances at the national level. The idea of forming a party originated with a handful of Jaramillistas, but this organizational structure soon spread, first among the group who had taken up arms with Jaramillo, and then among people throughout the state who heeded the call of party representatives organizing in their home communities.

It is important to keep in mind the relationship between the electoral strategies pursued in 1946 and 1952 and the armed resistance that took place at other intervals in the history of the Jaramillistas. Considering the elections first and then analyzing the guerrilla actions allows us to better highlight certain frameworks that accompanied each mobilization. The two episodes of electoral participation illustrate the importance of the Cardenista legacy and the Jaramillistas' continued willingness, despite the government's use of fraud and repression, to play by the rules. The 1946 and 1952 campaigns represent the clearest example of the way the government blocked popular efforts to organize through legal channels. By using repression to confront peaceful, reformist movements, the government not only revealed its authoritarian nature but also provided some of the strongest rationale for armed struggle. In the end, government repression of these electoral campaigns pushed the group in a more radical direction. In this experience the Jaramillista movement reveals the extent to which guerrillas can trace their origins to the violence of those in power.

A Party of the Poor

The Jaramillistas formed their political party in the aftermath of President Ávila Camacho's counterrevolutionary reforms. Upon taking office in 1940,

3. Jaramillistas at 1952 election rally, Cuernavaca, Morelos. *Archivo General de la Nación, Fondo Hermanos Mayo, Jaramillo.*

the new president amended a series of laws that marked a change in the revolution's course; he abandoned Cárdenas's strong economic nationalism and the populist policies designed to temper the exploitation inherent in capitalism and instead adopted a system that encouraged private investment and openly embraced a foreign-driven modernization. Moreover, the state sought to use agricultural production to finance and support industrialization by providing the urban sector with cheap food.[4] Increasingly, government policy accommodated private property and export agriculture, often to the detriment of the ejido or subsistence *minifundios* (small farms). In 1942, for example, Ávila Camacho implemented an agrarian reform law that eased former restrictions designed to alleviate land concentration. Cattle ranches and fields of key exports such as henequen, rubber, coconut, grapes, olives, vanilla, and quinine could extend beyond previous limits to as much as three hundred hectares.[5] Moreover, the accompanying Law of Agricultural Credit undermined the ejido by diminishing the funds available to its cultivators.

Thanks partly to state-subsidized inputs of production and infrastructure projects, agribusiness soon established its predominance in the Mexican countryside. In their haste to pursue an agricultural policy based on large-scale production, mechanization, and improved seeds and fertilizers, post-Cardenista governments never gave ejidos or small-scale farming a chance. Instead, new agribusiness sectors dominated by old hacendados and capital from the United States were hailed as the most efficient way to increase production. However, Mexico's Green Revolution, as the transformation in the agricultural sector became known, did not increase crop yields for domestic food consumption, as most of the efforts were geared towards exports such as animal feed, cotton, grapes, strawberries, and winter vegetables headed for North American markets.[6] As a result of this shift away from basic food crops, by 1970, Mexico—a country which a decade earlier boasted of its ability to feed its entire population—was importing 20 percent of its foodstuffs.[7]

In Morelos, the effects of these national economic policies began to be felt in 1940. While most of the population still made a living directly from agriculture, their ability to do so became increasingly precarious. The growing population, lack of irrigation projects, and the increasing costs of producing corn diminished rural dwellers' ability to support themselves through subsistence farming. Under this pressure, campesinos turned to commercial crops such as wheat, rice, and sugarcane. A few planted tomatoes, onions, and cantaloupes.[8] Such crops had a higher market yield than corn and had fairly predictable price fluctuations. But still, campesinos had to rely on a vast web of middlemen for seeds, fertilizers, and transportation. When all was said and done, even in a good year, campesinos had barely enough for subsistence.

Reflecting on his participation in the movement, one Jaramillista recalled, "The revolution ended, but what we fought for was not complete. We gained land, but not the means to work it. So the rich, the old hacendados, got together to see how they could make a profit. So even though the campesinos farmed their plot of land, who were they going to sell the products to? So the monopolists joined together to make large profits by offering the campesinos loans. As conditions for their loans we had to sell our crops back to them at half the [market] price."[9] While the Jaramillistas consistently presented themselves as heirs to the Zapatista tradition, as actors during a distinct historical moment facing profoundly transformed conditions, their battle was a different one. The Zapatistas did not seek to hold public office themselves so much as to ensure that elected officials were sympathetic to the campesino way of life.[10] When Zapatistas did exercise control of Morelos for a brief period during the revolution, they emphasized village leadership and repartitioned land with particular deference to communal customs.[11] Given Morelos's proximity to Mexico City, the Zapatistas most likely understood themselves to be part of the Mexican nations, but their immediate concerns were local and centered on the issue of land.[12] "In this insistent provincialism," Womack commented, "was the movement's strength and its weakness."[13]

The Jaramillistas, on the other hand, participated far more self-consciously in the national project, and the PAOM was founded on the goal of propelling campesinos to the state government. While their struggle was mostly limited to the state of Morelos, their rhetoric was consistently national. Seeking to elect a campesino as governor of Morelos, the PAOM began by noting that the poor had little chance of seeing their interests protected so long as state officials were not drawn from the popular classes. Printed on the lower right-hand corner of the PAOM stationery were the following words: "As long as the campesinos and workers have no access to public power, their interests will not be guaranteed."[14] This theme dominated both the 1946 and the 1952 gubernatorial campaigns. The Jaramillistas extended the principles of popular power to campaign financing; the one-peso bonds they sold to support the PAOM read, "The people of Morelos will be free from the crisis in which they live when they themselves voluntarily support the expenses of the civic electoral campaign of their representatives without the intervention of moneyed politicians or voracious financiers."[15] This statement encompasses the difference they saw between the official party and their own.

Although these campaigns were strongly influenced by Cardenista rhetoric, they also went beyond the system fashioned by the populist president by insisting on popular appropriation of government offices. When Bernabel Subdía, a campesino from Los Hornos, explained his support of Jaramillo's candidacy, he stated, "His ideals were going to be different. Yes. He was knowledgeable, he was a campesino, he knew the ways of the campesinos, their needs. He wanted to appropriate the position for the good of the campesino."[16] Subdía's assessment that Jaramillo wanted to "appropriate" the governor's position for the good of the campesinos reveals a view of the political offices as inherently working against, or at least being indifferent to, campesinos. These positions thus needed to be taken over by someone of goodwill, someone who knew the ways of the campesinos.[17] The Jaramillistas contrasted their own mobilizations to those carried out by politicians—even the FPPM (Federation of Parties of the Mexican People), Henríquez Guzmán's party, to which they were allied at the national level during the elections of 1952. Gorgonio Alonso's words describing the coalition between the FPPM and the PAOM is telling: "Here we formed two committees, one of the politicians, and the other one made up by us. . . . But they [the politicians] didn't do the work. So we organized all the towns and then they'd go make an appearance with the General [Henríquez Guzmán] and declare that the campaign was going wonderfully."[18] Alonso's statement reveals the tensions intrinsic in a mobilization strategy that combined Cárdenas's legacy and the ideals of grassroots organizing. From this alliance would emerge some of the residual contradictions born of the revolutionary compromise. The gulf that existed between the elite and popular groups became especially evident after the 1952 elections, when top Henriquista leaders were offered government posts and the poor were demobilized through repression.

The PAOM organized support for its candidate by forming one- or two-person committees that were assigned to visit towns throughout the state of Morelos. The party financed itself almost completely through membership dues and financial support from preexisting social networks, especially during the first campaign. It also collected donations at demonstrations. Members of the organizing committees often traveled throughout the state and stayed at the homes of relatives, compadres, friends, or members of the party. Some recruiters carried a letter of introduction from Jaramillo asking the hosts to provide them room and board. The women of the household cooked for the visitors, while the men sent their children to notify specific people about the meeting. These gatherings were usually held under cover of darkness. According to many accounts, more men than women attended these small gatherings. Rural social codes held that politicking should be left to the men. In addition, husbands often explicitly prohibited their wives from attending, under the pretext that they would not be able to keep the meetings a secret. Still, at public demonstrations, women were always very visible supporters.

The Jaramillistas campaigned against the incomplete nature of revolutionary reforms, the pervasive poverty in the countryside, and the persistent exclusion of campesinos from the decisionmaking process. The following passage is representative of the way in which they framed their grievances: "It is no use that we work until we are exhausted, it is no use that the revolution gave us land, it is no use that they give us credit if, in the end, the product of our labor is not enough to satisfy our most urgent necessities. . . . Furthermore, while campesinos work themselves to death, our exploiters sit in their comfortable offices without a care. From there they conjure up numbers and make calculations as to the immense quantities that each of our harvests should leave them." The same document called on campesinos to unite and secure their rights by placing "their own" in power. "In this manner," it explained, "we will triumph and will have fulfilled our duty as free, conscious, revolutionary citizens and as men of dignity."[19] During the 1946 campaign, and even more so in 1952, the Jaramillistas challenged the official party's claim over the revolution. Emerging from Jaramillista proposals was an attempt to keep alive the strands of the revolution which had the potential to empower campesinos. In fact, taken to their logical conclusion, the PAOM asserted, these principles mandated that workers and campesinos assume the reins of power, an idea fundamentally different from the bourgeois democracy set up by the 1917 constitution.

Thus, although the PAOM's political platform presented reformist propositions that differed from the structural transformation demanded in the

Plan de Cerro Prieto, the Jaramillistas were still appealing to previous notions of class struggle popularized during the 1920s and 1930s. Such language "politicized rural people's understanding of class and citizenship," not only in the countryside, but among the urban proletariat.[20] Still, the party as a whole shied away from explicitly Marxist language and instead emphasized Cardenismo and the revolution. As Jaramillo declared during one demonstration, "The Zapatista ideals and the best principles of the Mexican Revolution itself are being undermined."[21] These appeals resounded against Ávila Camacho's move to tone down revolutionary rhetoric and instead promote a doctrine of national unity. Arguing that a unified nation was necessary in the context of the Second World War, the Mexican government used this rhetoric in confronting social groups—especially labor—who sought concessions from the state. It is no surprise, therefore, that in the Plan de Cerro Prieto, the Jaramillistas had proclaimed themselves fiercely against Mexico's involvement in the war. When the Jaramillistas began their political campaign in 1945, the war was close to over, but the policies justified under the ideology of national unity were only just beginning. Thus, while the PAOM's platform toned down the demands made in the Plan de Cerro Prieto for the purposes of the electoral struggle, it nevertheless expressed an opposition, based largely on the Cardenista legacy, to Ávila Camacho's rollback of revolutionary reforms.

In this vein, for the 1946 elections the PAOM issued its "Minimum Program for Political Action and Governance," outlining a fifty-one-point proposal for agrarian, labor, economic, and educational policy. The document called for the preservation of the ejido, not as a relic of some past agrarian utopia, but as a way for campesinos to subsist in a modernizing world. The PAOM attempted to ameliorate campesino vulnerability by seeking to place technological advances in the hands of smallholders. The program called for machinery and transportation to support intense ejido agriculture, as well as irrigation projects, road construction, storage facilities, fertilizers, accessible credit under ejidal control, and small industrial annexes.[22] The Jaramillistas directly took on the idea of modernization, stating "no progress is truly revolutionary nor integrally democratic and popular, if it does not at the same time assure the masses an increasing economic well-being [and] a higher standard of living."[23] Their vision went beyond electoral democracy and linked political rights to economic ones. Whereas post-1940 government policies assumed—or at least stated—that the needs of workers and campesinos would be met automatically by a modern industrializing economy, the PAOM espoused the principle that progress was defined through the well-being of the masses. The PAOM thus did not oppose industrialization. On the contrary, several of its points promoted the idea of a modern industrialized nation. But its strategy made the ejido, not the latifundio, the basic unit of production, and campesinos, rather than capitalists, were to be in control of this production.

The principle of organizing around popular needs also applied to the industrial sector. While the party was not as clear on how factories should be run, it was very explicit that they should be organized to meet the needs of workers. The PAOM called for the establishment of local laws that would calculate living expenses in each region and use this figure as a base to establish an adjustable salary that guaranteed the basic necessities and economic improvement of workers. Point 2 of the section on labor of the PAOM's political program reads: "The party will push to conduct a study regarding the cost of living in each region so that the worker's economy and available resources for life may be improved."[24] The Jaramillistas also called for the establishment of good, clean, affordable housing, health care centers, recreational and sports facilities, libraries and day-care centers where women could leave their children during work hours. The demand for day-care centers is remarkable, as it suggests a social organization in which it was not assumed that women would stay home caring for their children. The PAOM did not present a socialist platform advocating ownership of the means of production, but it did emphasize the need for mechanisms by which workers could protect their rights.[25] Notably, it recognized the working class as the agent of genuine social change, stating, "The Mexican Revolution had, from its beginning, a definite class sense. It is the proletariat which predominates in the popular masses, and whose liberation constitutes the immediate objective fundamental to Revolution. The working class is, by definition, the revolutionary class, and, because of its organization, represents the most important factor in social and economic transformation."[26] This declaration again appears in explicit contrast to the policies of Ávila Camacho, whose taming of the revolution involved a deliberate campaign against organized labor. Citing World War II as rationale, not only did the president enact legislation severely restricting the right to strike, but Mexico's National Labor Confederation (part of the official party) voluntarily relinquished its right to strike. In the face of an official policy increasingly hostile to labor, the

Jaramillistas appealed to the class essence of the Mexican Revolution and to labor as agents of social change. These stances reflected the way the Jaramillistas, who were overwhelmingly of campesino extraction, sought to forge links with workers. Zacatepec laborers and rural schoolteachers, many of whom espoused socialist or communist ideologies, participated actively in the formation of the PAOM, and much of the party's language reveals their influence in developing its vision.

The PAOM proposed the establishment of a unified state coalition of workers as a way to avoid division among various labor organizations. This coalition would institute job-placement programs for the unemployed and regulate local labor laws so that all decisions regarding severance pay would be resolved in no more than a week.[27] Unlike the Plan de Cerro Prieto, which called for the formation of a national council of workers and campesinos to administer all social goods, the PAOM's platform was of a more populist nature, calling for a strong interventionist state, a hallmark of Cardenismo. The Jaramillistas' ideas on the economy again demonstrated a desire to resolve some of the population's basic needs. The first point in this section called on the government to place publicly owned real estate not serving a social function at the disposal of "class organizations for collective use."[28] Other provisions called for vacant land to be divided and sold to campesinos in plots no larger than six hectares for the creation of small farms. The party called for the creation of credit organizations for workers and campesinos that would charge no more than 3 percent interest, the organization of consumer cooperatives in all industrial workplaces, and the revision of tax laws to alleviate the fiscal burden of the poor. The PAOM promised to extend electricity to the entire state of Morelos as a means to promote its industrialization and pledged to "fight for the total reorganization of the Zacatepec complex, to change it back to the original norms corresponding with the vision of General Lázaro Cárdenas, who created it."[29] The Zacatepec cooperative figured prominently in the party's platform, its design serving as a model of production that could benefit campesinos within the context of industrial modernization. Finally, the PAOM made a firm point against economic imperialism, stating that all monopolies should be abolished and "imperialist capital" prevented from owning economic resources.

Interestingly, the Jaramillistas' proposals on education are the most extensive—yet another indication of the important role of rural teachers in the movement. These proposals demonstrate the legacy of Cardenismo and the extent to which the Jaramillistas embraced notions of progress associated with the educational system. Schools represented a source of cultural empowerment and economic mobility. Moreover, conscious of the ways in which the written word had historically been used against illiterate populations, learning how to read and write was seen as a tool with which campesinos could defend their rights. The PAOM proposed a doubling of schools in rural areas and a 10 percent increase in urban centers. These schools were to comply with their "social function of cultural and economic orientation appropriate to each region in order that their educational influence might also reach adults and achieve the most rapid progress for the Morelos population."[30] The government was to provide scholarships for poor elementary school students who obtained good grades.

Part of the educational reforms included an emphasis on the training of new teachers. For example, the PAOM called for the creation of rural *normales* (teacher training schools), where instructors would be trained "in accordance with the social tendencies of the revolution." In addition, the party proposed periodic courses for instructors to keep them abreast of the latest pedagogical innovations, and annual conferences where teachers from the entire country would come together and learn from each other's experiences. In order to expose the population to a wide range of knowledge, the government was to create mobile libraries stocked with material accessible to the population, as well as promote artistic groups that would give "open-air performances portraying social dramas."[31] As in the Plan de Cerro Prieto, this party platform devoted attention to the cultivation of the human spirit.

The PAOM proposed to provide schools with the appropriate equipment and personnel to impart technical skills, as well as to establish regional educational institutions capable of conducting technological experimentation. The party would "form missionary brigades that would travel to the most remote regions of the state, to provide basic industry courses to promote campesino initiative in the production of local crafts."[32] In this manner, campesinos could commercialize products unique to their region without being at the mercy of caciques and price gougers. Such programs were aimed at protecting campesino autonomy and eliminating some of the new structures that contributed to their poverty.

While the Plan of Cerro Prieto called for the end of the "capitalist-imperialist" system of exploitation, a new type of government, and a new constitution, the PAOM's platform could be fully implemented within Mexico's existing political and economic system. The PAOM presented their program within the framework bequeathed by the revolution, stating, "The party will maintain a close relationship with all revolutionary associations in the country and will fight for the maintenance and commitment to the principles of the Mexican Revolution."[33] Yet, the fact that they labeled their list of principles a "minimum program" indicates that their goals went beyond the more reformist policies enumerated in this document.

The Elections

Appeals to the revolution resonated differently depending on the region. In Morelos, they were translated into the familiar language of Zapatismo. Jaramillo's popularity lay partly in his connection to this struggle during the revolution. As one Jaramillista stated, "When he [Jaramillo] launched his campaign in 1945, we heard people talk about him, but we didn't know him. People said he was fighting for the ideals of the revolution, that the land would be free to cultivate whatever one wanted, not what the men [in power] wanted."[34] Jaramillo's appeal stemmed from Zapata's principles of "tierra y libertad" and the resentment increasingly felt in the countryside by campesinos who found themselves bearing the costs of Mexico's economic miracle.

Despite local sympathy, the PAOM faced an uphill battle in the electoral process. The party failed to register Jaramillo's candidacy by the January 30 deadline in 1946 and was thus technically disqualified from campaigning. It is unclear why the PAOM leaders did not register their party and candidate on time, but, as novices in the electoral system, most likely they were not aware of this stipulation. The president and secretary of the party did attempt to register the PAOM candidate on March 8, 1946.[35] Upon receiving the PAOM's application, state authorities sent a letter to the minister of the interior requesting his "esteemed opinion on the case so they could resolve the matter in a way that the office not be surprised by unwarranted complaints."[36] The memo reported that the PAOM had not yet presented the necessary documentation to prove its candidate met the prerequisites and that, even if the candidate did meet such requirements, "there was a strike against him [Jaramillo] in that he was a leader in the 1943 subversive movement and the state constitution strictly prohibits citizens who have taken part in that type of movement from running for public office." Federal authorities must have recommended that Jaramillo be allowed to run regardless, because the governor's office soon announced the registration of party and candidate, "keeping in mind that our constitutional regime is based on democratic principles, and we hope that this government will not receive unjustifiable charges that it intends to curtail the civic rights of citizens."[37] Such democratic principles, however, vanished by election day, which was sullied by numerous complaints of irregularities, the violation of electoral laws, and outright fraud.

Three parties competed for the governorship of Morelos in 1946: Ernesto Escobar Muñoz for the official party, Vicente Peralta for the Partido de Unificación Morelense (the Morelos Unification Party), and Jaramillo for the PAOM. There were many objections from PAOM members regarding the electoral process. In Xoxocotla, Zacatepec, Jojutla, and Tlaquiltenango (areas where Jaramillo drew his greatest support), citizens were prevented from casting their votes, and entire ballot boxes disappeared. In Zacatepec, for example, a letter to the president with fifty-seven signatures informed him that the ballot boxes were stolen by a colonel and federal soldiers.[38] A letter from Xoxocotla, signed by seventy people, complained that those in charge of the polls had "disappeared the election documents," preventing them from voting for their candidate Rubén Jaramillo.[39] By show of armed force, in Jojutla, civil and military authorities prevented voters in favor of Jaramillo from casting their ballots.[40] A particularly long list of irregularities was sent by seventy-six PAOM representatives from the most populated voting districts—Cuernavaca and Cuautla. They documented examples of fraud at forty-six polling stations. Among the most flagrant violations were polls watched by gunmen known to be in the pay of local authorities, PRI members who took ballots to their homes so they could cast "as many votes as pleased them," and the declaration of the official party's triumph in one poll location with a number of votes greater than the amount of registered voters in the area.[41]

The Morelense Unification Party, the third challenging party, also submitted complaints. Peralta's constituents pointed out that the voting authorities named by the Electoral Council were all loyalists of the PRI candidate,

Escobar. In Tetecala, two Peraltistas were prevented from assuming their duty as polling presidents. In addition, voters reported that many polls did not use rosters; instead, voters were just asked to sign their names, permitting people to vote in several locations.[42] Despite protest from both Peraltistas and Jaramillistas, official candidate Escobar Muñoz was declared governor elect. In response, Jaramillo wrote to President Ávila Camacho requesting a meeting to personally specify the violations that caused him to lose the elections.[43] Moreover, the president of the PAOM's executive committee, Trinidad Pérez Miranda, and party representatives from nine municipalities in Morelos wrote to the minister of the interior enumerating the irregularities in the voting process throughout the state. They offered to demonstrate, in whatever way the ministry requested, that Jaramillo had the support of the vast majority of the population of Morelos. The letter made an appeal to the minister's sense of revolutionary duty, stating, "We understand Mr. Minister, as a revolutionary government, one of the main duties that the very revolution imposes, is to guard its gains, and it is obvious that one of those gains, perhaps the most costly, is respect for the public vote."[44] The Jaramillistas also held public demonstrations objecting to the election results and demanding the release of those who had been detained for participating in Jaramillo's campaign.[45]

These accounts of voter fraud remain vivid in popular memory. Testimonies of Jaramillistas detail the various ways in which the governorship was stolen from Jaramillo. One campesino described how aside from padding voting rosters with lists of people previously deceased, soldiers were stationed all day on the roof of the church to observe the elections taking place in the town square below. That evening when the polls closed, they came down, grabbed the ballot boxes, and took them away. Another Jaramillista stated, "We all knew that they cheated, just like today: what the PRI says, that's what goes. Those who the PRI names, they're the ones [who take office]. Even if the people vote for another person, they don't make it [the vote] valid."[46] These words say as much about the official party's use of fraud as they do about the lack of accountability the rural poor saw in their government.

It is no secret to most of the Mexican population that the PRI commonly rigged local, state, and national elections. The ruling party had already turned to fraudulent measures in the 1940 federal elections when it faced a challenge from the conservative candidate Juan Andreu Almazán. In addition to the typical irregularities that characterized election day in Mexico—illegal pressure on voters, paid contingencies voting in various polling places, theft of ballot boxes—in 1940 there were also a number of violent confrontations that provoked dozens of deaths.[47] The PRM most likely won the 1940 federal elections fraudulently.[48] Various levels of irregularities would continue to characterize the elections to come.

While it is unlikely that anyone will ever prove which gubernatorial candidate actually received the majority of votes, it is possible to document the extensive fraud. That the government felt compelled to rig the elections speaks to the effective nature of the Jaramillista campaign. The fraud on election day was one in a series of actions stifling the voice of campesinos, and it was another example of the injustice of the system and the betrayal of the revolution. The belief that Jaramillo was illegitimately defeated has been reinforced by the memories of the vast number of people who attended his political rallies. Said one participant, "I attended a demonstration in Cuernavaca, on Morelos Avenue. There were huge crowds of people, at least three or four thousand, filling several blocks."[49]

Its dictatorial tendencies notwithstanding, the official party at times showed a tolerance and even a willingness to accept electoral challenges (by granting the PAOM's registration even after the deadline, for example). After all, the presence of such opposition enhanced the country's democratic image. But after election day, a wave of government repression against the Jaramillistas clearly laid out the limits of its tolerance. Jaramillo and other prominent PAOM members were forced to go underground due to this repression. From 1946 to 1951 they organized clandestinely throughout the Morelos countryside. During these years the Jaramillistas operated in a national context of increased hostility towards popular organizing. The new president, Miguel Alemán, intensified Ávila Camacho's counterrevolutionary reforms. Alemán moved to eliminate leftist elements within the official party and in 1948 achieved the famous *charrazo*, by which he deposed independent labor leaders. Despite the war's end, he fortified the doctrine of national unity by replacing it with the notion of *mexicanidad*, the rejection of any values foreign to Mexican culture. Which values were declared foreign was up to the PRI's discretion, but communism and leftist ideologies in general were the main targets. Meanwhile, the government openly embraced foreign investment and private enterprise as the mechanisms through which Mexico would achieve modernity. President Alemán even considered the idea of running for reelection—a sacrilege for a party whose democratic image lay in the transfer of executive power every six years. But such measures generated their own contradictions—not only with popular sectors, especially labor, that continued to mount strikes, but within the official party itself. As the 1952 elections approached, the Cardenista elements, which had been increasingly alienated within the official party, broke with party discipline and mounted their own campaign against the PRI. Seeing in them potential allies, the Jaramillistas joined this faction and again ran Jaramillo for governor of Morelos.

The Jaramillistas' Second Electoral Campaign

In 1951, the PAOM decided to take advantage of the political space opened by the FPPM, which ran Miguel Henríquez Guzmán for president. The FPPM was formed by several disenchanted members of the more leftist or Cardenista faction of the PRI. The Jaramillistas joined the Henriquistas (as FPPM members became known) in their efforts to defeat the PRI. This union was more a marriage of convenience than of ideals. Nevertheless, it gave the Jaramillistas the opportunity to transcend local politics, and, thanks to Jaramillo, the Henriquistas gained a significant following in rural Morelos.

Until the elections of 1988, Henriquismo represented the most serious split within the ruling party.[50] Henríquez Guzmán had been a revolutionary general with a long history in the ruling party and had twice been passed up as the party's nominee. The high-ranking members who joined him had seen their ability to move up in official party ranks blocked by the increasing dominance of university-trained, civilian bureaucrats.[51] Henriquistas did not present a fundamentally different economic or social program from the PRI; instead, they pointed to the corruption within the ranks of the ruling party and played on the discontent fostered by the government's rollback of social reforms. The FPPM based its platform on the idea that the revolution had been betrayed and that they would set it back on the track intended by Cárdenas. The Henriquistas' main criticisms against the ruling party centered around the severe poverty suffered by most Mexicans, the limited application of agrarian reforms, the stifling atmosphere faced by the workers' movement, and the lack of respect shown for democratic procedures. But the FPPM made no proposals for structural reforms. While it supported the breakup and distribution of latifundios, it did not even call for greater state intervention in the economy. As a leftist organization, the FPPM did not reach very far.[52] Rather, "Henriquismo represented the banner that justified the revolutionary movement and specifically tried to rescue Cardenismo as a political alternative and current within the government."[53] Whether the FPPM had the support of Cárdenas himself is a matter of debate. There is some evidence that Cárdenas encouraged Henríquez Guzmán to run for president.[54] Henríquez Guzmán held long meetings with the ex-president, and many high-ranking Henriquistas maintain that Cárdenas wanted Henríquez Guzmán to run to counterbalance Miguel Alemán's intention to perpetuate himself in power.[55] The FPPM certainly attempted to give the impression of Cárdenas's support. But, although some members of the Cárdenas family did openly appear at Henriquista events, Cárdenas himself remained conspicuous in his absence.

Even without Cárdenas's personal involvement, many Henriquista supporters saw the FPPM as the party that would continue his reforms and be true to the revolution's hard-fought ideals. The ideology of Henriquismo differed from that of the PRI almost exclusively in their criticism of the regime's abuses. Such was the dissatisfaction with the PRI among the citizenry, however, that the lack of an alternative program did not seem to hinder its ability to gain votes. The FPPM garnered enough followers to present a formidable challenge to the ruling party. Moreover, Henríquez Guzmán received encouragement from the Mexican Communist Party, whose support was split between the FPPM candidate and Vicente Lombardo Toledano, the candidate of the Popular Party.[56] A statement by General Francisco J. Mújica, a Cardenista and member of the ruling party who joined the Henriquista campaign, is typical of the FPPM's critique of the regime: "The institutions in Mexico are no longer institutions, but whims of one man that transmits himself through government organizations and institutional means to pressure the will of the citizenry."[57]

As can be seen from the PAOM's "Minimum Program for Political Action," the Jaramillistas' platform was more extensive and ideologically leftist than that of the FPPM. Still, an alliance with the FPPM could not be passed up, as it represented an opportunity for the PAOM to achieve national stature. For this reason the Jaramillistas could temporarily overlook some of their party's ideological incongruities with the FPPM. José Rodríguez, a PAOM leader, described the reason for the alliance with the FPPM: "Henríquez Guzmán was not the candidate that the PAOM wished for, but still he was the best from the regional and national revolutionary point of view. That was useful to us as a way of being in touch with other people from other states in the conventions or in the rallies that were held. Henríquez was not the candidate that we wanted, but of the ones available, Henríquez was the best, and according to us, the most revolutionary."[58]

In Morelos, the Jaramillistas took the same approach to organizing they had employed during the 1946 campaign. But this time their affiliation to a major national party gave them more access to campaign resources, including greater press coverage. They acquired a pickup truck, which they named "*la cotorra*" (the parrot), attached a loudspeaker to it, and drove throughout the state promoting Jaramillo's candidacy. Building upon organizing networks created during the 1946 elections, the PAOM extended the scope of Jaramillo's political campaign, emphasizing the official betrayal of the revolution. The Henriquistas, in turn, portrayed themselves as the legitimate heirs to Cardenismo, a message that resonated heavily with a rural population who had, for more than a decade, witnessed a halt and even the reversal of land redistribution. The political struggle of the FPPM became an important forum to discuss Mexico's agrarian problems. At no other point since Cárdenas's 1934 campaign had agrarian issues been so central to the national electoral debate.[59]

FPPM and PAOM speeches emphasized the need to rescue the revolution from the wrong turn it had taken under recent leadership. This meant restoring Cárdenas's policies. A PAOM manifesto put out early in 1951, signed by the president, secretary, and treasurer of the party declared, "The program of Henríquez Guzmán is the program of Lázaro Cárdenas, and this program has already proved its efficiency by embodying the desires of the great masses of workers of the cities and the countryside and by achieving the material and cultural progress of Mexico."[60] The theme of Henríquez Guzmán as Cárdenas's rightful heir is prevalent throughout Jaramillo's speeches and the PAOM campaign literature. But when speaking about his own candidacy for state governor, Jaramillo turned from the question of leadership to the need for campesinos to ascend to governmental positions: "Since it is campesinos that form the majority of the citizens, it is completely unjust that we continue to be ruled by elements that are neither campesinos nor workers."[61] This appeal reached many poor rural dwellers who were aware of the gulf separating them from those who claimed to represent their

4. Rubén Jaramillo and Miguel Henríquez in front of a statue of Zapata.
Archivo General de la Nación, Fondo Hermanos Mayo, Jaramillo.

interests. For example, when two of Jaramillo's supporters were detained for posting PAOM literature in Cuernavaca, they were interrogated by the governor of Morelos himself, who asked,

What is your relationship to Jaramillo?
We're supporters.
Of what?
Well, of his struggle.
Struggle for what?
Struggle for governor of the state, he's a candidate.
And you want him to win?
Well yes.
Why?
Because he's poor, just like us.[62]

During his campaign, Jaramillo placed a constant emphasis on the organizing process itself, condemning the government's "guided democracy" designed by corrupt politicians who justified their hold on power by arguing that "the people were incapable of choosing and would elect their own enemies."[63] He saw the electoral campaign as a means to organize the rural population and to raise awareness of the power they possessed collectively. Campesinos time and again related the sense of empowerment they felt during such mobilizations. "Even if we don't win," explained one Jaramillista, "at least the children will hear us talking, organizing against the rich."[64] Jaramillo well understood that government officials would not work in the interest of the poor unless pushed to do so. Another Jaramillista framed their goals this way: "Let's say we don't win, we will at least open a space politically so that we may win when the time is right. And we will be able to give guidance to the people so that they don't believe those men who come in search of us when they need us and show us contempt when they don't."[65] Another piece of PAOM literature proposed to "turn the electoral campaign of Henríquez Guzmán into a brave struggle to conquer bread, land, a decent wage, school, liberty, and democratic rights."[66] In this sense, an alliance with a party that had national scope was a crucial step in realizing and attaining broad-based power. One PAOM militant said, "It seems to me that the measures we adopted to inform people helped them a lot in gaining consciousness about what we were fighting for. Only for the electoral struggle? No, it was a social issue. . . . It is very important that this be made known, because it wasn't about Henriquismo. It wasn't merely an electoral struggle to support Henríquez, but rather meant to take advantage of that juncture, to make known the social struggle that Jaramillo had been building that was also recognized at a national level outside of Henriquismo, that is, before Henriquismo."[67]

The Cardenista legacy was the thread that linked the PAOM and the Henriquistas. The Jaramillistas attempted to build on the hope and empowerment experienced in the countryside during the Cardenista period. PAOM strategy placed campesinos at the forefront of the struggle, arguing that only in this manner would their needs to be met. At an organizing meeting early in the campaign process, Jaramillo declared, "Only by taking the power away from those who enslave and exploit the people, will the people have justice, bread, and liberty. As campesinos, we are the ones who should be at the head of this struggle because we are the only ones capable of giving everything for a just cause."[68] While these words were presumably directed at those in power, they in fact foreshadowed the different paths the Jaramillistas and Henriquista leadership would take after the elections.

One new aspect of the Jaramillistas' 1952 campaign was its explicit attention to the needs and rights of women, as evidenced by the formation of a "Sector Femenil." Interestingly, although women still did not have the right to vote in national elections in 1952, suffrage rights did not constitute the key issue for the women who organized this group. Their demands instead centered around household production, and they legitimized their appeal based on their relationship to men, a reflection of an agrarian policy in which the male head of household was the official beneficiary. Still, women also argued their case based on the right they believed they inherited from the revolution: "It is precisely us, the campesina women, who recognize and participate in the sacrifice realized by the men of the countryside to achieve the economic recovery of the country. . . . We, more than anyone, resolve to make the land bequeathed to us by the revolution produce everything necessary for the lives of our people, for the nourishment of our children." In this way, the Sector Feminil not only expressed the need to protect the revolution's legacy but also counterposed the knowledge and traditions of campesinas and campesinos to the technocratic solutions offered "precisely by those who did not work hard and lived like kings." Clearly, they objected to the government instructing them on the best way to make the land productive. President Alemán's policy that the countryside needed to produce more for the betterment of the whole nation was particularly insulting to them, since they viewed the rich as an exploitative class that made its wealth off the productive labor of the popular classes.[69] Women's participation was especially visible in this electoral campaign. Various pictures reveal an attempt to make their presence as women known. In one march, women appear at the center, flanked by two columns of men. Other photos depict a group of women with Jaramillo at the center. While such images still legitimize female participation with regard to Jaramillo, the male leader, they constitute a visible attempt to document their involvement.

The Henriquistas and Jaramillistas held demonstrations with hundreds, and sometimes thousands, of participants in the major cities of Morelos, such as Cuernavaca, Jojutla, and Cuautla, as well as in smaller cities like Yautepec, Tlaquiltenango, Zacatepec, Tetecala, Axochiapan, and Xoxocotla. The national newspaper *El Universal* estimated that over twenty thousand people attended one such rally in Jojutla.[70] This number is doubly impressive, given that the population in the state of Morelos at that time was slightly over 270,000.[71] The significance of such popular mobilizations to a party not accustomed to electoral challenges cannot be underestimated, especially because the PRI had spent the years since World War II attempting to rein in autonomous popular organizing. The government had virtually crushed the independent labor movement in the late 1940s, laying the foundations for sustained economic growth under a model based on labor's discipline.[72] In what one historian called the "modernization of authoritarianism," the Alemán administration had acted on a three-pronged strategy to establish PRI hegemony: making state governors adhere to a strict political discipline, eliminating the Left and labor militants from unions and reorienting the national ideology against communism.[73] The last policy fell in line with the 1947 Truman doctrine to contain communism by any means. The Henriquistas' ideology was far from communist, but official propaganda often attempted to portray it as such, using the Red scare to sway public opinion against them. For example, a 1951 headline in *El Universal* reported, "Henríquez Guzmán branded a communist."[74] While the Mexican Communist Party did support the candidacy of Henríquez Guzmán for a short time, the real threat of the FPPM was not its communism—of which it professed none—but its ability to destabilize the PRI's carefully greased electoral machine.

The government thus kept a watchful eye on all the opposition's activities. State spies sent detailed reports to the minister of the interior regarding

5. Women were prominent participants during the 1952 Jaramillista campaign.
Archivo General de la Nación, Fondo Hermanos Mayo, Jaramillo.

6. Jaramillista and Henriquista march during the 1952 campaign.
Archivo General de la Nación, Fondo Hermanos Mayo, Jaramillo.

Henriquista and Jaramillista activity. Judging from documents on Jaramillo, one of their main concerns was his ability to mobilize sustained numbers in Morelos. The informants constantly highlighted Jaramillo's appeals for campesino unity. They showed special alarm when he cited the revolution as an example of the power campesinos had when armed. These memos detailed a situation in which there would be an armed uprising after the elections if the results did not favor the opposition. Whether or not the agents faithfully reported on reality is less significant than the fact that, as the government's eyes and ears, they shaped the state's official version of events. Many leaders of the FPPM did allude to the need to make the government conform to the ideals of the revolution by whatever means necessary. The theme of armed struggle appeared consistently in Henriquista speeches. For example, in a rally in Cuernavaca, FPPM leader Graciano Sánchez directed himself to the government headquarters and declared, "With full knowledge of our responsibility, we make it known that when the people are fired up, they will follow the example of Zapata, and they will put an end to all the false revolutionaries and all their hypocrisies. . . . We have to save the revolution for what it has done in the countryside, and we have to save it, whatever the cost and whoever may fall."[75] At another Henriquista rally in Axochiapan, former governor of Morelos, Vicente Estrada Cajigal warned, "To believe that the population is calm is a delusion, because this peace is the calm before the storm. Hopefully the vote will be respected and the storm won't come."[76] Henríquez Guzmán himself often implied that he would lead workers, and especially campesinos—since he drew his greatest support in the countryside—in an armed movement if that was the majority's will. For example, at an extensive rally in Jojutla, he stated, "It will be the people who will determine the actions that I should take to ensure the vote is respected."[77]

In this tense climate, government agents following the campaign in Morelos repeatedly warned of an armed uprising. This fear seemed to have been especially acute in Morelos, given the popularity that Jaramillo achieved and the knowledge of his previous armed resistance. For example, after attending one rally, a government spy wrote, "Given the above speeches, what has been said previously can be confirmed, that Rubén Jaramillo will be one of the first to launch a rebellion."[78] A memo sent a few days later noted that throughout Henríquez Guzmán's tour of Morelos, Jaramillo had held a "very significant place" and that "those present at the rallies regarded him as governor elect and the most important opposition leader." More alarmingly, this memo surmised, "there already exists a premeditated plan by Jaramillo, with the approval of Miguel Henríquez Guzmán, to rise up in arms, when the circumstances require it." At this point, government agents concluded, campesinos in Morelos could count on the support of their neighbors in Puebla and on some former Zapatista leaders not affiliated with the PRI.[79] For the PRI, the PAOM's mobilization was reaching critical dimensions, not necessarily because of a potential military strength but because of the serious challenge to the PRI's legitimacy in its claims over the revolution. Campesinos operated with the living memory of their revolution, drawing resolve from the option of an armed uprising. This challenge to its legitimacy the government could not take lightly.

Both the local and federal governments tried their best to neutralize much of the opposition. Early on in the campaign, the governor of Morelos disbanded a rally planned by the Federación Campesina Morelense. This organization had split from the National Campesino Confederation to support Henríquez Guzmán's candidacy.[80] The Henriquistas also charged local authorities with blowing up a bridge on the Cuautla-Cuernavaca road to prevent a huge campesino contingency from arriving to welcome Henríquez Guzmán.[81] The PAOM also presented a formal complaint to the federal government protesting the ransacking of their Cuautla offices by uniformed police, who stole their campaign literature and kidnapped the individual in charge of watching the office.[82] PAOM member José Rodríguez related, "We were like Juárez," the Mexican executive who had been pursued during the 1862 French invasion, "running all over the place with the presidential offices."[83]

For all of the government's fear of campesino violence, during the 1952 campaign the sabotage, murder, and theft came from the state itself. Government agents received instructions to neutralize Henriquista mobilization and undermine their meetings through existing official organizations such as the CNC and the League of Agrarian Communities. For instance, they instructed CNC representatives to call meetings on the same day as events planned by the Henriquistas. In addition, the representatives of these organizations were advised to "dedicate themselves solely to their work, without distracting themselves with political matters, or premature agitation."[84] Elisa Servín, author of a detailed study of Henriquismo, found that the PRI operated in similar ways throughout the country.[85]

To these tactics the government also added a wave of assassinations. Henriquistas became accustomed to the appearance of bodies of FPPM militants on the road between Mexico City and Cuernavaca.[86] Such murders were so common in Morelos that the population referred to them as *carreterazos*—the highway killings. Likewise, during this political campaign a number of Jaramillo's followers were kidnapped, tortured, and killed. "We witnessed so much in those days," remembered Pedro Herminio, an indigenous campesino from Xoxocotla. "Young people were disappeared, then we'd find them dead. . . . That's what happened to people who struggled, they were killed."[87] State authorities generally resorted to violence to silence the PAOM's more visible members. The experience of Pedro García Vázquez and Luis Olmedo Miranda, two vocal PAOM militants, is a case in point. When returning from the Cuernavaca party offices one afternoon in July 1952, they were both abducted, taken to an unknown location, and interrogated the entire night. The following evening, their kidnappers forced them into a car and during the journey stabbed García and Olmedo with an ice pick. The two Jaramillistas were then left naked on the side of a road near the border with the State of Mexico.[88] Luis Olmedo died as a result of his injuries, but Pedro García, initially taken for dead, survived his nine stab wounds. To protect himself, he went into hiding and did not make his survival known for several months, giving him the nickname ever since of "El Muerto." Jaramillistas relate other instances of kidnapping and violent breakups of local PAOM assemblies. Another Jaramillista was brutally killed with a machete in his own home.[89] While such repressive measures were not uncommon in the months of political campaigning, the most severe cases of state violence would come after the elections. In the days just before July 7, instances of violence against Henriquistas increased throughout the country, with alarming reports from Jalisco, Tamaulipas, Puebla, and Veracruz. On election day, the country was under a virtual state of siege, with over eighty thousand soldiers and police sent to voting sites around the country.[90]

The 1952 Elections

The 1952 elections, both in Morelos and throughout the country, were characterized by large popular mobilizations and a backlash of state repression. The elections for governor of Morelos were held in April 1952, two and a half months before the presidential ones. Participants recall as many or even more irregularities during these elections as in the ones six years earlier. One PAOM member stated, "Many people were not allowed to vote. Many ballot boxes were stolen, and in those polling places there was no oversight. Many ballots were not registered by the Electoral Commission, and so they were annulled [FPPM] votes. . . . The military and police themselves would take the ballot boxes."[91] Another campesino related, "A lot of people voted. We believed that he [Jaramillo] won. Henríquez Guzmán also had a lot of people behind him [in Morelos] thanks to Jaramillo. The same thing must have happened that happened with Cuauhtémoc [Cárdenas], when he won."[92] Likewise, Pablo Ortiz explains, "Jaramillo had so many supporters around here and won as governor. But the PRI wins even if it gets only one vote."[93] Regardless of the actual number of votes received by the PRI, such fraudulent measures contributed to a view that not only was its victory illegitimate, but that even its massive efforts to repress the opposition had not prevented Jaramillo from receiving the majority of votes. Magnified by the PRI's fraudulent practices throughout subsequent decades, numerous Morelenses still hold that Jaramillo was the actual winner of the gubernatorial race.

The Jaramillistas protested the results, and Jaramillo, declaring himself governor elect, accompanied Henríquez Guzmán in his campaign throughout the state of Morelos. The presidential elections were scheduled for July 6, 1952, and the Jaramillistas continued to mobilize people for the FPPM. Still, at the close of election day, the National Electoral Commission declared PRI candidate Adolfo Ruiz Cortines the presidential winner, giving the FPPM only 16 percent of the vote.[94] This would be the highest percentage accorded to any opposition presidential candidate until 1982. But the Henriquistas rejected this number as fraudulent, and the day after the elections they called for a demonstration in Mexico City's Alameda Central.

Early that morning the government issued warnings on the radio prohibiting political gatherings. But still, people began to congregate in the Alameda Central, surrounded by growing numbers of riot police. When the crowd of at least five thousand Henriquistas refused to leave, authorities proceeded to forcibly remove the demonstrators. The official show of force was extensive. One newspaper described how "secret agents, uniformed police—both mounted and on foot—swat teams, members of the Department of National Security as well as the Judicial police all confronted the crowd in a fight that radiated outward."[95] The police eventually dispersed the crowd and in the process left many dead, many more injured, and at least five hundred people detained.[96] Based on accounts from eyewitnesses and hospital attendants, the U.S. embassy reported that at least twenty people had been killed.[97] Other sources place the number dead at one hundred.[98] Henriquistas refer to the day's events as a massacre. And yet this demonstration, and the state's response, virtually disappeared from the historical record. Two decades later, essayists Manuel Aguilar Mora and Carlos Monsiváis wrote, "The massacre of the Alameda is one of the least documented events in our recent political history. Many eyewitnesses and people who 'know' estimate the number [of dead] to be five hundred. For their part, official declarations—with the supreme optimism that would lead them to declare twenty-one dead in Tlatelolco in 1968—shrank the number down to seven. . . . It is enough to contemplate the pictures to discern the amplitude of the repression. And yet, the massacre has disappeared, almost literally, from our contemporary political memory."[99]

The violence in Mexico City offered Jaramillistas a glimpse of the repression that would follow in Morelos. In the months after July, state authorities unleashed a wave of violence against the PAOM activists. One campesino recounted, "We found out that they killed those protesting [in Mexico City], and from then on, the persecution was unleashed in many states. López de Nava [the governor of Morelos] took charge of the carreterazos here." Two other Jaramillistas, Luis Tapia and a campesino whose last name was Ortiz, were killed after the elections for publicly insisting Jaramillo had won.[100] Many of the murdered Jaramillista bodies also showed signs of torture. Eliut Hernández recalled the gruesome fate of her father, Eleuterio Sánchez, a campesino and active participant in the PAOM:

> They found him in Jiutepec; that's where they'd held him after he was kidnapped. They tortured him in the most horrible ways, they sliced off his heels and castrated him. They tied a rope around his neck and hanged him. When his body was found he was tied by his feet to a railroad track. He had disappeared two or three weeks before, and when they found him he had been dead for about three days. My mother had been looking for him. It wasn't until a woman who was searching for her son and husband told her that my father was in a morgue in Jiutepec and . . . he was about to be deposited in a mass grave. There were so many dead, that they were buried just like that in a mass grave; that's how much repression there was at that time.[101]

It is uncertain how many people died as a result of official repression, but the level of violence remains vivid in the memories of those who challenged the PRI. Pedro García recalled how "all these people began to get killed, then they [the police] would make it look like it was just personal conflicts, but they weren't; they would kill them for being Jaramillistas."[102] This was the government's response to legal mobilizations.

"Por las buenas no se puede"

Campesino accounts of such commonplace brutality provide further evidence of the extensive violence undergirding the PRI's rule and stand as an urgent call for a close examination of the state's repressive apparatus during the party's heyday. That opponents organized and operated from within the legal political framework made little difference to the government, and its repression forced many Jaramillistas into hiding in the months after the elections. Jaramillo again declared that he was taking up arms and, together with a group of about twenty people, fled to the sierra of Morelos. With legal channels closed, the Jaramillistas began to make plans for armed actions. One party militant recalled, "We had the superior organization among campesinos here in the state, and that was the motive for the worsening of the persecution! The conclusion that we came to was that by the rules [*por las buenas*], the PRI will never accept a loss."[103] The small armed cadre remained in hiding for seven years and, in conjunction with other Jaramillistas, continued to organize in name of the PAOM, which became a party of "permanent struggle and action" that operated until Jaramillo's assassination in 1962. In 1959, when Jaramillistas began to compile a formal registry, the PAOM's list numbered 3,068 members, including 31 in Puebla, 23 in Guerrero, 5 in Mexico City, and 2 in the State of Mexico.[104] According to Jaramillo's autobiography, at its peak the PAOM had 15,000 members.[105]

As for their Henriquista allies, the Jaramillistas quickly came to realize that the FPPM's declarations to have the will of the people respected "by any means necessary" were only rhetorical statements made in the heat of the moment. In commenting on Henríquez Guzmán, one Jaramillista stated, "We don't know if he resigned, backed out, or sold out; we're not sure what happened."[106] Many FPPM leaders accepted posts in the Ruiz Cortines administration, while others retired to private professional life. Remaining political ambitions were channeled into a new opposition party, the Authentic Party of the Mexican Revolution (PARM), which Ruiz Cortines helped create "specifically to give a safe outlet to those of the armed forces who wished to participate politically."[107] Early in 1954 the government revoked the FPPM's registration, under the pretext that it was partaking in acts of a subversive character and engaging in social agitation.[108] And, to minimize the reoccurrence of such challenges, the Ministry of the Interior changed the electoral laws, doubling the number of members necessary to register a political party. The Ruiz Cortines administration simultaneously attempted to increase its popularity by implementing anticorruption legislation and expanding suffrage rights to women. Through selective incorporation and repression the PRI preserved its hold on power, but it did not succeed in imposing social peace.

The state's reaction to the Jaramillista movement displayed the PRI's combination of flexibility and authoritarianism. That the government opted to rely more heavily on repression once it had declared the PRI victorious reveals this dual nature. The election and the political campaigns which preceded it lent legitimacy to the PRI's rule, and in this spirit the government was willing to tolerate and even be lenient with the PAOM—for example, in overlooking the late registration. But after the election ritual, the state sent a clear message as to where the boundaries lay. By repressing the Jaramillistas when they attempted to organize legally, the government once again pushed them into armed struggle, actions which were again accompanied by more radicalized assessment of Mexico's political system and the need to transform it.

CHAPTER FIVE

"They Made Him into a Rebel"

Government repression during the 1946 and 1952 electoral campaigns pushed the Jaramillistas to take up arms. During the two armed phases following each fraudulent election, the Jaramillistas employed a series of radicalizing strategies. Seeing their reformist demands blocked once again, the Jaramillistas reissued an updated version of the Plan de Cerro Prieto during the 1952 uprising, this time calling for a new revolution. The old one, they held, had been corrupted beyond the point of repair. Similarly, their previous measures of self-defense now turned into offensive strategies, such as plans to take over key municipalities in Morelos. As the PAOM saw more and more of its members murdered, Jaramillo and some of his men decided to take justice into their own hands against particularly ruthless *pistoleros* (hired gunmen) and local police chiefs. State terror such as the massacre of Henriquistas in Mexico City and the carreterazos in Morelos drove Jaramillistas into clandestine organizing, not only because legal channels proved useless, but because they were dangerous.

The second armed episode in 1946 and the third one in 1952 make evident the Jaramillistas' gradual radicalization. The 1952 electoral struggle that separates the two uprisings served to confirm the rationale for more drastic measures. Rather than abandon Morelos because of state repression, the

Jaramillistas took up arms, demonstrating their level of determination to challenge the political status quo. Each time they went underground, they found support not only from previous allies but also from new groups angry at the state's increasingly authoritarian nature. In 1946, the Jaramillistas joined with campesinos protesting the government's slaughter of diseased cattle, and in 1952 they formed part of the general unrest created after the Henriquista campaign. In their vision and tactics after 1952, the Jaramillistas moved farther away from Zapata's agrarismo and Cárdenas's populism, and their language increasingly resembled that of guerrilla groups that would appear in the latter part of the twentieth century.

The first of these subsequent armed uprisings came in 1946, shortly after Jaramillo's first campaign for governor. Jaramillo called a meeting of ejidatarios in Panchimalco, a town in the district of Jojutla, to strategize organizing tactics for sugarcane farmers. At this public meeting that drew three hundred people, Jaramillo denounced the abuses occurring at the Zacatepec cooperative: the low prices paid for the sugarcane, the fraud in the weighing system, the extent to which cooperative members were denied participation in the running of the refinery, and the general repression practiced against those who spoke out about the abuses.[1] The discussion had gone on for about two hours when several men from the rural federal defense made their way into the meeting and attempted to detain and disarm Jaramillo, who had become accustomed to carrying a gun. Knowing there was a price on his head, Jaramillo refused to go down without a fight. So he—together with his companion Maximino Casales Torres and his wife, who was also armed—opened fire and fled to take refuge in a nearby house.[2] According to Jaramillo's autobiography, the confrontation resulted in the deaths of three rural defense guards including a commander: Miguel Serrano, Ignacio Hernández, and Serafín Dorates. Raúl Ramos Cerda, manager of the Zacatepec refinery, had paid the men ten thousand pesos to assassinate Jaramillo.[3]

The "Panchimalco incident" would become a memorable and highly symbolic event. It stood as another example of Jaramillo's attempts to use legal channels to mobilize campesinos, and of the government's violent response. Jaramillo had already been illegally ousted from the Zacatepec cooperative. Many believed that the 1946 gubernatorial election had been stolen from him. Now, when he was advising campesinos to defend their rights in a peaceful public forum, local authorities stood poised to detain or even kill him as if he were committing a crime. For those who had any doubt, the repressive nature of the state apparatus was unmasked before their eyes. At the same time, by using force to protect himself, Jaramillo demonstrated that he did not easily cower before the state. This incident exemplified the Jaramillista strategy of using legal channels to demand their rights, but not hesitating to use force when more peaceful tactics were thwarted.

"Armed Hiding," 1946–1951

During most of Alemán's presidency, the Jaramillistas engaged in a practice of "armed hiding"—wielding arms in self-defense from clandestine locations without actively taking on the government in a declared uprising. The resort to armed self-defense during this interval was a response not only to direct government repression of the Jaramillistas but also to the specifically authoritarian tenor of the Alemán administration. This climate not only created an environment hostile to organizing but also resulted in policies that directly impinged upon campesino livelihood and indirectly fed the Jaramillista movement.

When the Jaramillistas attempted to organize through legal channels during the 1946 elections, local authorities continuously harassed its party members. For example, during the campaign, the judicial police detained two Jaramillistas, Antonio Mendoza Flores and Pablo Brígido Sánchez, in Cuautla, where they were handing out literature in favor of Enrique Calderón, an opposition presidential candidate with whom the PAOM was allied. They possessed, local authorities charged, "propaganda about a revolutionary movement" and "incendiary" literature. The Plan de Cerro Prieto, with which Mendoza and Brígido "claimed to be in full agreement," stood as the most damning evidence of their seditious acts. Natives of Mitepec, a town in Puebla near the Morelos border, both men had taken up arms with Jaramillo back in 1943 but, along with Jaramillo, had received an official amnesty one year later. Local authorities charged Mendoza and Brígido, as well as Jaramillo, whom they arrested one week later, with treason, conspiracy, seditious association, and abuse of the nation's symbols. However, as an example of the flexibility the Mexican state sometimes exhibited, a federal judge ordered them released due to the lack of evidence and the 1944 amnesty.[4]

These tensions between state and federal authorities recurred at various stages of the Jaramillista movement. As discussed in the previous chapter, during Jaramillo's 1946 gubernatorial race the state governor had sought to disqualify Jaramillo for not registering his candidacy on time, but the federal Minister of the Interior revoked this decision. In short, Morelos authorities reacted more harshly to the Jaramillistas than their counterparts at the federal level. This aggressive response stemmed from the local nature of Jaramillista goals. Even though the Plan de Cerro Prieto presented a vision of national state reconstruction, the Jaramillistas did not possess the strength to carry out such a revolution. The significance of this document stemmed from its view of local injustices as rooted in national and international structures of exploitation. But local authorities faced the messy task of controlling the Jaramillistas and silencing the attention they brought to unlawful practices, corruption, and repression. While the federal government also used repressive measures, these were always selectively applied, in a practice that halted some abuses and ignored others, ensuring the effective functioning of the national PRI apparatus. State authorities released Brígido and Mendoza but clearly revealed a low tolerance for independent political organizing. By closing off political options, the PRI effectively forced the Jaramillistas to opt for more drastic, clandestine measures. Intermittent federal flexibility notwithstanding, national policy provoked sympathy for Jaramillo during this period.

Even more than Ávila Camacho, Alemán's *sexenio* (six-year term), which began in 1946, marked a more drastic move away from revolutionary reforms. Alemán had been Minister of the Interior during the previous administration, an office that acquired great power through policies justified as wartime emergencies. In an effort to maintain a social peace that would make Mexico attractive to foreign investors, Alemán brought with him to the presidency heavy-handed tactics that took shape as Mexico moved to conform with the 1947 Truman doctrine. President Harry Truman's declaration about the need to contain communism throughout the world had a quick and noticeable effect in Mexico. Anticommunist measures had already become standard practice in Mexico, but they now became official policy. Moreover, the government increasingly labeled popular organizing or independent unionism "communist," and in 1947 created Mexico's national security agency (Dirección Federal de Seguridad), which spent much of its resources spying on domestic groups, including the Jaramillistas. The law of social dissolution, implemented during World War II to combat Axis activity in Mexico, was not only kept on the books but was used almost exclusively to jail social activists. The Communist Party, previously hopeful about working with Alemán, by 1949 formally condemned the administration's policies.

President Alemán also established a much closer relationship with the United States, one whose early signs are perhaps best symbolized in the countries' joint venture to combat aphthous fever (more commonly known as hoof-and-mouth disease) among Mexican cattle. The Mexican government, upon the urging of the United States, opted for the most drastic solution—the slaughter of all infected or potentially infected animals. This decision angered the rural population and worked to accentuate an already palpable discontent in the countryside. What to health officials in Washington may have seemed like unproblematic measures had devastating effects on Mexican farmers and rekindled nationalist sentiments. Thus, when Jaramillo went underground in 1946, he found support among the rural population incensed at the government's policy of slaughtering cattle infected with hoof-and-mouth disease. Desperately trying to defend their animals, campesinos were not averse to taking up arms. Conscious of the hardship the loss of an animal represented to poor rural dwellers, Jaramillo began to speak out against the *"rifle sanitario"* (sanitary rifle), as the government's solution to the disease became known. It didn't help matters that the team carrying out the animal killings counted on the very visible participation of American advisers. The government's program became so unpopular that, in some cases, the soldiers on the execution teams refused outright to perform their duties, and the government had to replace them on a continuous basis. To make matters worse, the remuneration promised by the government for the slaughtered animals was either slow in coming, never arrived, or had portions skimmed off through corruption. Not only did this policy adversely affect the campesinos' household economy; it represented a complete lack of sensitivity towards rural culture. An editorial in a left-wing journal movingly captured the effect of such a policy: "It was not a question of a few pesos more, a few pesos less. It was something more personal, more depressing, more intolerable. The patient and sober ox does not represent for our most humble campesinos the hope of eating meat. It is an instrument of work, an irreplaceable source of savings, a companion in misery and privation. The sanitary rifle spit fire and left in the hands of the Indian a few pesos that could not in any way replace the painful loss."[5]

Many campesinos felt, as they had during the 1942 forced military conscription, that the only way to confront these drastic government measures was rifle in hand. The teams carrying out the slaughter paid the price. In Michoacán, one confrontation led to the death of a veterinarian, an army captain, and six soldiers, as well as eight campesinos. Fifty others were incarcerated. Several officials from the United States working on the campaign were killed as well. In the region of the Bajío, campesinos and small farmers "locked their cattle up and asserted that they would defend their livestock 'no matter what.' Many campesinos fled with their animals to the mountains, leaving their fields unharvested."[6] The campesinos' reaction in Morelos was no different. In Tepalcingo, one ex-Zapatista general declared that he preferred to take up arms rather than permit the slaughter of his livestock. Some cattle ranchers also actively opposed the campaign and encouraged campesinos to fight and resist the government.[7] When Agustín Leyva, a former Zapatista from Coatetelco, heard that his cows would be sacrificed, he went in search of Jaramillo to ask for help. An experienced rifleman from the revolution, Agustín ended up joining Jaramillo's armed cadre.[8]

By choosing to deal with hoof-and-mouth disease by means of the rifle sanitario, the Mexican government seemed to indicate to campesinos that it was more concerned with demands from Washington than with the needs of its rural population. In popular circles it became a truism to affirm that the campaign's aim was not to treat the sick Mexican livestock but rather to "cure the North Americans of their fears of aphthous fever."[9] But Mexico, pointed out one scholar, "is not Texas, and cattle is not filet but a fundamental element of the rural economy. Cultivators have their cows and their team of oxen to work the land. Campesinos work with their cattle, they live from their cattle." An attack on these animals was an attack on agriculture.[10] So senseless was this campaign in the minds of many campesinos that rumors began to circulate that aphthous fever was actually a conspiracy by the United States to steal Mexican beef and sell it at low prices in Europe, where people were left starving after the war. According to this version, many local caciques were active participants in the conspiracy. What else was done with the meat after the cow was shot? Why didn't the government allow the use of home remedies that cured the disease? Why were veterinarians who could cure the animals persecuted?[11] These were the questions posed by campesinos as they witnessed the senseless slaughter of their animals. As he had done with the forced military draft, Jaramillo spoke out against the rifle sanitario. In a letter he sent to the governor of Morelos, he movingly captured the effects of this policy: "You should know that one does not kill the sick, one cares for them; that's why we have veterinary science." Jaramillo had just returned from Michoacán, where he had "seen men weep when their animal collapsed from the bullets of the tragically renowned sanitary rifle."[12] This policy elicited the ire of the rural population and in the process increased the popularity of Jaramillo as a defender of the rural poor. Many participants in this armed phase joined him in response to this newest attack on their livelihood.

Jaramillo's actions between 1946 and 1951 can be classified more as an "armed hiding" than an armed uprising. He did not formally rebel against the government and instead provided clandestine support for popular mobilizations, such as protests against the rifle sanitario and the 1948 strike at the Emiliano Zapata sugar mill. In each case, Jaramillo contributed to organizing efforts based on his own experience in past struggles. At this point, the Jaramillistas were not a guerrilla group, but rather a political movement forced into armed struggle. As Jaramillista Reyes Aranda put it, "He was the leader of the campesinos, and he'd be called to attend all the popular assemblies. He provided the counterweight [to the government], since he would make public what wasn't right, and that's why the government became his enemy."[13] Aranda's words vividly portray the process by which Jaramillo's popularity grew. Each time Jaramillo spoke out, he exposed the state as increasingly anathema to justice in the countryside. Rather than mend "what wasn't right," the state made an enemy of those who spoke out. As an armed cadre, Jaramillo's group thus became the branch of the popular movement that defended people from the violent reprisals of local police, hired gunmen, or even detrimental government policy.

"Otra vez las armas": 1952–1958

Jaramillo remained armed and in hiding until 1951, when he once again ran for governor of Morelos. Pushed into clandestine action to defend himself, he was anxious to once again become a public figure. As Jaramillistas participated in the 1952 elections and formed alliances with other groups, they achieved wide-scale mobilizations. The government combated this popular organizing through force, pushing the Jaramillistas into armed struggle for the third time. Jaramillo considered this persecution a strategy to isolate him in the mountains, contain his popular organizing, and freely abuse campesinos. As one Jaramillista put it, "Every time Rubén took up arms they [the politicians, caciques, the rich people of the state] would be happy, even though they were attentive to his actions in the mountains. But they felt better about carrying out all those maneuvers to benefit from the sweat of others. That's why, each time, Rubén accepted amnesty. It wasn't because he agreed with the government or because he was playing their game. It was because he wanted to be with the people, to struggle at their side."[14]

When Jaramillo took up arms in 1952, however, he did not confine his actions to self-defense and instead sought to join with other groups in hopes of provoking a generalized uprising throughout the region. Because the Henriquistas had made such a strong showing at the national level during the 1952 campaign, they had raised hopes for defeating the PRI. The extensive irregularities and illegal measures in the months leading to the elections, and especially on election day, turned this hope into rage. Small armed actions began to break out throughout the country. Spearheaded by the Jaramillistas, Morelos experienced several attacks on municipal offices throughout the state. Jaramillo's orders, given in a particularly cryptic style, are worth quoting for the contrasts between their tone and that of declarations he made while operating legally: "I make it urgently known to the leaders of each district of Cuernavaca, Morelos, that, based on the calculations we have made, any counterorder that might lead us to make a mistake and fail in our plans is not permitted. Thus, you should capture any person or persons who have such intentions and decree the punishment you deem necessary. Likewise, this should be the policy towards those bosses or soldiers who show cowardice and try to sow alarm or fear among the people who should operate in our struggle."[15]

Following this call, in the towns of Emiliano Zapata and Jiutepec on the outskirts of Cuernavaca, sixty armed Jaramillistas attacked police stations and took weapons and dynamite cartridges.[16] The Jaramillistas called for the resignation of the state governor, Rodolfo López de Nava (1952–58), for violating several articles of the Mexican Constitution and showing hostility to "the people, their rights, justice, liberty, and the Constitutional order." Even in these instances of armed rebellion, the Jaramillistas appealed to the law. The document, signed by Jaramillo and 704 delegates from different towns throughout Morelos, gave the governor an ultimatum to leave office within eleven days, or else the people could make use of their rights granted under Article 39 of the Mexican Constitution and "exercise their autonomy, in which case you will be the one responsible for all that may happen."[17]

In the southern part of Morelos, Jaramillistas also attempted to surround and take over the cities of Jojutla, Zacatepec, and Tlaquiltenango.[18] A participant in the action recalled, "Those of us here were told to meet in Zacatepec. More came from Alpuyeca and Tlacholoaya, and we left from here around ten or eleven at night—all of us with our armaments hidden in between the bundles of firewood we each carried. . . . There were about forty of us. It was drizzling all night. We had the place surrounded; we were just waiting for the signal: a shot or fireworks."[19] But the signal never came. The attack failed due to a combination of cold feet, lack of coordination, and small numbers. Although they enjoyed considerable popular support, when it came to a generalized armed uprising the Jaramillistas could not count on the same level of participation. This is an indication that despite extensive popular protest during these decades, militarily, the state was not under direct threat. Rather, the significance behind such ambitious plans lies in the level of frustration and anger brewing in the countryside following the crushing of popular demands in the 1952 elections. One campesino recalled, "We kept going to protest in Mexico [City], to press the Federation [FPPM]. Finally we had a meeting attended by people from many states. We agreed that there was no other choice but to openly declare ourselves against the government. They just do not listen to petitions or protests."[20] During the campaign, Jaramillo had expressed a similar sentiment, "Now, I am once again in the struggle, because I know that Mexico's campesinos, my compañeros, have a hunger and thirst for justice; because our ejidos are being snatched from us, because the CNC that we formed has betrayed us . . . and those lands we obtained with the blood of our brothers who died in the revolution."[21] Such statements reveal at once a frustration with the revolution, whose institutionalization meant a hijacking of its popular origins, and an appeal to combat this process through outright rebellion.

One of these rebellions would be led by Celestino Gasca, a high-ranking Henriquista, who had spent time gathering support in the countryside for the FPPM. Faced with Henríquez Guzmán's inaction in the months after the election, Gasca decided to take advantage of the smoldering discontent caused by the PRI's fraud and repression during the 1952 election. In subsequent years he spoke widely of an armed uprising that would erupt throughout Mexico and positioned himself as the leader. But his ideological program differed fundamentally from Jaramillo's, illustrating the wide social network brought together under the Henriquista umbrella. Gasca advocated private ownership of land, and he declared himself to be fiercely opposed to the ejido system, which ran counter to the capitalist system he favored.[22] According to Jaramillista testimonies, Gasca had originally agreed to send support for Jaramillo's planned uprising in Morelos, but the men he promised never arrived. After that, "Jaramillo would have nothing to do with Gasca."[23] In the years to come, Gasca continuously threatened to lead an armed uprising, but he waited until 1961, by which time he had lost momentum and support. What resulted from Gasca's efforts almost a decade after the elections were a series of municipal office takeovers by campesinos in Puebla, Veracruz, Guerrero, Chiapas, Coahuila, Oaxaca, and the State of Mexico. These actions left about one thousand people detained, several dead, and a state of siege in the respective municipalities.[24]

In any case, Jaramillistas, without the help of Gasca, did move against the authorities responsible for the intense repression that marked Jaramillo's electoral campaign. One party militant described how "there were times in which towns would reach an agreement to defend themselves. When action was taken and a cacique or a hired gunman was eliminated, the party [the PAOM] would endorse such acts. The people would discuss what measures to take; it was always in self-defense."[25] Jaramillistas speak only vaguely about the instances in which they avenged campesino murders. The execution of pistoleros or authorities with particularly ruthless records against the local population was one of the strategies by which the Jaramillistas sought to protect themselves. Such executions were rare, but they demonstrated to the local population the Jaramillistas' willingness to act against clear and identifiable enemies. They were an attempt to mete out justice in a system whose authorities acted with complete impunity. In this way, Jaramillo and his armed cadre constituted the "mobile and indispensable branch of the territorial struggle, the needed defense against official acts of violence. Jaramillo was simultaneously a *justiciero* [one who imparts justice] and what we might designate an 'organic vanguard' of the region's movement."[26] For all that the Jaramillistas relied on their leader, what emerges from campesino voices is the extent to which Jaramillo was a recourse to help carry out the will of a disempowered and vulnerable sector of Morelos. Jaramillo was thus a channel to organize and direct campesino discontent.

In their pursuit of Jaramillo, government forces used counterinsurgency measures that would become increasingly systematic during the 1970s dirty war. Campesinos in Jojutla complained to the president that these soldiers acted abusively and arbitrarily towards the general population, threatening "poor and defenseless people" who had nothing to do with Jaramillo. The government forces mistreated women and held up bars, stores, and even fruit stands.[27] One report complained that a campesino from Jojutla was kidnapped by the police for his alleged ties to Jaramillo and was found dead in the local hospital by his relatives.[28] Ricarda Juárez relates that her husband, Enrique Pérez Ramírez, also suffered persecution and torture at the hands of authorities. Pérez, a participant in the Jaramillista struggle, was abducted from his home in the middle of the night and mysteriously died in jail a few days later.[29] Jaramillistas recount other instances of state violence. An anonymous Jaramillista described how he, his brother, and three others were taken by the judicial police and questioned as to the whereabouts of Jaramillo. In the presence of the police chief, this campesino was beaten and tortured with electric shocks. "They put electric cables on my head. Then they took off my sandals and put water on my feet to make more contact. There were four of them writing down what I said."[30] Torture appears as a consistent method through which authorities attempted to disarticulate the Jaramillistas.

In response, the group's leadership would again act both to defend themselves and to impart some measure of justice in the face of a government that ignored the rule of law. With legal channels closed and federal authorities unresponsive, Jaramillistas thus avenged the death of Eleuterio Sánchez, a Jaramillista who was tortured and slain by Ticumán police chief Ermenengildo Barberi.[31] As described in Chapter 4, Sánchez had been castrated and the heels of his feet sliced off, and he had been forced to walk along railroad tracks. The press reported on the Jaramillista retaliations, but not on the government's torture. A report compiled from dispatches of United Press and the Associated Press, headlined "Continuing Strife between the Henriquistas and President Ruiz Cortines," stated that Jaramillo led an attack of thirty men on the town of Ticumán, "killing three government political leaders and wounding a policeman."[32] During this attack, according to another source, the Jaramillistas held a quick trial in the central plaza, after which they decided to execute the town's mayor, the chief of police, and two merchants responsible for Sánchez's torture.[33] The government sent federal troops, who chased the Jaramillistas into the mountains, killing eleven of Jaramillo's men. In the process, however, the army lost an even higher number of soldiers to Jaramillista fire.[34]

With such actions, we should not be surprised by Jaramillo's growing reputation as a ruthless bandit, on the one hand, and as a defender of the poor, on the other. Government propaganda not withstanding, Jaramillo enjoyed a tremendous amount of legitimacy in his own state. Moreover, the agrarian leader continuously made a point to defend himself from government sources that painted him as a mere *revoltoso* (troublemaker). He put out declarations explaining his actions, one of which read, "No citizen of the state of Morelos should believe the bad things that the government and its allies say about us, its opposition. We proclaim unconditional respect for the rights, freedom, life, and interests of the people." Jaramillo then inverted the government's argument that the rebels were enemies of the people; rather, the Jaramillistas were enemies of the real enemies of the people, "those who have governed with all kinds of crimes and injustices." Jaramillo insisted that his "politics were peaceful, clear, and irrevocably in favor of the poor and disenfranchised." He distinguished between the democratic principles he espoused and those practices the government falsely claimed to be democratic. In the "democracy" practiced by the state, said Jaramillo, there was only room for the "governing groups who then placed every obstacle before the people, thus effectively preventing them from exercising even their most basic civil rights."[35]

Much of the language of this document attempts to reclaim the Zapatista revolution from the state that had appropriated it. "We are agraristas from the heart," read Point 5 of the declaration, which went on to explain that the Jaramillistas were condemning a government that had left the ejidatarios to live in misery. The Jaramillistas had fought against the caciques of the "ranches, colonias, towns, and cities." The regional bosses, he explained, were an integral part of the power structure that denied the population its sovereignty. The declaration ended with an urgent appeal to the people to draw on their experience in various battles and recognize the nature of their enemies, reminding readers of Article 39 of the Mexican Constitution.[36] Jaramillo wanted to make it clear that his movement was lawful and based on constitutional rights. Not only was he defending the rights of the people against an abusive government; he was also reminding the population that their rights and liberties had come about only through hard-fought battles waged by those who in their time had also been labeled bandits.

The Modern Attila

The Jaramillistas faced a state apparatus which exercised its power at many levels, including control of information through the local and national press. Newspapers partook in the government's efforts to crush the Left by maintaining a fiercely anticommunist line.[37] Between 1940 and 1960, the press's hysteria against the "communist menace" grew to comprise leftist members of the PRI, including former president Cárdenas and former head of the state's official labor union Vicente Lombardo Toledano. While labeling groups communist was the easiest way to vilify them, newspapers often showed themselves quite creative in their characterizations of campesino groups such as the Jaramillistas. Rather than labeling them pawns of the Soviet Union, newspapers relied on notions of barbarism long held about Mexico's indigenous or rural poor. The majority of press coverage on Jaramillo portrayed him as a dangerous bandit, a delinquent, and an evildoer who sowed terror in the countryside.

The close relationship between the state and media is best illustrated in the reports of embedded *El Universal* journalists. Accompanying the "noble soldiers" who exercised their duty with "admirable precision amidst the thorny vegetation and inhospitable terrain," one article's author described Jaramillo as a "fierce enemy of the people" and marveled at community members' reluctance to reveal his whereabouts. "The indigenous people, dry and unexpressive, say nothing of their fellow villager. . . . Children and elders alike remain silent, refusing to understand any question that is posed to them. . . . No one knows anything."[38] It was this complicity, the article lamented, that allowed the Jaramillista armed group to thrive in the sierra, where they hid in caves and followed paths known only to wild animals.[39] Media portrayals of Jaramillo, moreover, are throughout tinged by a racist characterization of this peasant who dared defy the rule of law. One report, for example, stated, "Jaramillo is, at first glance, a repulsive individual, and his manner reflects a certain conceit, a somewhat natural tendency in a rustic individual who has managed to polish himself a bit by interacting with relatively cultured people."[40] In this vein, another report characterizes the four women who were part of Jaramillo's armed group as "old, ugly, and unspeakably dirty."[41] Overall, in Jaramillo the press of the 1950s sought to construct the archetype of evil.

National newspapers made it a special point to bring up Jaramillo's Methodist background, which, an *Excélsior* article commented, he used to "terrorize and exploit" the campesinos of Morelos.[42] The report offers no concrete examples of the relationship between Jaramillo's religion and this control over the population, but other newspapers, too, attribute to his Methodism some sort of mystical power with which he conducted "spiritual cleansings through weird gestures and phrases that permit[ted] him to seduce a great number of people who follow him."[43] Such reports labeled Jaramillo not only a bandit, but also an outcast, one associated with mysterious forces. By emphasizing Jaramillo's Methodism, the press sought to portray him as an alien element in an overwhelmingly Catholic society, even though he actually enjoyed a great degree of legitimacy in the state.

It is interesting, given the emphasis of the Truman doctrine on the communist threat and the extent to which other groups were denounced under this guise, that Jaramillo was not yet labeled a Red. This would change, however, after the 1959 triumph of the Cuban Revolution. Still, newspapers did portray Jaramillo as a national security threat, branding him "Public enemy number 1." Reports noted that he made use of guerrilla strategies and that he consistently avoided battling the army head on.[44]

Overall, national press coverage of the Jaramillistas employed a framework that juxtaposed the civilized, urban middle class to the poor, barbaric, rural masses. In this way, national newspapers gave voice to elite anxiety surrounding popular mobilizations. Similar characterizations had been made of Zapata, whom the press had christened a "modern Attila" during the revolution. This sentiment was especially acute when Zapatista and Villista forces took over Mexico City and acted with complete disregard to established class norms—daring, for example, to dine in elegant establishments such as the exclusive Casa de los Azulejos. Womack captures the double standard with which violence was judged: "Revolutionary executions were always distressing, but if the executioners were recognizably 'white' and dressed like civilized beings in pants, boots, and shirts, their deeds remained human. That the 'plebes' should execute victims was 'Indian,' subhuman, monstrous."[45]

Decades later and in circumstances of apparent stability, this sentiment was reproduced almost exactly in Mexico's national press with respect to the Jaramillistas. When the group tried and executed a particularly brutal Morelos police chief, the wrath of the civilized made itself heard, as various articles and editorials called for Jaramillo's assassination, to be carried out within or outside legal norms. One *Excélsior* editorial, in direct allusion to Jaramillo, stated, "We cannot recall if the death penalty exists within the Morelos legal code. But we believe that, as was done during the past war [the revolution], the federal government should reestablish it for cases involving assault or rape along roads. It should be done now with this type of bandits whose only goal is crime and theft."[46] Another editorial published a few days later expressed, "Just because we live in a regime that tries to respect civic life and to conform to judicial norms, does not mean that we should refrain from an authoritarian and firm policy to ensure compliance with the republic's laws."[47] The author's unabashed call for authoritarian principles appears revealingly candid of elite disdain for the poor.

Local newspaper reports seemed to reflect yellow journalism rather than outright racism. A 1950 article on the Jaramillistas appearing in *El Sol de Morelos*, for example, stated that five hundred "perfectly armed men" operated along the fringes of the state bordering Guerrero and Puebla. The reporter admitted he had no actual contact with the rebels and was basing his information on rumors that were credible, "given the quantity of information" they carried with them.[48] By citing the elevated figure of five hundred "perfectly armed men"—a number that surpassed even the highest estimates made by the Jaramillistas themselves and the most exaggerated reports from Ministry of the Interior agents—the newspaper helped justify a militarization of Morelos. In such a small state, this number of armed men practically suggested an imminent war. The presence of a small, highly mobile rebel army that might gain the sympathy of the rural poor—if it didn't already have it—jeopardized the state's unfolding economic projects of tourism and vast housing developments, not to mention the power of local caciques. While there were high levels of illiteracy, and even greater numbers of people who did not buy newspapers, such reports helped spread rumors about the "dangerous" nature of Jaramillo's actions. For example, one woman who would later join the Jaramillistas remembered her initial impressions about Jaramillo based on newspaper articles: "In my neighborhood in Cuernavaca someone would buy a newspaper and people would gather around to hear what it said about Jaramillo. . . . They lashed out against him badly, very badly. That he was a bandit, they said, that he had invaded such and such a town, that he stole from here and from there, that he robbed cattle."[49]

Two months later, the same newspaper published an account of an attack on the notorious head of the state police, Mario Olea. Campesinos, as well as agents of the Ministry of the Interior, often discussed Olea's ruthless qualities and the fact that he doubled as a hit man for both Zacatepec managers and Morelos governors.[50] The assault on Olea occurred the evening of April 6, 1950, near Chinameca, in the district of Jojutla. Olea stated that the attack, which left two of his men dead, involved between twenty-five and thirty-five men under the direction of Jaramillo, who was already "responsible for numerous subversive acts against the state government," had "on previous occasions declared himself in open rebellion," and had "been identified by many as the invisible head of the rebel groups throughout the state."[51] Olea had many enemies, however, and this was not the first attempt on his life. Pedro García, a Jaramillista, recalled, "Mario Olea was not the personal pistolero of one [Zacatepec] manager; he was the permanent pistolero of the refinery's management. Whoever was manager used him as a hit man. He also worked for the governor, whoever was in office. . . . But then Mario Olea stopped obeying the politicians' orders; still, they had little control over him because he knew all their secrets."[52]

A week after this incident, *El Sol de Morelos* published a letter from Jaramillo denying any involvement in the incident. Jaramillo declared that he had never attempted to assassinate the police chief; rather, Olea's accusations resulted from Jaramillo's uncompromising position as a defender of the poor. While Jaramillo opened his letter by stating that he turned to armed struggle in self-defense, he ended by justifying the causes for rebellion: "It is the bad acts of the authorities in charge of imparting justice that create rebels. . . . The submissive and meek, the cowards, have not been the ones who have helped the population; it has been those who rebelled against tyrannies and oppression." Jaramillo then invited Olea to act justly and fairly and guaranteed that if he did so, he would lose the support of the politicians.[53] Such declarations, which pointed to the government's responsibility in eliciting armed movements, inverted official arguments that branded the Jaramillistas as bandits. Jaramillista declarations in the press were actually quite rare, but in their literature the rebels explicitly defended themselves against the charges of banditry by citing official repression, authorities' illicit enrichment, and Article 39 of the constitution, which decreed that the people had, at all times, the right to change their form of government.

The Second Plan de Cerro Prieto

While the press attempted to discredit the Jaramillistas by portraying their military operations as the acts of savage barbarians, the rebels created a different impression among the residents of the Morelos countryside. The fact that Jaramillo eluded capture during the thirteen years he operated outside the law speaks to a significant degree of sympathy and complicity among the state's rural population. Participants remember the support which allowed them to survive during their clandestine years: "There was not a thing that smelled or seemed bad, or was rumored, that Rubén didn't already know. That shows that the people were with him and that they protected him."[54] Crescencio Castillo, another Jaramillista, stated, "Even within the gobierno, there were people that were on Rubén's side. Among the judicial police, a soldier or two were in contact with him. That's why anything that happened we already knew about."[55] Even within its own forces the government could not control the sympathy Jaramillo's struggle elicited. Building upon such popular support for their movement, during the 1952 armed phase the Jaramillistas engaged in a campaign of grassroots organizing throughout the rural landscape. The Plan de Cerro Prieto, modified according to the increasing radicalism of the movement, would become a key organizing tool.

Most of the Jaramillista actions during this armed phase consisted of traveling throughout the state creating support for their program. In fact, given the extent to which the Jaramillistas suffered persecution even during their electoral mobilizations, there was considerable overlap between their armed and legal actions. Cirilo García recalled how they went "from town to town, or to rancherías, and even bigger places like Jojutla, Cuautla, or Cuernavaca. We had meetings to advise people about the government's actions, about what it did to stay in power. And we would look for ways to struggle against government abuses, to present the people's complaints all together and in writing. That's how we carried out the struggle then."[56] In the process, many campesinos, including García, who originally joined Jaramillo in an act of self-defense began to relate their situation to a broader systemic injustice. There was thus an important development of consciousness in people who did not originally join Jaramillo for explicitly political motivations. For example, García first decided to join Jaramillo to protect himself after two of his uncles were killed for speaking out against Zacatepec's fraudulent weighing system. His account of Jaramillo's words provides an example of the process by which campesinos became politicized:

> I didn't know anything about him, but from the time I joined him, he talked about his struggle: "It is because of this, the abuse undertaken by caciques and the government against campesinos. What is happening to your family, that's because they defended the rights of campesinos. It is not in the interests of those in power to have people defend campesinos. And that's not only happening to your uncles; it happens to many in the entire state. My job is to help guide, to help campesinos use legal channels even if we are so often ignored, because if we don't protest, it's worse. So one has to protest, one has to denounce, even if we make them mad, even if they persecute us."[57]

Jaramillo's words, as remembered by García, are a clear indication of the meaning participants ascribed to their actions, a struggle which, despite the repression, was necessary, since without protest "it was worse." Along with their weapons, food, and water supplies, the Jaramillistas carried a typewriter on which Jaramillo composed petitions and wrote up grievances on behalf of the local population. Federal archival records contain many of Jaramillo's appeals urging a favorable resolution to specific acts of injustice. Such actions established a solid foundation for later mobilizations that supported Jaramillo during his electoral campaign. One participant described how, when they decided to create a party, "the movement was already there, because since [Jaramillo] had taken up arms he'd been organizing the people. When the party was formed there was already a structure with which to work peacefully."[58] The same structure through which the Jaramillistas worked in times of peace provided cover in times of war.

During the uprising of 1952 the Jaramillistas reissued the Plan de Cerro Prieto, updating their grievances and political vision. In many ways this plan paralleled the version issued in 1943. Both expressed a vision of political change that went beyond the reformist calls of the electoral campaigns and advocated a redistribution of wealth and an organization of society that eliminated the class structures. Yet the later document is far more explicit in condemning Mexico's social order and reflects a profound disillusionment with the political system and the economic project that it oversaw.

The ten years that had elapsed since the writing of the first plan provided additional elements from which to condemn the regime and the consequences of approving a constitution that did not place power firmly in the hands of rural and urban laborers—the majority of the population. This tone provides a glimpse into the increasing radicalized stance that the Jaramillistas would ultimately adopt.[59] Federal and state authorities had responded to the Jaramillistas' 1946 and 1952 political campaigns with fraud, but the authorities did more than just keep Jaramillo from winning the governorship. They used repression in an attempt to disarticulate their mobilization in Morelos. Therefore, the first point of the 1952 Plan de Cerro Prieto stated, "The Mexican people, in their long revolutionary trajectory since 1810 until the present, have always rejected tyranny."[60] The Jaramillistas thus placed their rebellion within the history of national battles that dated back to the war of independence. Several of the points that followed called attention to the ways in which the Mexican Constitution had been "trampled on." The document acknowledged that this constitution embraced Zapata's Plan de Ayala; however, since the government had failed to uphold the constitution and had resorted to force to stay in power, it was responsible for the crime of high treason. At the same time, the plan declared, the government continued to find ways—in open violation of democratic principles—to impose rulers. The plan stated that the first twenty-nine articles of the Mexican Constitution—those guaranteeing individual rights and liberties—had become a dead letter and in practice only facilitated abuses by the "press, clergy, and the capitalist bourgeoisie."[61] The 1910 revolution had been betrayed, and its protagonists had "given way to a new group of rich people who, in conjunction with foreign companies, continuously exploited the workers."[62] Thus the "bourgeois-capitalist regime" had taken possession of the resources that rightfully belonged to the people. In addition, foreigners under the aegis of the good neighbor policy had built monopolies which extracted the nation's wealth and exacerbated Mexico's condition as an exporter of raw materials and a consumer of industrial products. As they had done in their earlier plan, the Jaramillistas condemned the relationship of economic imperialism that conditioned Mexico's underdevelopment. In this relationship, declared the plan, the government was actively complicit.[63]

The plan also denounced the mechanisms through which the PRI maintained control of the population. It singled out monopolistic official unions. These unions included workers in every industry; even the garbage scavengers belonged to an official union, which, in the words of the plan, demonstrated how "we don't even have a right to the garbage."[64] The PRI also maintained control by imposing politicians at all levels of government, including senators, representatives, state governors, and mayors. Through such measures, the state dealt with its population as if it were the enemy. This type of treatment, stated the plan, was to be expected, since Mexico did not have a government of the people.

The document pointed out that the system of individual property ownership which existed in the country fostered a relationship of exploitation "of men by men," and thus the control of land, mountains, and water had to be reorganized to promote collective ownership. Again, the Jaramillistas called for an intensification of agricultural production and an end to exports of products needed by the Mexican population. The plan claimed that the 1910 revolution had been primarily agrarian and called for this New Revolution to extend its purview to include the factories so that they could be turned over to the workers.[65] The plan ended by announcing that it did not recognize the current rulers as legitimate, then declared that since the people were never heard unless they were armed, they would fight to achieve the triumph of the Plan de Cerro Prieto. Once the new revolution had triumphed, a junta of new leaders would draft a new constitution.

Jaramillo and many of his followers came from Zapata's agrarian revolutionary tradition. Yet in the decades after 1940 they faced a fundamentally different political situation. To the agrarian demands made by Zapata's Plan de Ayala, Jaramillo's Plan de Cerro Prieto added a vision that sought a drastic change in Mexico's class structure. One scholar even characterized Jaramillo as a political heir to the anarcho-syndicalist tradition of Ricardo and Enrique Flores Magón, who in the years before the revolution organized around principles that workers should own the factories in which they labored and peasants should own the land they tilled.[66] Certainly, the Plan de Cerro Prieto presented several anarcho-syndicalist elements, as in its call for a governing council of workers and campesinos, as well as their ownership of public goods and the elimination of businessmen.[67] Like Zapata's Plan de Ayala, the Plan de Cerro Prieto is consistent with the Magonista vision in which the masses are both the subjects and agents of change.[68] During the revolution, leaders such as Madero, Carranza, and Obregón sought to keep workers and campesinos on a short leash in order to control the extent of political change which resulted from popular mobilizations. These sectors were then to give up their arms and wait while the leaders enacted promised reforms. The struggles waged by Zapata, Villa, and the Flores Magón brothers, on the other hand, had profound implications for popular power. Mass mobilization was part and parcel of implementing political and economic change. Jaramillo's Plan de Cerro Prieto appealed to this bottom-up construction of the state in Point 15, which read, "A NATIONAL COUNCIL OF WORKERS that is born from the bottom up will administer all benefits for the good of the people."[69] In contrast to their electoral mobilizations, which placed hope in particular individuals, this document ultimately called for a restructuring of society that placed workers and campesinos at its head.

While the Zapatistas' main concerns centered around land, both plans shared the basic principle that the people were entitled to the means of subsistence. Yet, the Plan de Cerro Prieto presented both agrarista goals and a program that responded to Mexico's industrialization process. In their thinking about the ownership of land and the means to make it produce, as well as the entitlement to articles of basic human necessity, the Jaramillistas planned a socialist society. Absent from this vision were the earlier reformist appeals that had so marked Jaramillo's electoral campaign. Jaramillo shared with subsequent guerrilla movements the notion that the PRI had betrayed the ideals of the revolution as set forth in the 1917 constitution, especially Article 7, protecting freedom of speech and expression; Article 27, guaranteeing land rights and national sovereignty; and Article 123, establishing labor rights. Like rebel groups that came later, Jaramillo turned to armed struggle after exhausting legal channels. And, as did later guerrilla groups, this document placed no faith in Mexico's political system. The tone of the second Plan de Cerro Prieto revealed outrage at the authoritarian nature of the Mexican state and, unlike the first plan, called for a different constitution and a new revolution.

Jaramillo always justified his use of arms. The subtitle of a manifesto put out by the Jaramillistas in November 1956 and directed to "The Public Opinion of the Mexican Republic" read, "Arms should be used to defend the sovereignty, independence, and rights of the People and not to harm them." In a clear allusion to the revolution's popular generals, the manifesto pictured Jaramillo with a rifle in his hands, bandoliers criss-crossing his chest. The text condemned the ruling party for exacting increasing hardships on the Mexican population; it then proceeded to remind Mexicans that if they remained passive, they would be further subjugated. Jaramillo made an appeal to the people to stop legitimizing the ruling party by selling their vote and allowing themselves to be transported to PRI-sponsored rallies in exchange for perqs (such bought-off "supporters" were known as *acarreados*, or "shipped in").[70] Like the Plan de Cerro Prieto, this document emphasized that workers and campesinos were the source of the national wealth, and therefore they should be the ones "ruling, rather than obeying."[71] Therefore, the document concluded, it was high time that all workers unite and act as one to ensure their sovereignty. After all, wrote Jaramillo, Article 39 of the constitution guaranteed that right.

Although during this phase the Jaramillistas engaged in confrontations with the military and police forces (they even once used ransom money to finance themselves), they primarily acted in self-defense and encouraged the local population to stand up for their rights.[72] Despite their turn to armed struggle, the Jaramillistas had emerged with a broad, strong popular base and a comprehensive vision of the nation that they sought to re-create, all in accordance with the historical struggles of their ancestors and legitimized by the ideals of the Mexican Constitution. By citing the constitution's Article 39, they gave a legal foundation to their actions, insofar as the government's abuse of power and contempt for the rights of the people had rendered it illegitimate. The Jaramillistas were defending the Mexican Constitution, the document that guaranteed the rights of the people. As one Jaramillista put it, "[Most of the time] we weren't up in arms against the government. We were just defending ourselves. . . . We also had a political program, which was the same as the government's, except they weren't adhering to their own laws."[73] The logic here was powerfully simple: "We are fighting for the principles from which our rulers claim legitimacy but which they have completely betrayed. It is they who are operating outside the law."

CHAPTER SIX

Gender, Community, and Struggle

The situation of women in the Jaramillista movement underscores a common contradiction in social movements that pursue political and economic rights but constrain women's participation. Women Jaramillistas took on a double fight: they struggled against the structural forces that oppressed campesinos, and they challenged—through a variety of mechanisms—sexist practices which held that women should stay out of politics. Those who did participate shouldered the triple burden as organizers, workers, and family caretakers. Women were key to the movement's organizational structure and longevity, but they were rarely part of the leadership, nor were their opinions solicited or taken into account as much as men's were. It would be anachronistic to expect otherwise in the Mexico of the 1940s or 1950s—especially in the countryside. Nonetheless women acted. Initially they did so in a manner consistent with their socially assigned role as caregivers. Soon, however, the exigencies of the movement changed the nature of their tasks and pushed women into uncommon grounds, ones that clashed with the traditional rural norms guarding gender. This clash between theory and practice provides an opportunity to examine women's agency in the context of both rural society generally and social mobilizations in particular.

The experiences of Jaramillo's first and second wives reflect the ways gender dynamics unfolded within the Jaramillista movement. Little is known about Epifania Ramírez, Jaramillo's first wife, who died of unknown causes in the late 1930s or early in 1940. Some Jaramillistas affirm that her frail health was worsened by the constant and aggressive visits of gunmen in search of Jaramillo. The following description is typical of how Ramírez is remembered: "We knew Doña Epifania well; she married appropriately with a religious and civil ceremony. They were from Tlaquiltenango. I got to know her well. I'd visit her once Rubén left. She'd wash clothes for a living. . . . Poor thing! She soon died, fear stricken. . . . When she died, the gobierno surrounded the entire cemetery. They thought Jaramillo would come to her burial, but no. She never left her home, though many urged her. Sometimes at twelve at night the government would come and kick the door down thinking Jaramillo would be there. My *comadre* suffered a lot."[1] Ramírez, enshrined in a self-sacrificing aura, is remembered as Jaramillo's "real" wife, who taught him how to read and helped him become a Methodist pastor. The Jaramillistas lamented her suffering but admired her patience and selfless devotion to her husband.

Jaramillo's second wife, whose first name, coincidentally, was also Epifania, joined Jaramillo in the mountains. Epifania Zúñiga, a rural schoolteacher, lived in Los Hornos, from where she provided material support for the Jaramillistas during their first armed uprising. The Jaramillistas also used her house to store much of the movement's materiel. In the late months of 1943, the military invaded her home looking for Jaramillo, and she fled to the mountains, leaving her four children (all between the ages of six years and three months) with her mother.[2] Zúñiga is remembered as always carrying a weapon hidden in her *rebozo* (shawl). She is said to have saved Jaramillo's life on at least two occasions by shooting at soldiers or local authorities. While Jaramillistas praised such actions, a controversial air surrounds Zúñiga's memory. Some Jaramillistas accuse her of exerting excessive control over Jaramillo in the last few years of their lives. A few Jaramillistas speak of how, in the days prior to their assassination, when there were rumors that the government intended to kill Jaramillo, she prevented him from going into hiding as he had in the past.[3] She convinced him, some say, that with their presidential pardons they would be safe. A leader in her own right, Zúñiga was then planning to start a cooperative for other women using sewing machines promised by the first lady, Eva Sámano. Some of these negative views about Zúñiga stem, at least in part, from the extent to which she overstepped her assigned gender role.[4] The differing legacies surrounding Ramírez and Zúñiga are emblematic of some of the contradictions of a movement which called attention to the needs and rights of women but upheld gender codes that subjugated them.

Despite such social practices and even backlash, women's key role in the Jaramillista movement is undeniable, and today it is remembered by men and women alike. More importantly, while women's involvement tended to follow traditional gender lines, the dynamic of the movement and the exigencies of a life of struggle eased some patriarchal norms in ways that opened up the possibility of addressing female subjugation. In this way, Jaramillista conceptions of justice as they relate to gender act as a gateway to understanding peasant consciousness within a postrevolutionary peasant movement. Bringing to light the role of female Jaramillistas at once exposes women's traditionally overlooked experiences and uncovers the dynamic of female participation in a movement dominated by men. Women sustained the Jaramillista movement by providing food and shelter, serving as messengers, spies, and bodyguards, and often by linking the armed group to the general populace in Morelos. This behind-the-scenes participation leaves fewer historical records, and since women do not always conceive of such actions as political, reconstructing their participation is a complicated task. Today, female participants are less likely to self-identify as Jaramillistas than are male participants. Even so, their visible and active participation made the Jaramillistas one of the few postrevolutionary campesino movements to explicitly draw attention to the needs and rights of women. The Jaramillistas extended their criticism of injustice to a condemnation of the additional burden that poverty placed on women. While women have always played active roles in popular upheavals, rarely did their activities translate into gender-specific demands.[5]

Within the Jaramillista movement, gender roles followed historic patterns of participation in rural uprisings and also drew from the political project unfolding as a result of Mexico's revolutionary consolidation, which bowed to patriarchal lines. Official rhetoric emphasized women's innate moral qualities in the home and assigned them "the vital task of pacifying unruly male behavior and stabilizing the revolution."[6] Women constituted an essential part of the revolution's modernizing project, as they would be responsible

for transmitting and reproducing the new set of values.[7] Government officials hailed women's "maternal sacrifice" as an "indisputable characteristic of
the Mexican home."[8] Thus, appealing to the gendered notions of justice espoused by the revolutionary regime was a double-edged sword. On the one
hand, some aspects of Mexico's consolidation as a modern state provided a
source of empowerment for women: for example, the emergence of schools
that created "a direct linkage between [women] as household managers and
socializers of children and the state."[9] The introduction of technical advancements such as the corn mill—part of the state's attempts to turn women into
"modern, market-oriented homemakers"—shortened the hours of domestic
labor and provided women greater opportunities to enter the public sphere
of politics.[10]

On the other hand, agrarian reform, by upholding the peasant household
as a unit with gender-specific roles, reinforced rural patriarchy.[11] Indeed,
the government used state agencies such as the Agrarian Department to
instruct women on their proper role. For example, one of their pamphlets
read, "Dedicate all your attention to your husband, who arrives from the
field tired from work, looking for the tranquility of your home, and with
good appetite. Serve him and be amiable with him, making sure to listen to
him and never reveal a bad mood. Be an agreeable wife and self-sacrificing
mother."[12] But, as Jocelyn Olcott has shown in her study on women's organizing during the Cárdenas years, while the state sought to harness female
mobilization for its own reform project, women were not simple receptacles
and transmitters of the state's will. Women who participated in government-
sponsored associations inevitably helped shape them and often pushed beyond the institutional confines towards more radical proposals.[13]

A similar dynamic is evident among women participants in the Jaramillista movement. Traditional gender roles at first determined the ways
in which Jaramillista women supported the movement, and the demands
they voiced corresponded to the state's gendered notions about the family
unit. However, the immediate needs of the movement at times overrode
rural gender constraints, thus providing a greater space for women to assert themselves. The Jaramillistas did not seek to revolutionize gender roles;
many of their appeals simply sought to relieve the strains poverty placed
on a woman's ability to care for her family. However, the recognition that
women were subjected to an additional layer of hardship, and the Jaramillistas' proposals to ameliorate this condition, at once stand as a testament

to women's participation in the movement and evince the Jaramillistas' gendered conceptions of justice.

Women and Social Change

The history of women's political organizing during the Mexican Miracle remains largely unexplored.[14] From the little that has been written for the early decades of this period, it is possible to discern three principal currents that would mark the course of Mexico's feminist movement. Of these three currents, the one followed by women associated with the Mexican Communist Party most closely resembles the appeals voiced by the Jaramillistas. Although these women linked their exploitation to capitalism, they faced limitations in their ability to organize because male party members downplayed the need to address sexist practices within the party. Instead, women's rights were subsumed within the analysis of class struggle. Other currents of the feminist movement in Mexico reflected a different view. Women within the official party sought to compete equally with men, both within the state apparatus and the party structure. The capitalist economic system was not an issue. A third current argued for the need to form female organizations independent of state and party structures and made demands specifically based on biological differences. While their demands aimed at easing women's household responsibilities, such proposals reinforced a gendered division of labor by differentiating between women and men's social responsibilities and their economic and political rights.[15] Upper- or middle-class women, whose worlds differed greatly from those of poor women, spearheaded each of these three movements.

The poverty which characterized campesino households placed an additional strain on women, who not only performed domestic duties but also often had to find a source of income to supplement that of their husbands. As the pressures on campesino families became more acute during the period of the Mexican Miracle, the rural population had to produce more with less. They accomplished this by diversifying income sources and working harder for longer hours.[16] In addition to raising market and subsistence crops, campesinos and campesinas worked as domestics or peons on large farms or in nearby urban centers. Others made and sold crafts at local markets, and some women earned a small income as *curanderas* (traditional healers) or midwives. To survive, the entire family labored. Although such work by women and children is often rendered invisible, it constitutes one of the most important inputs for the peasant economy. The gendered division of labor assigned women the task of household reproduction, which in the countryside is far more arduous than in cities.[17] After studying rural Morelos, the anthropologist Arturo Warman found that women and children, "besides undertaking in tasks that are not strictly productive but save expenditures," contributed thousands of workdays to peasant production, enabling households to survive on an "income that statistically, would be not merely insufficient but ridiculous."[18]

Moreover, campesino labor and income was appropriated at various levels. With limited access to urban centers, small-scale producers depended heavily on intermediaries who siphoned off much of the profits by charging high transportation costs or paying low prices. Because the Mexican government prioritized city dwellers, it kept prices low on the dietary staples destined for urban markets. Small-scale farmers thus subsidized urban consumption. During the Mexican Miracle, as Warman put it, "agricultural growth fell upon relatively fewer and fewer people, who necessarily worked more. In many senses, the true miracle of Mexican development was located in agriculture, in the countryside and in its people."[19] For campesinas, this situation translated into harsher exploitation of family labor. In addition to their paid work, the laborious processes of making food, cleaning, and taking care of the children absorbed most of the remaining hours in the day. In the countryside, women were expected to perform these chores, and men rarely, if ever, helped.

While women exerted varying degrees of influence in family decisions, a belief in male superiority ultimately upheld men's power, which found expression in physical coercion and sexual violence. Women thus experienced the structures of exploitation more acutely, and challenging them required action on several levels. To participate in the political movement, women had to break with stereotypes of passivity and assigned roles of nurturing caretakers. Women whose actions contradicted those expectations and entered the "male" world of politics faced a severe backlash from their husbands, and society in general. This was the case with Epifania Zúñiga, who was not only a strong leader of Jaramillista women but in the movement itself.

As an analytical tool, gender provides a window into relations of power and speaks to the egalitarian character of a movement, regime, or national project. In her analysis of gender and sociopolitical change, the historian Sandra McGee Deutsch employs gender as a tool to measure the extent of social change put forth by a specific political regime. By looking at revolutionary Mexico (1910–24), the first Peronist administration in Argentina (1946–55), Cuba under Fidel Castro (1959–2008), and the Unidad Popular period in Chile (1970–73), she found that the degree of social change sought in each case could be measured by the expressed attitudes on gender. She noted that "egalitarian gender policies and in some cases gendered rhetoric expressed and symbolized their overall aims."[20] The more conservative projects—such as Perón's, Carranza's, and Pinochet's—sought to naturalize gender subordination and the ensuing division of labor. This, McGee Deutsch argues, stems from the fact that "the essence of the political right is its belief in a given order of things, in the immutability of the social hierarchy, the economic system, and the definitions of manhood and womanhood." The political Left, on the other hand, "does not accept the status quo as natural or given, and it seeks to reshape existing institutions and ideas to construct a more egalitarian and just society."[21]

The Jaramillistas accepted a gendered division of labor that assigned women to the domestic sphere and men the role of providers and ultimate household authorities. But what the Jaramillistas did not accept was a situation of poverty that rendered such roles impossible to fulfill. To understand the part Jaramillista women played in the movement, it is therefore useful to employ the distinction between "strategic" and "practical" gender interests.[22] The former, in Maxine Molyneux's formulation, derives "from the analysis of women's subordination and from the formulation of an alternative, more satisfactory set of arrangements to those which exist."[23] These more radical demands could include, but are not limited to, the "abolition of the sexual division of labor, the alleviation of the burden of domestic labor and childcare, the removal of institutionalized forms of discrimination, the establishment of political equality, freedom of choice over childbearing, and measures against male violence and control over women."[24] Practical gender interests, on the other hand, stem from the specific conditions faced by women due to the gendered division of labor. "Practical interests are usually a response to an immediate perceived need and they do not generally entail a strategic goal such as women's emancipation or gender equality." Key to understanding the specific ways in which women come together and organize, then, are the threats they face in the process of household maintenance and reproduction. While some women may accept a gendered division of labor, when conditions become such that they are unable to perform their socially assigned roles, this pressure can become a catalyst for political action. These mobilizations are inextricably tied to class interests, as, by definition, poorer women will have a harder time providing basic sustenance for their families. While "these practical interests do not in themselves challenge the prevailing forms of gender subordination, . . . they arise directly out of them."[25] In the process of organizing, women's political actions—in the streets, on the picket lines, or in public demonstrations—challenge social conventions that view them as passive, servile, or as self-sacrificing victims.

Since women in rural areas are generally socialized from a young age to be caregivers and are ultimately responsible for household maintenance, their immediate concerns may not appear political in nature. On the contrary, because traditional forms of political participation can threaten women's ability to sustain the household and thus their socially ascribed role, women may hold a conservative position vis-à-vis overt political action. They may react negatively to the initial consequences of men's participation in political activities. Threats of violence, the diversion of resources away from the family, and the time commitments demanded by political organizing often place women in the difficult position of choosing between the short-term needs of their families and the long-term goals of political action. As family protectors, women often react against members of their family who chose to join a political movement, particularly in an atmosphere hostile to independent organizing. Many women associated with the Jaramillistas were thus skeptical or opposed to participation at first; once involved, however, they were among the most loyal supporters.

Las Jaramillistas

Just as the Jaramillistas engaged in a variety of tactical and ideological forms of struggle, so too did gender-based demands change depending on the particular facet of the movement. Jaramillista militants expressed the most progressive notions of gender-based equality during the armed uprisings, when their espoused ideology was the most radical. For example, the Plan de Cerro Prieto dealt with issues of gender in three different ways. It declared women to be equal before the law, called for an end to specific practices that subjugated women, and stipulated that women should have the same opportunities as men. In its demand for a six-hour work day, it was explicit that such conditions apply to both sexes.[26] Such proclamations appeared in 1943, during the first armed uprising, and bear the mark of an anarchist proclamation made by the Flores Magón brothers in the early 1900s. Ricardo Flores Magón's *Semilla Libertaria* was an important text to the Jaramillista leadership, which may explain why, at times, the movement espoused notions based on this anarchist tradition. While other Jaramillista declarations on the rights of women originated from women themselves and emerged from their own organizations, the Plan de Cerro Prieto was written in 1943 during the first few years of the struggle, before women formed their own committees. It is difficult to state with certainty that this point on the liberation of women came from a *Magonista* text, however there are some parallels with the views expressed in *Regeneración*, the anarchist newspaper published by the Flores Magón brothers. An article in 1910 entitled "A la Mujer," for example, stated, "Women's misfortune is so ancient that its origin is lost in the shadow of the legend."[27] Both texts argue for the need to change the conditions that led women into prostitution. Ricardo Flores Magón's declaration, for example, reads, "The salary of women is so low that she is often forced to prostitute herself to provide for her own."[28] A fundamental point of comparison between Jaramillista and Magonista ideology is that each saw women's exploitation as originating from their class position.

Despite its declaration of equality between the sexes, the Plan de Cerro Prieto treats women as subjects vulnerable to "masculine desires," which leave them pregnant and without resources for their children. Like the Magonista text, it particularly condemned circumstance that led women into prostitution. For example, the plan called for the protection of "maternity to prevent immorality and prostitution." Childcare centers were to be established even in the smallest villages so that poor parents could ensure their children's full physical development.[29] While an obvious paternalistic tone pervades the Plan de Cerro Prieto, and the text does not analyze the social relations of power that have historically made it possible or acceptable for men to walk out on their children, it does address the social needs of poor women, an issue rarely discussed in women's suffrage movements of the time or in many feminist agendas in general. The plan thus attacks female oppression from a class perspective.

Finally, Point 18 expresses the notion that, in order to liberate women from their historic "condition of slavery," they should have access to resources that "cultivate all areas of knowledge and of industry, so that she can sustain herself with work that will represent for her a decorous, honest, and satisfying means of making a living. In this way, hunger won't force her to sell herself and her modesty to the highest bidder on her flesh."[30] This demand comes closest to depicting women as agents of their own liberation, although it is still charged with a strong moralistic tone, portraying modesty as a natural and necessary virtue of the female sex, a characteristic which must be viewed within the pervading mores of the Latin American countryside during this time period. While many Jaramillistas conformed to sexist practices, the movement's appeals for sexual equality are an important indicator of its social project. The Jaramillistas were political heirs to a legacy that was at once anarchist, Zapatista, and Cardenista. Of these currents, only anarchists proclaimed the equality of men and women—albeit in theory more than in practice. While Zapatista and Cardenista elements were certainly more dominant, the leadership, who self-consciously attended to their ideological formation, read and at times invoked ideas from the Flores Magón publication. It is not surprising, therefore, to see explicit or implicit parallels in proclamations that described their political vision.

As the movement unfolded, women's participation became increasingly central and would ultimately give concrete grounding to some of the abstract proclamations on women's equality. Through their participation, moreover, women asserted their capabilities as political, social, and revolutionary actors. As the *soldaderas* had done during the revolution, Jaramillista women were willing to carry weapons, plant explosives, and protect Jaramillo with their lives. They were crucial militants in the struggle. One Jaramillista woman described how she was able to get access to the soldiers' barracks by pretending to sell food. "We'd be sent to try to find out what was going on. . . . I would buy lots of oranges and fill my basket up. And we'd go try to sell oranges wherever there were soldiers, or lots of guards."[31] On another occasion, when Jaramillo's group was in the mountains, they received repeated reports of a man wishing to join them. Jaramillo, however, was suspicious. Thanks to a woman sympathizer from a nearby community who got the man drunk and led him to confess his true intentions, Jaramillo found out that he'd been paid by the manager of the Zacatepec refinery to infiltrate the group and assassinate him. "Can you believe this?" exclaimed Pedro García as he related the story. "It was a woman who did this!"[32] Couched in paternalism, such comments illustrate at once the amazement and the admiration with which Jaramillista men viewed the women's actions, which not only aided their cause but also protected their lives. The disbelief in such capabilities stemmed, in part, from the fact that women (especially poor rural women) were not seen as political actors in their own right. The terminology of a government report inadvertently revealed this view when it noted that Jaramillo traveled with "several individuals and a women, all armed with guns."[33] This reference portray's Jaramillo's wife Zúñiga as a separate entity, rather than as a part of the "individuals" involved in the struggle, a distinction that reveals the government agent's own sense of wonder about female participation.

"To do the work society assigns them," writes Temma Kaplan, "women have pursued social rather than narrowly political goals. When it appears that the survival of the community is at stake, women activate their networks to fight anyone—left or right, male or female—whom they think interferes with their ability to preserve life as they know it."[34] Once women became involved in the Jaramillista movement, their commitment was unbreakable. For example, one woman who knew Jaramillo from his days as a Methodist pastor became one of his most loyal providers and protectors. Without her husband's knowledge, she would gather and send as much food as she could to Jaramillo's group. When Jaramillo was in Cuernavaca and needed money, she sold the few animals in her possession and gave him the earnings. On her deathbed she instructed her children, "Don't ever abandon Jaramillo; take care of him. And after him others will come. Others will have to come when Jaramillo is gone, and you should never turn the other way, never. This is as important as religion."[35] This woman demonstrated an uncompromising commitment to the struggle Jaramillo led, as well as a broader vision of social change. While her initial words center around the figure of Jaramillo, she concludes with a far more extensive sentiment: "Others will have to come." This statement affirmed the continued need for struggle and the obligation of participating in its ranks. By passing this responsibility on to her children, she sought to keep her own resistance alive. That she equated the Jaramillista movement with religion reveals her overriding faith in the just nature of their cause. Her self-perception as a caregiver encompassed deeply revolutionary qualities, tendencies exhibited by feminist activists throughout history.

This uncompromising commitment is evident even among women who initially expressed fear about the implications of participating politically. Paula Batalla, one of the most prominent Jaramillista women, recalled how she initially feared Jaramillo, for she had heard he was a bandit. When she found out that her son Daniel attended Jaramillista meetings, she scolded him, saying, "Look, that man is just deceiving people. He's a bandit, he's compromising people. Why are you getting involved?" But Daniel continued to participate, making up excuses for his absences. Batalla finally confronted her son: "'Do you know how many people they've hanged just for taking that man a taco? And you're getting involved.' I would try to give him advice. 'You are risking your life. Think of your children, they are the ones who will suffer if something happens.'" [36] Batalla's initial fears reflected the repression suffered by the Jaramillistas for their organizing efforts; she expressed hostility to the movement from the perspective of a mother and caregiver. Still, many Jaramillista women risked everything and often defied their husbands and families to join Jaramillo's struggle. Batalla, in fact, would herself soon hear Jaramillo speak. "Since the first time I heard him I liked what he said, because he fought for the poor." She soon became one of the most important Jaramillista delegates. Initially active solely in the women's committee formed during the 1952 elections, she later figured prominently in the movement as a whole. Batalla's home became a safe house, and since she was a traditional healer or curandera, she instructed Jaramillistas to pose as patients when they came to see her. In this way they avoided attracting unwanted attention. Batalla recalled how she provided shelter for numerous Jaramillistas: "We used my house as barracks. That little room over there, it's no more than nine meters [long]. Well, about forty or fifty men fit there during the rainy season. How did we do it? Who knows! But we all fit in there!" [37]

Women's actions in the 1948 strike in Zacatepec vividly demonstrate the central role of Jaramillista women, especially when it came to mobilizing the community. Mothers, wives, and daughters of the striking workers and campesinos organized to prevent scabs from entering the refinery. [38] By guarding the mill's gates, women provided a picture of the support networks sustaining the strikers. Likewise, they hoped their presence would shame those who crossed the picket line by calling attention to how the scabs' actions affected not only workers but entire families. Decisions to participate in these labor mobilizations arose out of women's own social networks and did not constitute tasks delegated to them by the male strike committee.

"We would hold our own assemblies, only women," recalled one Jaramillista. "There we would decide what actions we were going to carry out against the manager . . . he must have been so scared to see so many of us arrive at his house."[39] These words carry the sense of empowerment women experienced as they came together—they felt strong enough to take on one of the most powerful men in Morelos. During labor mobilizations, Jaramillista women embarrassed the Zacatepec manager by plastering his house with literature regarding the strikers' demands. One woman recalled how they would wait at the manager's house with tomatoes and eggs to publicly humiliate him for his treatment of the workers and ejidatarios.[40] Women's involvement in the strike was so visible that newspapers ran articles criticizing how they "sustained the agitation with insulting fliers."[41]

Through genuine grassroots organizing women recruited their friends, comadres, relatives, or other women they deemed sympathetic to support the strike and create an environment critical of managerial abuses. On one occasion they were able to prevent the detention of Mónico Rodríguez, a worker at the Zacatepec refinery and one of the main strike leaders. Alberta Galarza, Rodríguez's wife, found out that the Zacatepec authorities were searching for her husband, so she quickly sought the help of the other women on her street. Together they went to the house where Rodríguez was hiding. The guards at the door were under strict instructions not to let any man in or out of the house while the police chief went to get the search warrant demanded by the homeowner. In the meantime, taking advantage of the guard's expectations of female docility, the women dressed Rodríguez up in a skirt, blouse, and shawl, surrounded him, and escorted him from the house without the guard's knowledge. When the police chief returned with a search warrant, Rodríguez was on his way out of Morelos.[42] Here, as in other struggles, women activated the social networks they created in their domestic life in order to protect the movement's leaders.

In this and other instances, women manipulated widespread beliefs in female passivity for the benefit of their struggle. Women, for example, acted as Jaramillo's bodyguards at public events, surrounding him in such a way that made him a difficult target. They performed this task in its fullest dimension, including carrying guns in their shawls or in bags of groceries, hidden among the various vegetables. While the Jaramillista women generally suffered less repression than their male counterparts, they were not immune from state violence. Paula Batalla, for example, recounts the brutality with which one Jaramillista, Rosa Ocampo, was treated for her participation in the movement: "They took her out at night and beat her. They wanted her to tell them all she knew about Jaramillo, or about the Party, about everyone. 'Where's Jaramillo' they asked, and she replied 'I don't know him, how am I going to tell you where he is.' They beat her, then they tied a rope around her neck, leaving it raw and scraped. I don't think they raped her because she would have told me but she didn't say anything about that."[43] In its campaign to eradicate the Jaramillistas, the government distinguished little between the armed group and the population that sheltered and concealed them. In this way, women Jaramillistas risked their life and livelihood when they chose to join or support the movement.

Women of the PAOM Speak

Jaramillista women were concerned with issues related to the survival of the family, and thus they demanded economic liberation rather than mere political inclusion. They objected to the post-Cardenista policies that sacrificed the campesino way of life in favor of large latifundios and export production. They challenged the government's rhetoric about efficiency in the countryside and pointed out that it was precisely campesino knowledge that would allow for the economic recovery of the country; it was they who knew how to make the land produce. Like the Jaramillistas as a whole, women emphasized the legal nature of their struggle for justice: "We are making use of our rights, protected under the law, to defend ourselves and our interests [which are] seriously threatened precisely by those who are lazy, who don't work, and who live like kings."[44] The dichotomy articulated in this statement—those who worked versus those who enjoyed the wealth created by the poor—was itself a common theme around which the Jaramillista movement organized. Addressing poverty lay at the core of the manifold ideologies that over time found expression in Jaramillista voices and documents. Women of the countryside suffered this marginalization and, propelled by the Jaramillista struggle as a whole, now mobilized to have a say in the political and economic system that governed their lives.

Women's active participation slowly began to translate into gender-specific demands. This was especially the case during the 1952 campaign, in which women played a particularly visible role. Epifania Zúñiga organized a women's committee in charge of mobilizing support for Henríquez Guzmán and Jaramillo. Composed of about forty women and known as the Sector Femenil (Women's Sector), Jaramillista women used this committee to call attention to their own rights and needs. In doing so, they made appeals based on gendered notions of their participation in the revolution. They thus vindicated their rights in the present: "The Morelense women who yesterday gave our brothers, our fathers, our husbands, and our sons to the agrarian revolution feel proud to participate in this electoral campaign because in this way we contribute to the effective economic liberation of all Mexicans and we position ourselves as part of a strategic plan to conquer the civic rights that all women in Mexico should have; women should have the same political rights as men."[45]

While this appeal is consistent with the state's gendered construction of nationalism, which viewed women as contributors to men's actions rather than as political actors themselves, women could use such notions to justify their participation in the "male" world of politics. Jaramillista women emphasized the centrality of female participation in the revolutionary war—it had been through the support and consent of mothers, wives, and sisters that men fought in the war. They now sought to participate and contribute in the postrevolutionary political struggle. They did not place civil rights as a priority, but instead treated them as part and parcel of the general social and economic transformation they sought. Thus, the "effective economic liberation of all Mexicans" appears inextricably linked to sexual equality. If we consider the link between class and gender oppression, then such demands present a more radical feminism than political rights shorn of economic equality. Jaramillista women demanded equality with men while denouncing the stark situation faced by those who lived in the Mexican countryside. Moreover, by establishing their own organizations as women, the Sector Femenil participated in the emerging tradition by which women asserted themselves as political actors in their own right and not just in relation to men, as had been the prevailing tendency in the early 1920s.[46]

The way the Jaramillistas directed attention to women's rights reveals a Cardenista legacy, insofar as his regime incorporated traditionally excluded sectors into the national project. Women made a special case for their own participation. In 1951 in Cuernavaca, Jaramillista women formed their own organization within the PAOM, laid out the effects of class exploitation on rural women, and put forth demands aimed at alleviating this situation.

Their initial participation as supporters transformed into an active role, and their demands further contributed to Jaramillista notions of justice. Male Jaramillistas rarely recognized their own power relations with regard to women. When they spoke about the difficult situation campesinas faced, it was always related to structural pressures placed on the family, and not specifically to women's patriarchal subjugation. And while female Jaramillistas mostly framed their grievances from the perspective of class, rather than gender, because their own experience was mediated by their condition as women, they could not help but foreground gender. In this way, their demands inextricably linked gender and class exploitation.

Jaramillista women framed these class-based demands within gendered notions of female moral superiority in the face of male corruption. These views prevailed across the social spectrum in Mexico. Moreover, they were naturalized and reinforced both by state rhetoric and by women themselves, who commonly articulated and assumed gendered perspectives to justify their political involvement to husbands, fathers, and brothers hostile to female participation in the male world of politics. It is not surprising, therefore, that in demanding equal rights, women asserted that they would make better use of them than many men, who "had become servile and conformist and had joined detestable and shameful political tendencies that betrayed and stole from the people."[47] To a certain extent, this argument paralleled the broader points made by the Jaramillistas when they asserted that they, unlike the government, followed the spirit and principles of the Mexican Constitution.

In this vein, female Jaramillistas defended the communal system of production, saying that they supported the Henriquista campaign because the movement was "not engaged in dirty politics" or in unrest that sought "to interrupt the proper function of the agricultural production" of their ejidos.[48] Women condemned the corruption of male politicians and, partly on that basis, argued for their necessary inclusion in the system. This is an example of the classic argument that women would "uplift" the "dirty" politics of men to a higher moral level, and it has been echoed by female participants in social movements across Latin America. To this women Jaramillistas added a sense of moral authority born of the sweat and toil involved in cultivating the land that would feed their families: "It is precisely us, the campesina women, who recognize and participate in the sacrifice made by the men of the countryside to achieve the economic recovery of the country. . . . We, more than anyone, are resolved to make the land bequeathed to us by the revolution produce everything necessary for the lives of our people, for the nourishment of our children."[49]

These statements demonstrate an important difference in the way women, as compared to Jaramillista men, discussed the merits of female participation. When a male leader—whether it be Jaramillo, Enrique Flores Magón, or another Jaramillista—praised female participants, they often expressed an admiration of the women's "male" qualities. The women themselves, on the other hand, framed the issue in terms of justice and integrity rather than strictly stereotyped images. In this respect, they presented a compelling argument against social notions of female inferiority: How could men charge women as incapable of carrying out certain tasks, when they themselves had done such a terrible job and become "servile and conformist"? When women portrayed themselves as worthier revolutionaries, they pointed out the absurdity of their exclusion.

Women's participation in the Jaramillista movement was most visible during the electoral campaign, precisely because they could act in accordance with existing models of female political participation, especially those that had emerged during the Cárdenas years. According to one Jaramillista, women made up 20 to 25 percent of PAOM members.[50] While women would not be allowed to vote in federal elections until 1953, they organized politically at all levels of society. For campesina women in Morelos, the formation of the PAOM stood as an important opportunity to support a campaign they believed would promote the interest of the campesinos and to make their own appeals as women. Indeed, the PAOM declared one of its principles to be "Equality of rights and conditions between men and women in the economic, political, and social spheres," since without such equality, continued the declaration, "it was impossible to have a true democracy, because one half of the population cannot be subjugated to the privilege of the other half."[51] In this way, the assertiveness of individual women generated organizations dedicated specifically to women's needs. Campesinas acted as PAOM representatives in various communities—something virtually unheard of at the time—and formed women's committees in others. One Jaramillista woman recalled, "We each had towns to go to. For example, one could be in charge of all of Atlacomulco and would have to look out for everything that went on there and then talk to him [Rubén]. . . . Don Rubén would tell me to go to Coatetelco and look for so and so's house, who would then give me the money to travel to Tetecala. And that's how we did it. In one day I would go to three or four towns."[52] Stated another woman, "I was in charge of organizing people, . . . giving them guidance; . . . then we would go to the office to get more instructions and report about what we had done, how we had worked. Those were our obligations." [53] It was this type of political organizing that helped create, maintain, and strengthen the PAOM, and women were essential actors in this process. In fact, because of their position as women, they often had better access to certain community networks, such as the marketplace and religious circles. Moreover, their active work in building the structures that sustained the party began to translate into more visible roles, such as making public declarations at speaking events. This was especially the case with Epifania Zúñiga, who spoke at many political rallies. Her words were no less emphatic than Jaramillo's. One newspaper describing an Henriquista rally in Cuautla reported that Jaramillo's words of welcome were followed with a "fiery" speech by Zúñiga.[54] At one rally in support of Cuba, she reportedly declared that communism was only detrimental to millionaires, but not to the poor, "whose hearts were with the Cuban people, since the revolution carried out there represents the liberation of Mexicans as well."[55]

Women Jaramillistas played a key role in the dissemination of information both about the ideals of the Jaramillista movement and the repression the state meted out. They raised their voices, for example, against official violence and tried to make public the repression ordered by Morelos governor Rodolfo López de Nava (1952–58). In a poster signed by eighty-seven women, the Jaramillistas declared that the judicial police, rather than guaranteeing the public peace, "sowed terror everywhere," and that it was impossible to keep living under this "detestable local dictatorship."[56] In his six-year period as governor, concluded the document, López de Nava would "surely destroy the Morelense family and its household economy."[57]

Women thus tried to create awareness about the nature of the Jaramillista struggle and sought to dispel government propaganda that treated Jaramillo as a steadfast bandit and criminal. For example, when government repression forced Jaramillo into armed hiding after the 1952 election, women distributed informational leaflets about his struggle. One of these documents

7. Jaramillo surrounded by his supporters. Archivo General de la Nación, Fondo Hermanos Mayo, Jaramillo.

read, "The rebelliousness of this man remains alive, not by wasting gunpowder and conducting random killings, but by punishing the enemies of the nation, and by keenly and justly educating people." They called for support for the "compañero Rubén Jaramillo and the disciplined and brave people who follow him" and asked "that citizens not lend themselves as soldiers to a government that exploits and oppresses" but instead "deny that government all that it asks."[58] Alarmed by the words of this flyer, the municipal president of Jojutla sent it to the police chief, the state governor, and the head of the judicial police.

While the Jaramillista women often made appeals specific to their gender, they concentrated on denouncing the injustices around them. These included repression, poverty, and the lack of political freedom. Jaramillista women thus made some specific gender-based demands, but most of their actions and appeals stemmed from a desire to transform a social reality detrimental to themselves, their families, and their community. In this way, argues Temma Kaplan, women's "commonsense analysis of what is wrong in the here-and-now grows from perceptions about concrete reality rather than from abstract rights."[59] However, expectations of what was and wasn't a woman's proper place constrained their participation. Some men prohibited their wives from attending strategy meetings, claiming that women could not keep the issues discussed there a secret. Ricarda Juárez, for example, whose husband always ordered her to the kitchen while the men held their meetings, was told not to listen to Jaramillista matters because she might gossip about them. This was one of the many ways women were excluded from the decision-making process. While women often complied with their husband's demands, some reflected self-critically about this dynamic which excluded them. Stated Eliodora Alvarado, "I don't know what they talked about because one couldn't be where there were only men talking. That's the problem with us women, men arrive and start discussing important issues and we don't go and listen."[60] And yet, women would always find ways of participating, with or without their husbands. Margarita Hernández recalls how during the 1959–1962 Jaramillista takeover of the Michapa and Guarín plains (discussed in detail in the next chapter), her mother, Leova Gutiérrez, would make her way to encampment despite her husband's explicit prohibition. Gutiérrez would wait for her husband to leave for work, and then she and her young daughter would join the other Jaramillistas who had begun to settle the land. "I remember women making bonfires in order to cook for the people there. I remember my mother was excited about the possibility of getting land. Then we'd make sure to return before my father was back."[61]

When they did not face the constraints of their husbands, women gave themselves wholeheartedly to the struggle. One night state authorities broke into the home of Enrique Pérez, a prominent Jaramillista, and kidnapped him. With the help of family members, his wife, Ricarda Juárez, soon located him in a Cuernavaca jail, where he later died under mysterious conditions.[62] Rather than be intimidated by her husband's incarceration and death, Juárez began to participate in her community's struggle for land, and she played an active role in local and national campesino organizing and in the mobilizations commemorating Jaramillo's death up until the late 1990s, when her frailty finally put an end to her political activism.

Single or widowed women often found it easier to join the movement in a more active manner. One such Jaramillista remarked, "If I had been married,

I would not have been able to participate."[63] Jaramillista men were quite aware and open about these limitations. For instance, when they approached one woman to be the delegate from her town, one of the arguments they used to persuade her was that since she did not have a husband, she could perform PAOM duties wherever and whenever they needed her.[64] As Paula Batalla reflected about her own participation, "If I had had a husband, what would I have told him? Wait for me here? And if my parents had been around what would they have said? 'Don't go there, something might happen to you.' No, no, no. It's better that I don't have them."[65] Batalla's words reveal the numerous ways traditional domestic units constrain women's participation in events outside the home. Such constraints created a gap between theory and practice regarding gender issues within the Jaramillista movement. While some Jaramillista men expressed concerns about the oppression of women, many reacted negatively to women's attempts to actively claim their rights by attending meetings or advocating their opinions. Jaramillista goals of full political equality for women existed alongside serious barriers erected by rural cultural norms.

"My Best Soldiers"

Jaramillo, for his part, attempted to address these issues and wrote about his strong confrontations "with the weakest in the group who, as men, did not know how to value the courage of women who think in a revolutionary manner and dedicate themselves to the principles that are the basis for the liberation of the oppressed, enslaved, and exploited people."[66] One woman recalled how Jaramillo, during his meeting with President López Mateos, publicly introduced the group of women accompanying him, stating, "These women . . . are my best soldiers, never mind that they are dressed as women . . . they are my best soldiers."[67] This statement at once conceded to and parodied the idea of women's purported weakness. Jaramillo also seems to be expressing his own admiration for the role women played and cautioning others not to belittle their actions or disrespect them on account of their gender. The women's role as bodyguards hearkened back to the legacy of women as soldaderas during the revolution, and Jaramillo's views are reminiscent of the pride Enrique Flores Magón expressed for women who participated in the revolution, reserving "his highest praise for 'nuestras revolucionarias' [our women revolutionaries]" whose skills smuggling arms, munitions, and literature had, he remarked, "exceeded many men's."[68] Jaramillo and Flores Magón spoke in a similar vein: each admired women when they displayed "male" characteristics of valor and strength.

When women exhibited such characteristics, however, they inherently threatened male authority and control. Epifania Zúñiga is the case in point. Jaramillo's defense of his partner in struggle reveals an emerging sensitivity to this dynamic. Wrote Jaramillo in his autobiography, "On many occasions she attended justly and sincerely to the compañeros, giving her advice and opinions about Jaramillo's ideas. In the midst of all the hardships, she never weakened nor lost hope. She always tried to give encouragement and strength to everyone, not paying attention to the many criticisms made by her compañeros in the struggle."[69] Although she was criticized by some, Zúñiga's contribution to the movement is difficult to deny, even by those who resented her influence. One Jaramillista even speculated, "If they would have left her alive, she would've mobilized people. But they killed her because they were afraid of her; she herself could have led another movement."[70] Zúñiga exercised political leadership and had shown courage and determination by arming herself and taking to the mountains. Moreover, she had specific plans to achieve women's self-determination and autonomy. Although her idea of establishing a sewing cooperative emphasized a task socially ascribed to women, it also combined notions of communalism and female autonomy and is consistent with projects presented by women throughout Mexico in an effort to empower themselves.[71] In the legacy of Jaramillismo, however, this initiative has not been recognized on its merits, and has instead been cited as the reason why Jaramillo did not go underground in 1962. Zúñiga's proposal stands not as a popular initiative stifled by state repression—like Jaramillo's—but as a negative influence on him. Remarkably, Zúñiga's actions reflected a revolutionary *compañerismo*, or companionship in struggle, that sexist practices have prevented from developing in most social movements. Because women are largely invisible in male accounts of the Jaramillista history, Zúñiga's role as one of Jaramillo's closest collaborators has not been appropriately recognized.[72] Rather than let her culturally assigned role as woman and caretaker constrain her, she instead sought to combine these responsibilities and dared to practice the equality Jaramillistas espoused. In the end, Zúñiga's desire to improve the economic situation of local women, their families, and their community came at the detriment of her role in protecting Jaramillo.

Within Jaramillismo, as with most social or armed movements, women participants faced numerous limitations. A product of the social mores that established male superiority, the Jaramillista movement generally upheld these gender codes, despite their explicit proclamations on women's rights. Jaramillista women were active militants who helped sustain, reproduce, and extend the movement throughout Morelos. Their actions were most often consistent with gender norms that ascribed to them the role of caregivers and providers. However, female Jaramillistas also took advantage of prevailing social notions of female docility to take on responsibilities that would have been more difficult or impossible for men to carry out. In the process of political organizing, women came together and formed their own groups that at once articulated campesino demands characteristic of the Jaramillista movement and issues specific to women. These concerns were always class based and often appeared mediated through anarchist or Cardenista tendencies that existed more broadly within the movement itself.

As a social construction, the concept of gender inherently carries numerous contradictions. When analyzed in the context of a movement fighting for social justice, these contradictions give way to a complex, painful, and at times even comical reality. Male Jaramillistas assumed that women's capabilities as fighters did not equal men's. In this belief, they acted in accordance with the patriarchal reality of rural Mexico and thus reproduced aspects of the very inequality they sought to combat. Despite these constraints, however, women fought sexism within the movement, as well as the gender exploitation embedded in poverty. In this way, female Jaramillistas demonstrated, often to the amazement of their male compañeros, the valor, determination, and creativity that were key to the movement's longevity. Thus we have Jaramillo's boastings about his best soldiers, "even if they're dressed as women," the ingenuity of female Jaramillistas saving Rodríguez by escorting him dressed in drag, and the countless other acts, both as militants and as caretakers, in which women engaged. And, remarkably, considering all the constraints, *las* Jaramillistas established their own organization within the movement through which their needs and rights might be addressed.

CHAPTER SEVEN

Judas's Embrace

In the early months of 1958, letters protesting the nomination of Norberto López Avelar as the PRI's candidate for governor of Morelos poured into the president's office.[1] López Avelar, a Carrancista soldier, had been one of the cadets who had triumphantly posed at the head of Zapata's slain body in the photograph publicizing the agrarian leader's assassination in 1919. "How is it possible," read one statement, "that someone who collaborated in the despicable assassination of General Emiliano Zapata now governs the cradle of the southern revolution?"[2] The state's murder of Jaramillo during the administration of López Avelar added yet another layer to a crime already shrouded in an aura of betrayal.

Typical of a party that claimed itself at once revolutionary and institutional, later that same year President López Mateos came to power wielding a revived agrarista rhetoric. The president's overtures to campesinos included the official pardon he extended to Jaramillo, who had remained underground since the 1952 elections. Jaramillo used the renewed political space to build popular strength, this time not through an electoral challenge but through a demand for land. Together with six thousand other campesinos, he initiated proceedings to establish a colonia on some vacant lands in western Morelos. Here the Jaramillistas applied current notions of development and progress and sought to participate in, and benefit from, the regime's proclaimed modernity. They added to the demand for land—a perennial campesinos request—a call for roads, adequate housing, and electricity. Such demands are remarkably similar to those that emerged in the 1970s and 1980s as inhabitants of shantytowns around major cities sought to regularize their settlements and gain access to urban infrastructure. The process of urbanization that had overtaken Mexico in the two decades since they began their mobilization was thus reflected in this last Jaramillista proposal.

The Jaramillistas continued to use the constitution as a basis to legitimize their demand for land from the Department of Agrarian Affairs and Colonization (DAAC). Zapatista and Cardenista frameworks emerged anew in the Jaramillista settlement proposal for Michapa and Guarín. However, the fact that this phase of the struggle occurred after the triumph of the Cuban Revolution added another dimension to the movement, both for the participants and for the state. The immediate distribution of wealth and full-fledged social reforms in Castro's Cuba brought the PRI's claims over the revolution further into question. For the Left, not only in Mexico, but across the Americas, the Cuban example set the stage for renewed possibilities of social transformation. While the Jaramillistas still framed their demands in terms of the Zapatista and Cardenista legacy, the Mexican government increasingly abandoned these constituting elements of the modern Mexican state—further exposing itself to popular challenges. The government was unwilling to accede to Jaramillista demands because they conflicted with the development strategies followed by post-1940 administrations. Despite President López Mateos's agrarista language, the state deepened its commitment to an economic model that made campesino existence increasingly precarious. Couched in the rhetoric of modernity, the development policy of the Mexican government privileged urban centers at the cost of the countryside.

The PRI battled the Jaramillista project on both political and economic grounds. Politically, the Jaramillistas exposed the contradictions between the PRI's revolutionary commitment and its repressive practices. The agrarian movement became a potentially acute problem for the Mexican government following the triumph of the Cuban Revolution. Jaramillo joined his voice to those of others in Mexico and throughout Latin America who defended Cuba against U.S. imperialism. But unlike the Mexican government (which maintained a cordial relationship with Fidel Castro), Jaramillo did not express solidarity with the Cuban Revolution solely to espouse a defense of national sovereignty. Rather, he admired Cuba's agrarian reform and hailed it as a model to be followed. This comparison highlighted the inadequacy of Mexico's agrarian law and its application.

On the economic front the Jaramillistas stood as a threat because they fought for land coveted by powerful entrepreneurs in Mexico City. As would happen increasingly in land struggles in decades to come, the government sided with private commercial interests against the Jaramillistas and made way for an industrial project in which campesinos were conceived of only as laborers. When the government sent the army to remove campesinos from land to which they were legally entitled, the Jaramillistas reconsidered the feasibility of operating through legal channels. In doing so, they no longer turned to strategies inherited from the Zapatista struggle and implemented during the Cárdenas years. Instead, they began to contemplate the lessons learned from Cuba and considered the ways that Maoist and Guevarist tactics might be put to use in Morelos.

The Struggle for Michapa and Guarín

The dry and rocky soil of the Michapa and Guarín plains seems, at first glance, an unlikely source of contention. Its potential, however, lay in the nearby Amacuzac River that could be used to irrigate the lands that extended into the municipalities of Coatlán del Río, Tetecala, Puente de Ixtla, Miacatlán, and Amacuzac. While most of the Michapa and Guarín plains had been distributed to campesinos during the Calles administration, they had remained uncultivated because the ejidatarios received no technical support and their attempts to work small portions of this land were blocked by nearby ranchers who appropriated the plains to graze cattle. In 1959, when a group of campesinos from the region learned of a private initiative to irrigate the area, they decided it was time to claim their rights and went in search of Jaramillo.[3]

The initiative soon became much more than an action to repossess an ejido. Under Jaramillo's leadership the ejidatarios, joined by landless campesinos from other parts of the state, formed a committee that devised an ambitious project seeking to create a population center and distribute the twenty-seven thousand hectares of land among six thousand campesinos.[4] The committee framed its demands in a way that emphasized campesino initiative and self-sufficiency. In their first appeal to the president, they asked for loans to begin the process of irrigation and distribution. They wished to hire a technical assistant to divide the land equitably and efficiently and emphasized campesino participation in the entire process. The Jaramillistas promised not to deplete government resources: they intended to use the credit efficiently and pay it back in a timely and honest manner. Moreover, they pointed out, this project would benefit numerous families, the state's economy, the federal government, and the entire plains region.[5] Jaramillo and the committee simultaneously worked out the legal details of the project with the DAAC, and in March 1960 they received approval from this institution. Federico Tafoya was assigned as the engineer responsible for providing technical assistance.[6]

The Jaramillistas named the population center after Otilio Montaño, one of Zapata's closest collaborators and the principal author of the Plan de Ayala. This choice in name was at once a claim over the Zapatista legacy and a reflection of the desire to implement Zapatismo in Morelos. The Jaramillista vision for this popular colonia combined elements of traditional campesino subsistence farming with modern commercial ventures. In addition to providing rural dwellers with individual plots of land where they would cultivate crops, the Jaramillistas proposed to construct canneries so that the community could commercialize tomatoes, cantaloupes, and watermelons. Likewise, they wanted to establish a sugar refinery and a rice-processing plant that would be run as cooperatives, so that their profits would benefit the community as a whole. In this way, the Otilio Montaño population center would be grounded in the "latest innovations offered by modern science."[7] Other projects for the community included the construction of dams to collect water from the Amacuzac River, reservoirs to gather rain water, and thirty kilometers of roadways. The planning committee also envisioned the construction of streets and modern houses for the inhabitants, the introduction of running water, electricity, telephone, and telegraph service, and all "other necessary facilities for a modern population center." This petition calculated the project's cost at $480 million pesos, an amount the participants proposed to pay back over a ten-year period at 7 percent interest.[8]

In establishing that each campesino family should have its own plot of land (one thousand square meters) while simultaneously calling for massive rice and sugar cooperatives and the commercialization of products such as tomatoes, the plans for Michapa and Guarín paralleled certain ideas presented in Zapata's Plan de Ayala. One Jaramillista actually character-ized their project for the plains as an updated version of the Plan de Ayala.[9] While they were, in fact, very different, Zapata himself had been conscious of the need to cultivate commercial crops. For example, the revolutionary leader had warned the residents of Villa de Ayala, "If you keep on grow-ing chile peppers, onions, and tomatoes you'll never get out of the state of poverty you've always lived in. That's why, as I advise you, you have to grow cane."[10] Where Zapata confiscated sugar mills and distributed the surround-ing lands, he insisted that the mills keep running, not as private property, but as public works.[11]

Despite the PRI's appropriation of the figure of Zapata and its monopoly over the revolution, the ideals that the Zapatistas had fought for continued to permeate Mexico's rural landscape and exposed the PRI's increasing al-liances with private and commercial interests. The two interest groups that competed with the Jaramillistas for these lands and thwarted their plans were the cattle ranchers who currently used the region and the develop-ers who planned to turn it into a mega-industrial and tourist complex. The government's backing of powerful economic actors over the campesinos further highlighted the gulf between the state's revolutionary claims and the economic and social realities overseen by the official party. In light of the state's abandonment of the revolution's agrarianism, the Jaramillistas came to embody an alternative in Morelos. They carried Zapata's flag and embraced modern proposals for popular development.

The Jaramillista plans for roads, schools, and recreation centers demon-strated an eye towards progress. Economic autonomy and self-sufficiency were two main goals for this population center. One participant, José Ro-dríguez, described how "the plan would give land to the campesinos, but in a more advanced way: with credit and guarantees. It was going to be a population center with technical direction. . . . That was the intention, to form an agricultural, industrial, and commercial center, because everything would be elaborated and produced there. And there would be work not only for the campesinos that were there but for those all over the state. The vision Jaramillo had was extensive."[12]

But one of the first obstacles the Jaramillistas faced came from nearby ranchers and caciques who had taken possession of part of the plains to pas-ture their cattle. These cattle owners began to mobilize some of the original ejidatarios in a campaign to discredit the Jaramillistas as outsiders and argued to the DAAC that these lands were legally constituted and functioning ejidos. In order to make the plains appear to be working ejidos, ranchers provided tractors and barbed wire to some of the very ejidatarios they previously prevented from farming these lands.[13] In response, Jaramillo invited authorities to see for themselves the patchy and haphazard nature of the cultivated areas, which revealed the false nature of the ranchers' claims.

When Jaramillo made his request for the Michapa and Guarín plains, he recognized that these lands had been distributed as ejidos. However, they had remained uncultivated for over three decades, and under agrarian law the original recipients had forfeited their legal rights over the land. As proof, Jaramillo and Tafoya sent aerial photos of the plains to show that they lay fallow.[14] Jaramillo also made numerous trips to Mexico City to obtain the final signature from Roberto Barrios, the head of the DAAC, so the Jaramillistas could prove to local rancheros, caciques, and *políticos*—as they referred to corrupt state authorities—that they had legal rights to the land. But Jaramillo's visits to the agrarian offices invariably resulted in long hours of waiting and unanswered requests. Due to pressure from the cattle ranchers or from the entrepreneurs wanting to use the plains for their own project, Barrios was clearly having second thoughts about his initial authorization to the Jaramillistas. One campesino recalled, "When we had everything fixed and ready, he [Barrios] must have felt the pressure; all of a sudden he turned on us. That was it! And from then on the only one who would see us was his secretary, Lazcano, who would tell us again and again, 'Mr. Barrios is out with López Mateos.'"[15] The symbolism in this recollection illustrates the degree of collaboration the campesinos witnessed between different government offices.

But after a year and a half of paperwork, trips to Mexico City, and unanswered petitions, the Jaramillistas were growing impatient. Jaramillo had filled out the necessary forms, paid numerous fees, and had an initial document signed by Barrios giving the Jaramillistas the go ahead. On February 5, 1961, the Jaramillistas thus began to settle and work the contested land. This time local ranchers reacted by paying campesinos twenty pesos each and providing them with food and alcohol in exchange for posing as the legitimate ejido owners. According to Jaramillistas, the Zacatepec manager helped out by sending three truckloads of mill workers to pose as ejidatarios.[16] Ejidal commissariats spearheaded complaints against Jaramillo and

Tafoya—the former charged with land invasion and the latter with falsifying documents.[17] The actions of local cattle ranchers, in conjunction with the Zacatepec manager and with the federal government's tacit approval, illustrate the power network stacked against campesino initiatives for land reform.

Jaramillo continued his appeal to various agrarian authorities, his tone revealing campesinos' swelling frustration: "I know that there are numerous vested interests whose parties are taking action, . . . backwards politicians and caciques of ranches and towns want to stop the people's will . . . but they will be unable to, because the needs of the people are greater than all the authorities, and all the laws. This is why it is indispensable that these needs be taken care of."[18] These petitions fell on deaf ears, and the DAAC reversed its original decision that provided the Jaramillistas the initial approval on the project. The executive secretary of the agrarian office now argued that these lands were ejidos and pequeñas propiedades and therefore could not be used to create a new population center. Instead, he offered the Jaramillistas territory in the state of Quintana Roo, a proposal that Jaramillo rejected.[19] As with previous government offers for land in Baja California, the campesinos were not willing to move. Barrios, then, made a deal with Jaramillo: if he could convince the campesinos to vacate the land, the DAAC would solve the conflict in favor of the Jaramillistas.[20] Jaramillo agreed and convinced campesinos to withdraw from Michapa and Guarín.

Jaramillo's decision sparked controversy among his followers. Although the Jaramillistas acquiesced, they were growing increasingly frustrated and began to talk of an armed invasion. Legal channels were getting them nowhere, and perhaps the government would be persuaded through more forceful measures. The following exchange illustrates the mood: "At one meeting of about one thousand campesinos we already had 800 weapons. People were saying [to Jaramillo] 'Jefe, we have to go in by force, give us the go ahead.'" Jaramillo found himself caught between his campesino supporters, who favored direct action, and his own desire to achieve the Jaramillista project legally. He opted to give legal channels another chance, stating, "We did not come as rebels, we came as settlers."[21] Jaramillo harbored hope in President López Mateos, who had expressed a commitment to agrarian ideals and had declared that during his rule no piece of land would remain uncultivated and no campesino would go without land. Moreover, the president had met personally with Jaramillo and granted him amnesty. Jaramillo

8. Jaramillo speaking before campesinos at Michapa and Guarín. *Archivo Fotográfico, Rodrigo Moya.*

understood the serious nature of resorting to an armed struggle and knew that it did not always represent a position of strength vis-à-vis the government. Apropos of the subject, he responded to a reporter's query: "That's what my enemies would want: that I take up arms so they can declare this movement illegal, separate me from the people and the land, and have me shot in the mountains. No, my struggle is here right now."[22]

So Jaramillo sent numerous appeals to the president in which he cited the abuses of Morelos authorities and asked for federal intervention in the matter.[23] But the president did nothing, and when Barrios failed to act on his promise, the Jaramillistas took over the Michapa and Guarín plains once again in the early days of February 1962, almost a year after the first attempted settlement. Three hundred men, women, and children began, for the second time, to build their houses and prepare the infrastructure. The Jaramillistas cleared the lands for a school building, administrative offices, and a recreational center. The process of struggle lent them further resolve. Participants described their experience in Michapa and Guarín with a sense of empowerment that was similar to the testimonies of those who participated in Jaramillo's campaign for governor. In the 1946 and 1952 state elections, campesinos had supported Jaramillo because his candidacy represented an opportunity to elect a governor who would prioritize the needs of the campesinos, or as one Jaramillista put it, "someone who enforced the law, who would actually institute the Federal Labor Law, and Agrarian codes."[24] Now, through the Otilio Montaño project, the Jaramillistas sought to put these laws into practice.

Indeed, the rising tensions over Michapa and Guarín illustrate the various issues at stake. The profit potential of this land had not gone unnoticed. Requests that the plains be irrigated dated back to the Ávila Camacho administration. The government had denied initial petitions, explaining that it was unable to allocate the necessary resources due to Mexico's war effort. But the project appeared anew when the ejidal commissariats made their second appeal in 1951, a request that also went unheeded.[25] But private entrepreneurs presented another proposal in 1959. This project called for the establishment of a hydroelectric plant and an irrigation system that would allow for the cultivation of coffee, avocados, nuts, and other products "that campesinos could be taught to farm." In addition, they proposed to set up several poultry and sheep farms. The project also included tourist ventures and the construction of industries designed to assist Mexico City with its production needs. This "Cuenca Sur" initiative would span the three bordering states—Morelos, Guerrero, and the State of Mexico.[26]

The campesinos' knowledge of commercial plans for Michapa and Guarín had initially propelled them to claim their rights to the land: if the government was finally going to irrigate the plains, then it should be for the benefit of rural dwellers, not for a project reportedly spearheaded by ex-president Miguel Alemán, the millionaire Alfredo del Mazo, and the former manager of the Zacatepec refinery Eugenio Prado.[27] Both projects, the Otilio Montaño colonia and the Cuenca Sur development, were framed in the context of progress and modernity, but their social visions differed dramatically. While the Jaramillistas sought to commercialize products such as sugar, rice, and cantaloupes, they also wanted campesinos to have access to individual plots of land to cultivate subsistence crops such as beans, corn, and chiles. Moreover, the commercial aspects of the Jaramillista project were still envisioned within a cooperative structure designed to benefit the entire population occupying the area. The Cuenca Sur proposal stood in obvious

9. Jaramillistas began to build makeshift houses as they settled in the Michapa and Guarín plains. *Archivo Fotográfico, Rodrigo Moya.*

contrast. While its architects stated that it would instruct local ejidatarios on how to farm certain commercial products, the profits would not be distributed collectively. Moreover, the proposed products—coffee, avocados, and nuts—were destined for outside commercial markets, a dynamic that in the previous two decades had resulted in increasing land concentration and an agricultural structure in which the peasant family had to invest ever more hours of labor just to ensure survival.[28] Likewise, the aspects of this project that catered to tourism and housing developments favored profit-generating enterprises characteristic of a state moving increasingly further from policies addressing the social needs of the countryside's population.

10. Jaramillistas at a communal meal at Michapa and Guarín plains. *Archivo Fotográfico, Rodrigo Moya.*

The Jaramillistas continued to face harassment by cattle ranchers and those paid to pose as ejidatarios. Jaramillo began to make plans to arm as many settlers as possible to defend themselves from these groups' aggression. The Jaramillistas only possessed a few weapons, but they were enough for self-defense. They agreed that if the authorities came to remove them and attempted to arrest the leaders, the people would engage in unarmed resistance while the leadership, armed and able to defend themselves, would elude capture. And authorities soon did arrive. They came in the middle of the night on February 13, 1962. Eyewitness accounts place the number of soldiers in the hundreds. They detained six people and charged them with possession of a deadly weapon and social dissolution.[29] Significantly, authorities reported their attempt to arrest Jaramillo directly to the Estado Mayor Presidencial, the president's military advisors, thus illustrating the president's concern in the matter.[30] Jaramillo, in the meantime, issued a complaint against the Morelos governor, the state *procurador de justicia*

11. Unidentified Jaramillista at Michapa and Guarín plains.
Archivo Fotográfico, Rodrigo Moya.

and the representative of the DAAC. But the state judge absolved all accused parties, citing the fact that the head of the twenty-fourth military zone (the zone corresponding to the state of Morelos), Pascual Cornejo Brun, had acted on orders from above.[31]

The federal government's involvement foreshadowed another round of state-sanctioned violence against the Jaramillistas. According to the PRI's operating logic, when co-option did not yield submission (and such attempt had proven futile since 1942), the party proceeded with repression. When the Jaramillistas applied, at the local level, notions of development framed in terms of the Zapatista and Cardenista legacies, they peeled away the layers shrouding a government policy ever more bereft of its constitutional mandates. The state's legitimizing framework rung hollow as the Jaramillistas revealed the endurance of popular local memory over an official history which could "only incorporate certain strands of regional mythology," making repression necessary in the end.[32] As the government attempted to appropriate or do away with popular radical alternatives, these would reappear in new and innovative ways.[33] In the case of Michapa and Guarín, the seeds were sown for renewed militant measures that in the past had been interpreted as a return to Zapata's armed agrarismo. After the triumph of the Cuban Revolution, however, the implications of tactics such as armed incursions would change, not only because the actions were themselves different, but because after 1959 any group with a tradition of armed struggle was necessarily seen through the lens of the successful July 26th Cuban movement.

"It Is in the Michapa Plains Where the Current Regime Will Define Itself"

The battle over Michapa and Guarín took place at a moment in which the successful Cuban Revolution at once rejuvenated Mexico's Left and forced the PRI to grapple with the legitimacy of its own institutionalized revolution. López Mateos masterfully undertook the task of at once reasserting an independent foreign policy vis-à-vis the United States and continuing to repress popular movements at home. The United States' aggressive stance against Cuba heightened feelings of nationalism and anti-imperialism throughout Latin America and in Mexico created a climate that allowed the Left to incorporate itself more directly into the nation's political life.[34] The formation of Movimiento de Liberación Nacional (National Liberation Movement, MLN) in 1961 was one of the clearest manifestations of this attempt to regroup. Former president Lázaro Cárdenas broke with tradition and re-entered the public light as a vocal defender of the Cuban Revolution and the most prominent leader of the MLN. Although it was short lived and of a reformist rather than revolutionary nature, the MLN nevertheless was a force to contend with, grouping a wide range of social actors that included certain leftist elements of the PRI, intellectuals, students, and some members of the Communist and Socialist parties. Seeing that the Mexican population had mobilized in support of Cuba and perceiving an opportunity to validate its own revolutionary credentials, López Mateos publicly defended Cuba's right to self-determination. In 1960, Mexico hosted Cuban president Osvaldo Dórticos, and López Mateos couched his praise for the Cuban Revolution in careful nationalist terms: "We are confident that as was the Mexican revolution, the Cuban Revolution will be another step towards the greatness of the Americas."[35] Mexico lent Cuba diplomatic support by opposing Washington's initiatives in the Organization of American States (OAS) to levy economic sanctions on the island. In 1964, Mexico would be the lone OAS member to maintain diplomatic ties with Havana.[36] Initially, U.S. diplomats reacted angrily to Mexico's defiance. In a July 1961 memo, the U.S. ambassador to Mexico, Thomas Mann, suggested that if Mexico did not remain receptive to Washington's recommendations on, among other issues, foreign investment and the battle against communism, the United States "could withdraw from discussions in friendliest and most relaxed manner, expressing understanding of Mexican policy, and then simply put a 'slow man' on [the] job of passing on Mexican requests for assistance."[37] In December of that same year, Mann reiterated this recommendation with evident frustration, adding that it needed to "dawn on Mexico that cooperation has to be a two-way street, and that Mexico needs [the] US more than we need Mexico. It is important that in the weeks ahead each statement by a US official and each action on loan applications be carefully considered in light of [the] probable effect on Mexican decisions."[38]

These initial frustrations, though, soon gave way to a mutual understanding between Washington and Mexico City. López Mateos made it clear to Washington that, while it was politically unfeasible to sever diplomatic ties with Cuba, "*when fundamental issues [were] at stake*" he was "willing to be *helpful.*"[39] Not only did Mexican authorities aid U.S. intelligence by supplying the American consulate in Mexico with detailed passenger lists of people traveling to Cuba, but under President Gustavo Díaz Ordaz (1964–70), Mexico's embassy in Havana shared intelligence information on Cuba's domestic situation with the United States.[40] Indeed, Washington reached an "informal understanding . . . at the highest levels to maintain relations with Cuba so one OAS country [could] have foot in door which might sometime be helpful."[41] While this level of cooperation remained highly classified, Mexico's policy of "double-dealing" could be detected in the ways the government sought to control domestic enthusiasm for the Cuban Revolution.[42]

Actions such as the repression of demonstrations against the Playa Girón invasion and the photographing and confiscation of materials from passengers returning from Cuba revealed the government's efforts to temper public support for the Cuban example.[43] In June of 1961, López Mateos—who had initially characterized his administration as "extreme left within the Constitution," now appeared to correct any unintended sympathies the Left might have gathered from his statement. He now declared his intention to "repress any demagogical excess that, whether from the left or the right, attempted, outside the constitutional framework, to disrupt national life."[44] This apparent centrist position was not borne out in policy. Not only were religious and anticommunist groups quick to praise such assertions, but pro-Castro demonstrations were often violently dispersed, while the state meted out no such response to the Right's mobilizations against Cuba.[45]

It was in this environment that the Jaramillistas joined the massive rallies staged by the MLN and added their voices to those of others in Mexico and throughout Latin America who defended Cuba against U.S. imperialism. Although Cárdenas and even López Mateos framed their defense of Cuba in nationalist terms, Jaramillo expressed admiration for Cuba's agrarian reform and hailed it as a model to be followed. As had been the case during the 1952 Henriquista campaign, there was a wide gap between the MLN leaders such as Cárdenas, who were ultimately accommodating to the political system, and the popular base willing to engage in radical action. In a 1961 interview, Jaramillo remarked, "The accomplishments of [the Cuban] revolution in terms of land redistribution coincide with our own revolutionary aspirations. . . . The campesinos in that revolution did things better than we did, and the Cubans with their government have the guarantees that we lack."[46] Recalled Pedro García, "Committees of women, workers, and campesinos visiting from Cuba would seek Jaramillo out. . . . I saw them here in Cuernavaca. It wasn't just because he defended Cuba; they admired Jaramillo's social struggle. But still, imagine, Jaramillo speaking in Cuernavaca, the recreational center of the North Americans."[47] Some Jaramillistas mention that Jaramillo received an invitation to visit Cuba. It is uncertain, however, whether such an invitation was actually extended. Castro's diplomatic ties with the Mexican government led him to follow a strict hands-off policy towards Mexican dissidents (much to the dismay of the Mexican Left). García's recollection nevertheless establishes the links many Jaramillistas perceived between Jaramillo and the Cuban Revolution.

During the Bay of Pigs invasion, Jaramillo spoke at a rally in Cuernavaca condemning U.S. aggression against Cuba. According to one Department of the Interior agent reporting on this rally, both Jaramillo and his wife Epifania Zúñiga spoke in favor of communism, hailing its potential for ameliorating the condition of poverty. While a redistribution of wealth such as the one taking place in Cuba would be detrimental to millionaires, it could represent a source of liberation for the Mexican people.[48] Such public proclamations about the virtues of communism appear somewhat anomalous, given that Jaramillo seldom made reference to this doctrine. Perhaps the context in which Jaramillo and Zúñiga alluded to Castro's economic system led the agent to simplify their declarations or to simply equate support for Cuba with support for communism. Certainly this was the attitude of U.S. intelligence sources, which, for example, viewed the MLN as a "rabidly anti-United States, Pro-Cuba Communist front."[49] Likewise, one CIA document characterized Jaramillo as a "communist agrarian leader."[50] Jaramillo, who had often been labeled a bandit by the local and national press, was now increasingly branded a communist. Paula Batalla recalled, "They started calling him a communist. I don't know what communism means, but that's what they accused him of and that's why they started persecuting him again."[51] Another Jaramillista reflected, "They are saying that we're what they call communists. Maybe we are. If demanding lands and saying that we don't want to be robbed anymore is communism, then maybe we're communists."[52] In this way, mobilizations leading up to the final episode in the Jaramillista struggle increasingly bore the imprint of the Cuban Revolution.[53]

These allusions to communism are an example of how the Cuban Revolution intensified Cold War politics and began to color mobilizations at the local level. While the Mexican government would consistently defend Castro's Cuba on the basis of self-determination, the island's economic project was anathema to Mexico's commitment to capitalism. As such, Cuba could be defended but not admired. When groups such as the Jaramillistas expressed admiration for the Cuban Revolution because of its success in redistributing wealth, they were implicitly criticizing Mexico's concentration of wealth overseen by the system of capitalist accumulation. The creation of the Otilio Montaño population center not only threatened local interests of the cattle ranchers who had taken control of the land; it also went against projects such as the Cuenca Sur that were typical of Mexico's development strategies during the Mexican miracle. No less threatening to the government was the example that the population center would set to other campesinos nation-wide. The Jaramillistas understood the larger significance of their grassroots project. One participant speculated, "If Rubén had organized that city, be-cause it would have been a city born completely from one moment to the next, with all the political and moral capacity that Rubén taught, it would have been a huge inspiration, maybe even for the entire nation."[54] The Jara-millistas had already proven their capacity to survive persecution from hired gunmen, state police, and army forces, and had mobilized massive numbers for their political campaign. For this reason the government could not take this renewed phase of the struggle lightly.

With the Otilio Montaño population center the Jaramillistas sought to participate in the national economy based on the cultivation of products with a long history and tradition in the state of Morelos. While the Jaramil-listas' proposal was large scale and involved the commercialization of local products, it stemmed from genuine grassroots initiative. More importantly, the projects of the Otilio Montaño population center were to be non–profit-making ventures administered as cooperatives whose revenue would remain in the hands of the local population. This proposal stemmed from a popular conception of development in the sense that it envisioned building houses and streets with access to water and electricity, and not tourist or industrial projects dictated by the wants and desires of Mexico City's population and industry. One participant in the land takeover recalled the speeches that Jaramillo delivered at Michapa and Guarín, affirming that Jaramillo's vision for the lands was socialist. "When the committee was formed I partici-pated and he would say 'The system of government here will be socialist. . . . Everyone will work and everyone will rest.'"[55] Such references to socialism were vague, but they indicated the influence of rural schoolteachers who had, since the Cárdenas administration, disseminated programs of socialist education. While Jaramillista references to socialism were rare, Jaramillo himself and some of those close to him such as Mónico Rodríguez and José Rodríguez espoused the need for workers' ownership of the means of pro-duction. These ideas of social and political justice were now reinforced by the triumph of the Cuban Revolution.

Thus when a Morelos newspaper headlined a story on the Jaramillista land takeover, "It Is in the Michapa and Guarín Plains Where the Current Regime Will Define Itself," it unwittingly captured the significance of the Jaramillista land takeover and the government's reaction to it. The Jaramillistas had long been a thorn in the government's side. As a campesino movement fighting in Zapata's homeland, the Jaramillistas both embodied the living legacy of the battle for *tierra y libertad* and stood as an implicit denunciation of the government's efforts to institutionalize the revolution. That the Jaramillistas were prevented at Michapa and Guarín from putting into practice projects which melded Zapatista and Cardenista ideals while Cuba underwent its socialist revolution renders their plans for a clandestine organization especially significant. That López Mateos oversaw the army's removal of the settlers and a few months later the assassination of the Jaramillo family lay bare the limits of Mexico's official defense for Cuba, one that the United States, as expressed by CIA documents, would come to appreciate.

From Self-Defense to Guerrilla Strategies

The Jaramillistas are a perfect example of the process by which state repression radicalized social actors. The Michapa and Guarín experience produced an all-too-familiar dynamic: López Mateos had pardoned Jaramillo, who had once again opted for legal channels. And still the Mexican government responded with force. Faced with this situation, there was a growing faction of Jaramillistas who advocated a new strategy of clandestine organizing to break this cycle. Initially prompted as a means to confront the new wave of repression, these plans were still in the beginning stages when the land invasion was put down. José Rodríguez, an advocate of this strategy, remembered warning Jaramillo, "The situation is more dangerous than before, precautions need to be doubled . . . you can't be publicly active. Things need to look quiet while the organizing is done in relays of three or five." [56] The idea was to take a different tack and "go about things the other way around," giving the impression that all was calm in the countryside while organizing clandestinely. People were to arrange small groups that would go to Jaramillo for help, training, or instructions and then return to their communities. Jaramillo would travel from place to place to meet with these commissions and in this way begin to set up a structure in Morelos by which the Jaramillistas could extend regionally and eventually nationally. [57] With these plans, the Jaramillistas were clearly entering a new phase, one that linked community development, political education, and armed resistance. Their goals were to construct small group cooperatives of about fifty people in the places where Jaramillo had strong support. This process would allow the Jaramillistas to "create a socialist region without calling it that or decreeing it as such."[58] Jaramillistas would use this strategy to establish their own style of socialism: "We would build our own blacksmith shop to make hoes and plows. We would also have a carpenter, pottery, and butcher's shop. Others would specialize in the cultivation of beans, corn, etc., until we are self-sufficient. But we would not stop interacting with the people, we would continue to be in the struggle."[59]

Local leaders would teach through example: "In many places people will see that they are poor because they live with individualist lifestyles, we will be setting an example. . . . We had read how in China there existed liberated zones in which the red army ruled and they carried out this type of thing."[60] Jaramillo was to initiate this plan by going completely underground. Operating clandestinely, he would form "truly revolutionary organizations" consisting of ten to twenty individuals, each from a different village of Morelos, Guerrero, or Puebla. The members of these organizations would receive a rigorous political education and be responsible for forming groups of about five people in their own village and transmit their political knowledge. This cell-based organizational structure would be the mechanism through which the basis of a revolutionary consciousness could be raised. The Jaramillistas also saw this strategy as a means to reduce their longstanding dependence on their leader, a crucial step in ensuring the continuation of the movement. The broad-based organization formed previously by the PAOM party structure would provide fertile ground for these highly trained secret groups to do their organizing. "The plan was to create many Rubéns," as one Jaramillista put it. Group members would work rigorously to link ideological formation and the solving of specific issues in the community. This advocate continued, "In all the towns these cells would establish the basis for revolutionary consciousness and analyze problems in a different way and disseminate that language and education so that people could see the solution to their problems differently. Once established, they would analyze the issues of land, water, industry, the high cost of living, everything. As a result of this program they would engage in struggle with the larger group to create widespread consciousness."[61]

Such a strategy was meant to generate the basis of a people's revolutionary army, one that would grow directly out of the community's effort to resolve material demands. Its proponents anticipated that local authorities would react with force to the first instances of such organizing. Local caciques might seek to disrupt popular assemblies or beat or incarcerate participants. Such provocations would force the town to organize and, ideally, lead them to community self-defense. "[T]hat's how well-trained armed groups would emerge. These small groups, trained in secret, could take the lead in defending the people."[62]

This plan was one in a series of strategies by which the Jaramillistas continually redefined themselves. It constituted an attempt by the Jaramillistas to persist in their popular organizing, despite government repression. But it was also another instance of state repression that elicited a more militant response. Given the triumph of the Cuban Revolution, it is impossible not to read Jaramillista proposals that included a cell structure organization, a people's revolutionary army, and calls for community socialism as a move towards the types of guerrilla groups that appeared throughout Latin America in the 1960s and the decades thereafter.

It is difficult to determine the extent to which the Mexican government was abreast of the proposed strategy. Its extensive intelligence apparatus, organized through the Federal Security Agency (Dirección General de Seguridad), kept a careful eye on the Jaramillistas, and it is therefore likely it had wind of the plan at some level. With the Cuban experience still fresh, the government could not overlook this looming organizing strategy, especially so close to the capital. When the federal government tried to arrest Jaramillo based on the charge of social dissolution, it added him to the long list of agrarian and labor leaders whose fight for social justice had been labeled a threat to national security. Persecution of the Jaramillistas was assumed under the familiar Cold War framework of communist containment, a mission that dramatically intensified with the triumph of the Cuban Revolution.

Moreover, not only were the Jaramillistas radicalizing their tactics of struggle; they were also building broader alliances. During this time Jaramillo and seventeen supporters also joined the Communist Party. Other Jaramillistas may have done so as well.[63] The membership of the Jaramillista leadership in the PCM reveals an important dynamic occurring within the movement. While there was a current propelling them towards clandestine militant actions, others within the group sought wider popular alliances. Such actions are indicative of the way the Jaramillistas attempted to expand their movement beyond a traditional agrarian one to a more broad-based popular, political, nationalist struggle. Jaramillo became increasingly explicit about the

12. Jaramillo at his home, speaking to campesinos and some visitors from Mexico City. *Archivo Fotográfico, Rodrigo Moya.*

relationship between the campesino fight for land and demands made by workers. He offered solidarity to striking teachers and railway workers, and on International Worker's Day he spoke against the government's co-option of this holiday through its official celebration, urging all workers to demand not only higher wages and fewer work hours but also the nationalization of all industries and of all sources of national wealth. It was necessary, he stated, to engage in a political fight to gain public and economic power as mandated by Article 39 of the Mexican Constitution.[64] Jaramillo had began to characterize his struggle in a different light compared to past electoral campaigns, stating that the PAOM was not a venue to gain political posts but rather "to resolve economic and social problems of its members," and that the party's struggle was "not about electoral politics but about political economy."[65] In this way, the Jaramillistas increasingly presented an alternative to an unresponsive and often violent state.

Ultimately, Jaramillo's relationship with the PCM was an attempt to extend the scope of the Jaramillista struggle and to imbue it with an institutional framework that might channel the energy and discontent of the campesinos into organizations of a national scale. While Jaramillo was cautious about his relationship to the PCM and demonstrated distrust of the leadership, the party was an important source of relationships with intellectuals in Mexico City. At the same time, PCM leaders were anxious to extend their influence in the countryside and saw Jaramillo as a potential channel for doing so. PCM leaders did not hesitate to exaggerate the ideological connections between themselves and the Jaramillistas. For example, an article published in the PCM's newspaper *La Voz de México* after Jaramillo's death stated, "In the last years of his life, Jaramillo did not limit his struggle to an immediate fight for land. Rather, he explained to campesinos that their complete liberation depended on the socialist transformation of society. He educated them in the Marxist-Leninist principles using the simplest forms."[66] The Michapa and Guarín land invasions are evidence of both the exaggerated nature of this statement and the gulf that separated the PCM leadership from its rural base. And it was precisely the more radical aspect of the popular base, as well as campesinos' willingness to engage in direct action, that elicited state repression. This had been the case after the defeat of the Henriquistas in 1952, when the FPPM leadership proved accommodating to the PRI. It had been the case when Lombardo Toledano and the Partido Popular turned their backs on campesinos engaged in land struggles in northern Mexico. And it was the case when the PCM (whose leadership often disdained popular organizing) expelled members unwilling to follow the party line, which was more a reflection of Comintern's guidelines than of Mexico's political reality.[67] As the Cuban Revolution grew increasingly radical in the 1960s, the Mexican government tempered its defense of Havana. The MLN, meanwhile, languished in a lack of programmatic action, and the PRI once again seemed to weather the storm. But the challenge to its institutionalized revolution would reemerge in a far more dramatic way in the 1968 student movement and the army's brutal assassination of hundreds of unarmed civilians in Mexico City's Tlatelolco Plaza. This massive show of force produced its own radicalized social actors, as in its aftermath significant numbers of students went into Mexico's countryside to join, form, or live among clandestine organizations.

The seeds of militant action had long existed in the Jaramillista movement. These were reflected in programs such as the Plan de Cerro Prieto, which had numerous socialist proposals, as well as in the Jaramillista cadre's willingness to engage in armed struggles on occasions past. And while some of the leadership read anarchist publications such as Flores Magón's *Semilla Libertaria*, their dependence on one leader, their consistent appeal to the Mexican Constitution, and their participation in elections belied the anarchist character attributed to the movement by Donald Hodges.[68] There existed, however, a type of organic quality to the relationship between Jaramillo and the movement's popular base. His familiarity with agrarian law, his determination to push forward to the highest level, and his refusal to be co-opted earned him the trust of Morelense campesinos. While the Jaramillista movement did not succeed in broadening its base to a national level, they consistently expressed their demands with reference to more generalized legitimating ideals inherent in the political projects of Zapatismo or Cardenismo. When these seemed too confining because of state co-option, Jaramillistas appealed to international principles of justice disseminated decades earlier by the Flores Magón brothers and renewed in the 1960s with the triumph of the Cuban Revolution. Since the Jaramillista leadership read, in addition to *Semilla Libertaria*, works by Mao and some historical studies on the Soviet Union, it is not surprising that many of their principles would be articulated in terms that resemble the frameworks found in these works. Ultimately, the Jaramillista's ability to educate people politically was disquieting to the government. The state may have appropriated the revolution, but to popular groups such as the Jaramillistas, the war had won them concrete rights that they continued to defend.[69] "Our problems are old, Sirs," replied one Jaramillista to journalists from *Siempre!* doing a story on Morelos. "They are the problems of all the campesinos on this land. We have been fighting for justice for a long time, so long, that we've even lost the fear we had when we began."[70]

These reporters had gone to Morelos to document the situation soon after another wave of government repression that finally succeeded in eliminating Jaramillo, an official crime that would become etched in popular memory and would be transmitted in numerous corridos. This verse of a corrido that circulated after his death captures the sentiment:

Cuidate, Jacinto López,
Escóndete, Arturo Orona.
No vaya el compadre López
—cara de buena persona—
después de un gran abrazote,
a darles caja y corona.

Beware, Jacinto López,
Hide, Arturo Orona.
It might be that the compadre López
—with the face of a good man—
after giving a great embrace
will also send a coffin and wreath.[71]

So clear was the state's message with the Jaramillo assassination that only a few months later, when a high-ranking military officer was dispatched to Mexicali to dissuade Alfonso Garzón (a popular peasant leader tied to the MLN) from running against the PRI in local elections, the officer gave Garzón two choices: "(1) either quieting down and fading into the background or (2) becoming a national figure in Mexico, along with Rubén Jaramillo. Garzón chose the first alternative, after some hesitation, being persuaded by the assurance that in his case, he would be made a martyr by hanging rather than simply being shot."[72] The offer was backed by a show of force, as troops were dispersed throughout the Mexicali Valley in the days preceding the confrontation.[73]

Jaramillo was not the first campesino leader to be assassinated by the state, and he was far from being the last. But the particularly blatant show of force surrounding his and his family's execution shocked even the official press. Upon news of the assassination, letters of protest poured into the president's office, and many local and national newspapers condemned the massacre and demanded that those responsible for the crime be prosecuted.[74] Organizations such as the Independent League of Agrarian Communities in Jalapa avowed to the president, "If this crime goes unpunished, history and the opinion of future generations will hold you directly responsible."[75] Another letter bitterly pointed out, "Yet another crime may be added to those committed by the revolutionary government."[76] Organizations from Cuba, El Salvador, and an international woman's organization also sent letters to the Mexican president urging justice in the death of the Jaramillo family.[77] Even the official press condemned the crime and called for an investigation, although it ignored the army's role in the assassination. An article in the national newspaper *Excélsior*, for example, characterized the killings as a "clumsy" and "stupid crime," and said that even though they may have given Jaramillo "a dose of his own medicine, the same cannot be said about his family, who however, were themselves not white doves."[78]

Despite the heavy military presence at the funeral, thousands of campesinos surrounded the five coffins mourning the loss of their leader and his family. Those closest to the Jaramillista leadership observed cautiously from a distance. Crescencio Castillo recalls how he and Pedro García went to a hill near the cemetery: "I had to watch, even if it was from afar. . . . A friend lent me his binoculars and with them I could see everything, all the movement, and how all around the cemetery were those rotten soldiers."[79] A group of reporters that included Carlos Fuentes went to Morelos shortly thereafter and were told by one Jaramillista, "There's a lot of gobierno these days prowling around Morelos. Now, after they killed Jaramillo, we are being watched more than ever, as if peasants as humble as we could be dangerous."[80] The campesino answered the *Siempre!* writers, "Who killed Jaramillo? I think you know. He was killed because of the fight he led for justice for the campesinos. Up there in Mexico City they talk a lot about freedom. Some kind of freedom."[81]

It is difficult to speculate with certainty who issued the order to kill Jaramillo. The day after the murder, an agent from Mexico's Federal Security Agency traveled to Morelos to confirm rumors of the assassination. The head of the state's public security forces in Cuernavaca informed him that, as far as they understood, the federal agents had been "complying with orders from the President."[82] Jaramillo had suffered numerous attempts on his life since 1942. However, aside from the army's persecution during his armed uprising, all of these came from hired gunmen or the local police force. In 1962, in contrast, it was the federal army who kidnapped and killed the Jaramillo family. The assassination of Jaramillo resulted from the logic of a state party that did not hesitate to use force when co-option bore no fruits. The Jaramillista struggle had long posed a political and economic threat to the state. By the early 1960s, Morelos was increasingly contemplated for its potential to meet the needs of the capital. The campesino lifestyle defended by Jaramillo, as well as the economic project the Jaramillistas proposed, were incompatible with investors and policymakers who saw it as the ideal place to establish industrial corridors such as CIVAC, construct housing developments, build tourist resorts, and—as in most of Mexico—farm commercial crops.

Politically, the Jaramillista struggle also stood as a threat. Jaramillo's charismatic leadership, ability to mobilize popular sectors, and his tradition of armed struggle became more difficult to ignore after the Cuban Revolution and the accompanying rejuvenation of the Mexican Left. That president López Mateos had, in a public act of reconciliation, embraced Jaramillo as a gesture of his will to work with the agrarian leader marked Jaramillo's assassination as an official act of betrayal. To this day, Jaramillistas refer to López Mateos's gesture as the *"abrazo de Judas"* (Judas's embrace), and his death came to symbolize the fate of those who laid down their arms and placed their trust in the government. For subsequent armed campesino groups, the lesson of Jaramillo's assassination would be acutely remembered and his name invoked in movements not only in Morelos but in other parts of Mexico, including the Chiapas rebellion.[83] The state's selective use of force would increasingly become standard practice. This trajectory would continue, but not end, with the much more widely recognized Tlatelolco massacre and the government's dirty war of the 1970s, today widely considered a crime against humanity.

Mexico's Left interpreted the official crime against the Jaramillo family within the framework of Cold War politics. Jaramillo's public condemnation of U.S. imperialism, combined with the fact that he was killed only a couple of months before Kennedy's visit to Mexico, would lead some to believe that the order came from Washington. According to this view, López Mateos acted on Washington's orders, or at least wanted to show that when it came to subversives—especially communists—Mexico stood firm.[84] One news magazine carried a full-page cartoon depicting Kennedy's welcoming committee (made up of clergymen, businessmen, and politicians) led by a military general handing Jaramillo's head to Kennedy on a silver platter.[85] The following version was echoed by many: "The order really came from the White House, since he [Jaramillo] gave his support to the Cuban revolutionary cause and gringo invasions were the order of the day. That really did him in because before, mostly due to his religious background, they almost trusted him. But once he declared himself in favor of Castro Ruz, they said, 'This one is not one of ours.'"[86]

My own inquiry into U.S. State Department records under the Freedom of Information Act yielded a report from the U.S. embassy in Mexico describing the assassination of Jaramillo and his family and a summary of the agrarian leader's struggle. The document speculated that a Mexican "federal government agency took the law into its hands and executed the five persons."[87] Interestingly, a State Department document dated May 6, 1962 (seventeen days before Jaramillo's assassination), was denied to me because it "contains security-classified information."[88] Wherever the actual order to assassinate Jaramillo originated, Cold War ideology provided a nationally and internationally legitimizing framework for government repression in Mexico and throughout Latin America. Leftist groups, likewise, interpreted this repression within the Cold War context and speculated about Washington's involvement. And this repression would serve to further radicalize leftist groups. While the pursuit of agrarian demands by means of legal petitioning, land invasions, and massive popular demonstrations by no means came to a halt in the second half of the twentieth century, many rural struggles in Mexico acquired a more militant tactical and programmatic nature in response to government repression. This trend would greatly accelerate after 1968, when the Tlatelolco massacre laid bare the state's repressive apparatus, and, through the exodus of a large contingent of students into Mexico's sierra, united militant sectors of the Left. To this dynamic—still under crucial need of study—the Jaramillista movement represented the historical prelude.

The Jaramillista Legacy

When President Carlos Salinas de Gortari came to power in 1988, he implemented a series of market-oriented reforms that required changing the Mexican Constitution. Undertaken as part of the neoliberal project that would later culminate in the North American Free Trade Agreement (NAFTA) signed by Mexico, the United States, and Canada, and due to go into effect on January 1, 1994, one of the most drastic measures was the dismantling of Article 27. This article, one of the Zapatistas' most important achievements, protected campesinos' right to land. Salinas's changes not only decreed the privatization of collectively held lands but also declared all pending land petitions null and void. As if to add insult to injury, the president proclaimed Zapata his personal hero, featuring the agrarian leader in the backdrop of many of his speeches and naming his son "Emiliano" and his personal jet "Zapata." His appropriation of Zapata fooled only those who believed that land privatization equaled modernization. Salinas's neoliberal reforms had a devastating effect on the social well-being of the general population and were characterized by a level of corruption that later made it necessary for the state to bail out some of the very sectors it had auctioned off. Salinas ended his term in disgrace and virtually had to go into exile.

Part of Salinas's unmaking came on January 1, 1994, the day when the indigenous peasants who founded the Zapatista Army of National Liberation rebelled against the federal government, declaring NAFTA a death sentence to indigenous people. The EZLN called for Mexicans throughout the country to join them in a popular uprising. Mexicans did not heed the call to arms but did stage massive demonstrations in protest against the army offensive the state leveled against the new generation of Zapatistas. After twelve days of fighting, the EZLN and the government established a ceasefire, an agreement the Zapatistas have honored even when the government has not and in the face of a widespread low-intensity warfare. This low-intensity warfare—which human rights organizations have more aptly termed "civilian-targeted warfare"—designed to wear down the EZLN's support base, has resulted in numerous human rights violations, illegal incarcerations, and a widespread militarization of the state. In its rawest form, the government response has included massacres such as the December 1997 paramilitary killing of forty-five indigenous persons, mostly women and children, as they prayed in a church in the highland community of Acteal.

This repression not withstanding, the Zapatistas have relied solely on peaceful venues to mobilize for their demands, which include indigenous and women's rights, land, local autonomy, and the right to basic services such as education and health care. Framed within a fervent opposition to neoliberalism, the Zapatistas' struggle and their call for a "world in which there is room for many worlds" resonated in distant corners of the globe, contradicting the claims of those who saw with the fall of the Berlin Wall the end of the inspiration for proposals not based within a capitalist order.[1] The Zapatista movement thus not only served to warn the Mexican government that its authoritarianism would not proceed unchecked but also reminded scholars that despite the now predominantly urban nature of Mexican society, the countryside continued to be a key arena of struggle, and campesinos key actors.

The indigenous rebels of this state adopted the Zapatista name because, as they put it, "Emiliano Zapata is the hero who best symbolizes the tradition of revolutionary struggle of the Mexican people."[2] The massive popular support lent to the 1994 Zapatista uprising is an important indication of the extent to which Zapata is still a hero squarely in the hands of the people. His legacy has been kept alive, in part, by rebel groups like the Jaramillistas who continued to fight in his name. Nor surprisingly, Jaramillista veterans were among those who responded to the Chiapas uprising and were in turn recognized by the EZLN as key predecessors of their struggle. Félix Serdán, for example, who has traveled to Chiapas on numerous occasions, was named an "honorary major" of the EZLN forces. On October 26, 1996, in front of six hundred delegates gathered for the National Indigenous Congress in Mexico City, Comandante Ramona of the EZLN turned over a Mexican flag to Serdán, who was then seventy-nine years old. In a 1943 skirmish between the army and the Jaramillistas, Serdán had been injured and captured. Soldiers confiscated from him the group's documents, a typewriter, and the Mexican flag that Félix was in charge of carrying. Estanislao Tapia, a Zapatista veteran from the revolution who later participated in the Zacatepec mobilizations led by Jaramillo, also traveled to Chiapas to participate in the 1994 National Aguascalientes Convention. Two years later, at the age of ninety-six, he was too frail to return for a second visit. He instead wrote a letter to the EZLN, which remarked, "It is of great satisfaction to me that you continue to fight. . . . I hope that the struggle will unfold in favor of the people. Don't lose hope. Continue to defend the ideals of my General Zapata."[3] Serdán later accompanied the Zapatistas in mobilizations such as the 1999 national referendum in which EZLN delegates consulted public opinion on indigenous rights and the Zapatista march to Mexico City in March 2001.[4] The 1999 EZLN visit to Morelos included a stop at Jaramillo's grave, where the two Chiapas rebels deposited a wreath on each of the family members' graves. The actions, words, experiences, and memories of such participants have succeeded in keeping alive the history of Zapata's struggle and are key to the ability of Mexico's lower classes to mount new battles. They also signal the continuities in the resistance movements of twentieth-century Mexico.

The Ghost of Jaramillo: Guerrilla Groups in Mexico

The Jaramillista struggle speaks to campesinos' unwillingness to bend to the will of the state, even in times of apparent peace. Its dynamism and longevity provide useful conceptual tools for understanding both the nature of an authoritarian state and the willingness of campesinos to resist and combat its domination. Two principal tendencies coexisted in the Jaramillista movement: Cardenismo, an institutionalized agrarian ideology that encouraged peaceful reformist demands for change, and Zapatismo, which emphasized bottom-up land distribution, the preservation of campesinos' subsistence lifestyles, and a willingness to take up arms to achieve these goals. These trends defined agrarian movements in Mexico for decades to come. These two tendencies developed and evolved in the trajectory of the Jaramillistas, sometimes in dialogue with one another and very often conditioned by the actions of the state. If the government had not reacted to the Jaramillistas with repression, the group's Cardenista elements would have likely prevailed. However, state violence forced the Jaramillistas into an armed struggle that—given the ideological polarization of the Cold War decades, especially after the triumph of the Cuban Revolution—led them to acquire the characteristics of modern guerrillas.

Scholars have devoted significant attention to when, why, and how peasants rebel, recognizing that agrarian revolts impelled major transformations worldwide.[5] Key to these studies are analyses of the characteristics each rebellion acquired: How did campesinos engage with, or confront, ruling institutions? When did they opt for open revolt? What was the nature of their ideology? What did such characteristics reveal about the cultural and political context from which they emerged? Such studies focus primarily on large-scale peasant rebellions that resulted in national regime changes. How, though, are we to interpret smaller peasant revolts? One way, as Steve Stern suggests, is to recognize peasants as "*continuous initiators* in political relations among themselves and with nonpeasants."[6] Our understanding is still incomplete, notes Stern, of "the manifold ways whereby peasants have continuously engaged their political worlds—in apparently quiescent as well as rebellious times, as initiators of change as well as reactors to it, as peoples simultaneously disposed to 'adapt' to objective forces beyond their control and to 'resist' inroads on hard-won rights and achievements."[7] Scholars of postrevolutionary Mexico have focused on popular culture in order to elucidate the ways in which ordinary people have resisted, participated, and shaped the process of state formation. In so doing, the PRI's hegemony appears far less complete. The Jaramillista movement confirms this perspective, not only because they engaged and sought to influence the state's project, but because when it acted to their detriment, they militantly confronted it.

Guerrilla movements in Mexico remain vastly understudied. And yet their presence in a country hailed for its political stability and the longevity of its ruling party speaks volumes about Mexico's political reality during the course of the twentieth century. The Jaramillistas provide a crucial link between rural rebellions rooted in the revolution, so meticulously studied by historians, and guerrilla struggles of the Cold War decades that pervaded the Mexican landscape but have been omitted from the official version of history and remain largely ignored by scholars.[8] To tell the story of the armed Left elucidates the nature of the PRI's rule, the depth of campesino consciousness, and the tenaciousness of rural dwellers in their insistence on living off the land, even as the government imposed a capitalist economic model that increasingly rendered their way of life obsolete.

From a strategic point of view, guerrilla warfare is not new. It has been used throughout the world by popular armies to offset the technological superiority of enemy forces—most often foreign invaders or occupying colonial powers. Fighting forces during Mexico's war of independence, the Reforma, the French invasion, and the revolution all employed forms of guerrilla warfare. Programmatically, however, guerrilla movements in the second half of the twentieth century differed from earlier peasant revolts that were characterized by narrowly defined objectives but coincided with or came to constitute major national upheavals. During the Cold War, campesino guerrillas acquired an increasingly socialist vision and defined their struggle as an explicit attack on the state. In Mexico, this occurred for two interrelated reasons. First of all, the national project born of the revolution bound disparate regions and their populations more firmly into the fabric of the nation-state. It was more likely, therefore, that grievances would be understood in a national and even international context. Second, and especially in the decades after 1968, schoolteachers with socialist ideals, as well as politically committed leftist university students, increasingly provided ideological tools to link local injustices with larger structural forces.

The Jaramillista movement embodied this transformation in campesino movements both in the years of its struggle and symbolically after it was repressed. The assassination of the Jaramillo family and the ensuing persecution against other participants ended the Jaramillista movement. But it did not end rural resistance in Morelos. On the contrary, it radicalized many campesinos, who—joined by workers, students, and schoolteachers— formed new associations that mobilized and sought a systemic change. A similar dynamic emerged throughout Mexico, its pace quickened by the 1968 massacre at Tlatelolco. Many of these groups were convinced of the need for armed action. Perhaps the most famous case was the guerrilla assault led by Arturo Gámiz and Pablo Gómez on the military headquarters of Ciudad Madera, Chihuahua, only three years after the assassination of the Jaramillo family. Such drastic measures actually had their origins in a long history of legal mobilizations by campesinos whose demands centered around land and water rights. Rather than hearing or solving such issues, the authorities in Chihuahua responded with repression, convincing many in the group that they would only be heard weapon in hand. The assault on Madera proved to be a complete failure and resulted in the death of eight of the thirty-two attackers. While the group's actions appeared as desperate measures undertaken by young idealists, the operation reflected the increasing willingness of many to embrace radical tactics in an effort to confront the state and seek its overthrow. This dynamic occurred in regions across Mexico, including Morelos, where veteran Jaramillistas participated in clandestine organizations, this time not to gain short-term economic concessions from the government but to eventually seek its overthrow. Such goals would be possible, as one militant put it, only through "simultaneous armed and violent actions in different parts of the country, using as an example some of the guerrilla activities that recently took place in the state of Chihuahua."[9]

While guerrilla groups remained largely localized, there existed some important temporal and regional continuities. The Jaramillista links to the guerrilla group in Guerrero headed by Lucio Cabañas and Genaro Vázquez, for example, represent an important continuum for armed movements in Mexico. Like the Jaramillistas' turn to arms, Guerrero's guerrilla group, the Party of the Poor (Partido de los Pobres, or PDLP), resulted from the continual repression of campesinos by local caciques and the judicial police. Cabañas took up arms in 1967 after state authorities violently repressed a peaceful demonstration in the Atoyac sierra of Guerrero. Once in the mountains, however, Cabañas refused to reconsider legal channels—in part because of Jaramillo's fate.[10] For seven years, the Party of the Poor engaged in the political education of campesinos in the Guerrero mountains (Cabañas called it "*hacer pueblo*," literally, "to make a people"). The region's population provided food and shelter for an armed cadre that began with three people and grew steadily to one hundred, with other support forces in different regions that numbered at least seventy.[11]

As far as we know, former Jaramillistas did not become combatants in Guerrero, but Cabañas did seek their advice. In this way, Cabañas's group benefited from the experience of more than two decades of Jaramillista struggle. Pedro García, one Jaramillista, described the process: "When Lucio was persecuted by the government, we had a contact and we went to the sierra with great difficulty, because it wasn't that easy to see him, just as with Jaramillo, the people protected him. But we had a contact and so we went . . . and we made a few recommendations, about some of the mistakes Jaramillo made."[12] According to García, their suggestions concerned the role of the Communist Party. Even though Jaramillo rejoined the PCM in 1961, he remained deeply distrustful of the national leadership, who had held that conditions were not ripe for an open confrontation with the state and instead advocated only peaceful actions. To campesinos—who faced both the violence of poverty and systematic repression by caciques, the judicial police, and the army—such a stance often rang hollow. So García recommended that, just as Jaramillo had done, Cabañas keep his distance from the PCM leadership. The Party of the Poor also sought connections with veteran Jaramillistas for strategic purposes. Because the state of Morelos bordered Guerrero, fleeing *Cabañistas* could use it as a place of refuge. Moreover, Morelos was a midway point to Mexico City, and therefore stood as a critical connecting link to militants stationed in the capital. Cabañas wanted Jaramillistas to provide food and shelter and run messages for the members of the Party of the Poor.[13]

The legacy of both regional and national insurgencies fortified subsequent struggles. Each new mobilization added a layer of experience and memory, and offered the opportunity to learn and strengthen their own movements. "I think it was fruitful to have talked with Lucio and the people who were with him," concluded García, "because in some ways, we had the experience of the Jaramillista movement here in Morelos even if things change from one region to another."[14] Intelligence sources alerted the government to the connections between the Jaramillista veterans and guerrilla groups in Guerrero, noting that throughout Mexico armed movements were acquiring strength, their ranks swelling because of the increasing militarization. This, related one report, "caus[ed] the formation of guerrilla groups in various parts of the republic, especially Chihuahua where there are approximately 3,000 *guerrilleros*, the majority rural schoolteachers who every day gain more strength."[15] This figure is an exaggeration, but it reflects the extent to which armed groups constituted part of Mexico's social landscape, a situation the government simply could not ignore. That the report noted the prominence of teachers is a sign of this group's militancy, not just in Chihuahua, but throughout Mexico.

Even after Jaramillo's assassination, the government kept a vigilant eye on groups in Morelos, where many Jaramillistas stayed active and formed new political organizations that included an analysis of their own history of struggle. In their reflections, the Jaramillistas realized how heavily they depended on their leader; one commented: "When they killed him, they killed a liberation movement."[16] Subsequent political discussions focused on ways of creating a decentralized but coordinated struggle. Some Jaramillista veterans came together with participants in the Revolutionary Teachers' Movement, calling themselves the Ho Chi Minh Sectional.[17] The language of the emerging group reflected several important tendencies: a radicalization stemming from the government repression, a reaction against the PCM's position that campesinos were neither the principal subjects nor agents of revolutionary change, and a marked anti-imperialism specifically targeted against the United States. So while they named themselves the Ho Chi Minh Sectional in solidarity with the Vietnamese struggle, they described themselves as Maoist. On participant recalled, "I joined a semiclandestine, Marxist, Maoist party. . . . In that party we were very excited about political discipline, a constant study of the economic, social, and political situation in the country, and the international situation as well. We analyzed the ideological experiences of China and the Soviet Union, we pronounced ourselves in favor of the Chinese. We became Maoist. And that led to a dynamic participation with popular groups in a way that was very characteristic of the Jaramillistas. That is, Maoism, almost in a natural way, connected with the thinking and praxis of the Jaramillistas."[18]

In their attempts to place the Jaramillista struggle into an international context, the Ho Chi Minh Sectional compared Jaramillo's assassination to that of Patrice Lumumba, "since it was carried out due to official orders and to protect the imperialist interests of North Americans."[19] For the sectional, the government's increased reliance on repression signaled that the official party had made common cause with an international alliance to crush left-wing movements. For this reason, it was more important than ever to "completely distrust the current government and any that constitutionally succeeded it."[20] The league's constant allusions to Jaramillismo indicated the centrality of his struggle in formulating new tactics of resistance and the enduring willingness to continue the fight in the countryside, regardless of state repression. The Ho Chi Minh Sectional sought to transcend the short-comings of the Jaramillista movement: its localized nature, its reliance on the leader, and its concentration on economic concessions rather than the overthrow of the state.[21]

The Cold War and State Violence

State violence did not succeed in eliminating popular opposition; instead, it wound up radicalizing their tactics and ideology. Groups originally fighting to hold the government accountable for social reforms mandated by the Mexican Constitution came to consider, and plan, direct attacks on the state. In a climate of heightened ideological polarization, the government immediately identified these groups as part of an international communist menace. With varying degrees of constitutional legitimacy, this paradigm appeared again and again throughout Latin America, and the United States willfully supplied weapons and resources to combat the Reds. The Mexican government's use of repression, then, became validated by imperial allies engaged in a broader struggle against communism. It is not surprising that, despite concrete evidence to the contrary, Mexico's intelligence apparatus continuously emphasized the armed Left's ties to Fidel Castro.

The reports written by government infiltrators were devoid of reliable analysis. It is often difficult to assess from these intelligence sources what information is an accurate reproduction of the discussions held by clandestine groups. The state's agents commonly made embellishments inflating the power of rebel groups to justify the important nature of their work.[22] But as a consequence, such reports resulted in increased government repression. In his study of the history of the Mexican intelligence apparatus, Sergio Aguayo argues that intelligence sources exaggerated the nature and extent of guerrilla groups to justify and expand their own institutions. It served the government to use these reports uncritically to justify repressive measures. For example, Fernando Gutiérrez Barrios, head of the Federal Security Agency, knew that there was no support from Cuba for clandestine groups in Mexico, and yet he fanned President Díaz Ordaz's paranoia without ever making a real assessment of the strength of armed groups.[23] "The Mexican guerrillas," Aguayo found, "had a limited capacity and were confined to specific regions. It was an irritation factor, not a threat to national security. They did, however, represent a potential danger, and from there stemmed the generalized perception that they constituted a threat."[24] The state's violence was out of proportion to reality, which, in turn, strengthened belief among social activists that peaceful means of struggle were futile.

In the late sixties, the movements that succeeded the Jaramillistas in Morelos consistently fell victim to this repression. The judicial police disarticulated the Ho Chi Minh Sectional by infiltrating it and capturing individual members. Reyes Aranda, a former Jaramillista, was the first to fall and disclose—very likely under torture—the whereabouts of José Allende, another Jaramillista veteran and group member. Allende was captured and, during his interrogation, ordered to identify various people in photographs. When he refused, his captors applied electric shocks to his eyes and testicles. The agents then demanded he reveal where the group hid its weapons. When Allende replied that the only weapons he had—the hoe, plow, and shovel— were in his shed, the agents beat him so hard that for the rest of his life his bones ached with cold weather.[25]

Intelligence documents detail the state's desire to eliminate armed groups, regardless of how much force the process required. In the early 1970s, the population of Guerrero suffered particular brutality under a policy recommending that "the state governor, a military officer by training, eliminate the guerrilla groups. [In this way] the next governor would not have to endure guerrilla actions since, by exterminating them, he would undercut any [groups] aspiring to imitate them."[26] Recovering the history of guerrilla groups in Mexico thus also reveals the nature and extent of the Mexican government's use of repression. Implicit in the myth of Mexico's social stability is the idea that official violence was relatively absent. While it certainly never reached the levels seen in many Central and South American military regimes, repression undergirded the PRI's rule. The eloquent summary of Arturo Warman, a lifelong scholar of rural Mexico who in the 1990s became a defender of the PRI regime, is worth quoting at length:

> Its magnitude, degree of violence, and illegality vary greatly, from the simple threat to individual persecution and imprisonment, to outright slaughter and destruction of settlements. The agents of repression also vary: pistoleros (hired guns), "white guards," local police, special police forces, or federal institutions. Repression is used to suppress what the system cannot absorb and the people it cannot co-opt. In contrast with forms of control applied to other groups in society,

in the rural areas repression is not the exception. It is a constant, surrounded by a wall of silence and indifference, concealed under the ambiguous and degrading term, "common crime." Due to its general extent and frequency, repression constitutes a complement to negotiation, absorption, and concession.[27]

Ongoing Resistance

Despite of the violence inflicted on hundreds of campesinos in Guerrero, Morelos, and throughout Mexico, and despite the radicalization of these groups during the 1960s and 1970s, by 1979 rural organizations once again came together in a movement that sought redress through legal channels. Seeking to rescue the Zapatista struggle, the Plan de Ayala National Confederation (Coordinadora Nacional Plan de Ayala, CNPA) brought together a nationwide independent campesino organization that broke with the government's traditional mode of corporatist control. In Morelos, campesinos became affiliated through the People's Union of Morelos (Unión de Pueblos de Morelos, UPM), which achieved extensive popular mobilization. Again, Jaramillista veterans figured prominently in the leadership. Through such organizations, campesinos accomplished what the Jaramillistas had been unable to achieve: unity with other campesino organizations across Mexico. Two thousand delegates representing more than forty local, regional, and national organizations arrived at the founding congress.[28] Land continued to be the central issue for the CNPA; its motto was "Today we fight for the land, tomorrow for power." In 1982 it was changed to "Today we fight for land and power."[29]

The legacy of Jaramillo and his movement in Morelos has been kept alive by its survivors, who continue to combine old and new forms of struggle. The Jaramillistas defied the state's economic project and legitimized their rebellion based on Morelos's history of resistance. The Zapatista experience during the revolution bequeathed a collective memory of armed struggle that future leaders would use to mobilize campesinos to protect and preserve their hard-won rights. Campesinos held on to the example and memory of Zapata, whose image inevitably acquired mythic proportions. And yet, as the revolutionary state drafted a new set of rules for its citizens, campesinos refashioned their forms of struggle and found creative ways of dealing with the terms and conditions set forth by the new rulers. As Jennie

Purnell found in her study on popular movements in Mexico, "Each time the Mexican state has attempted to redefine the relationship between peasant communities and the state, it has added a new layer to local legacies of agrarian and political conflict and has created possibilities for new alliances, new claims and new identities."[30] This pattern may be seen in the case of the Jaramillistas, who adopted and stood by Cardenismo as a means of participating in the national state project. In fact, the experience of Cardenas's rule led Jaramillistas to broaden their goals beyond traditional campesino demands for land, debunking the notion that the rural poor are inevitably and irrationally conservative. Cárdenas's populism profoundly influenced the Jaramillista movement and can help us understand the impact of his presidency and contribute to the ongoing debate regarding the nature and long-term impact of Cardenismo.

While campesinos in Morelos acted with a collective, often utopian memory of Zapatismo, policies under Cárdenas made their hard-fought goals viable. Infused with new ideological elements, Jaramillistas incorporated Cardenismo to the extent that it fortified the moral and legal basis of their struggle. It expanded their social movement beyond strict campesino demands for land and the means to work it. Even though Cárdenas organized popular sectors into separate institutional structures, the various elements of a socially responsible state—education, health care, fair prices, and adequate wages—could act as a rallying cry for otherwise disparate groups. In the Jaramillista movement, this unity played itself out through the alliance between workers and campesinos at Zacatepec, the formation of a political party calling for a return to the tenets of Cardenismo, and the idea for a community with modern infrastructure in Michapa and Guarín. In each of these instances, the populist state of the 1930s provided a historical precedent and, rather than succumb to the limitations imposed by subsequent rulers, the Jaramillistas developed a more radical vision.

Whether through a Cardenista, Zapatista, or socialist framework, campesinos articulated a profound sense of justice and challenged the policies of an authoritarian state. In this sense, while the PRI's ability to stay in power for seventy-one years speaks to the success of its ruling mechanisms, scholars, by concentrating on the state party, have neglected the numerous and constant forms of struggle that took place during the supposed Pax Priísta. The top-down scholarship that dominates the period of the Mexican Miracle has, in turn, led to the characterization of post-1968 struggles as "new social movements," a paradigm that more often than not abandons class as a unit of analysis, focuses on identity as an all encompassing explanation, and is blind to the diverse ways in which people organized historically to seek social justice.[31]

Acknowledging the continuities between past and present social movements enables us to see the fall of Mexico's one-party system as a product of popular resistance. While some of the mechanisms of control remain alive even after the PRI's electoral defeat, so too has popular resistance. Today this resistance is most vividly exemplified by the recent unrest in Oaxaca, historically a bastion of PRI rule, and in the hundreds of thousands of people who have filled the Mexico City *zócalo* (the city center) protesting the fraud of the July 2006 presidential elections. In defiance of the institutions that validated an electoral process riddled with irregularities, on November 20, the day that commemorates Mexico's revolution, supporters of the left-leaning candidate Andrés Manuel López Obrador declared him Mexico's legitimate president. However symbolic this gesture, almost a century after the revolution, the mobilizations in support of López Obrador are filled with its legacy, from demands that Article 39 of the constitution be respected, to reformulations of Madero's original declaration from "effective suffrage and no re-election" to "effective suffrage and no imposition." Popular mobilizations have been so great that former president Fox had to move the official celebration of Mexico's independence from the nation's capital to the state of Hidalgo and a month and a half later canceled the official commemoration of the revolution. In each instance, convened by López Obrador, hundreds of thousands of people filled the zócalo to mount an alternative celebration of these holidays. Unnerved by the unprecedented size of these mobilizations, president elect Enrique Calderón was hastily sworn in on December 1, 2006, with an equally unprecedented show of force.

The Jaramillistas stand as one of the many movements that eroded the regime's power and exposed its authoritarian nature. Because of the varied and continued protest during the Mexican Miracle, the PRI increasingly resorted to repression. It ultimately dealt with the Jaramillistas through force, just as it did with the Henriquistas and the labor movements of the 1940s and 1950s. This state terror, however, did not produce a generalized national and international outrage until 1968, when the army massacred workers and middle-class students peacefully demonstrating in Tlatelolco. While the PRI stands as the most enduring party regime of the twentieth century, the resistance it faced throughout its rule reveals the impossibility of exerting total domination over a people. Popular groups never ceased to defend their rights to land, just working conditions, and the preservation of their indigenous cultures. The Jaramillistas are an integral part of this tradition. In the long trajectory of their movement, they repeatedly adopted new forms of struggle, rescuing Zapatismo, refashioning Cardenismo, and contributing to the living history of resistance in Mexico.

NOTES

Abbreviations

AGA	Archivo General Agrario
AGN	Archivo General de la Nación
AGN/P	Archivo General de la Nación, Ramo Presidentes
ALM	Adolfo López Mateos
ARC	Adolfo Ruiz Cortines
BMLT-AE	Biblioteca Miguel Lerdo de Tejada, Archivo Económico
CCJM	Casa de la Cultura Jurídica de Morelos
CEMOS	Centro de Estudios del Movimiento Obrero y Socialista
DFS	Ramo Dirección Federal de Seguridad
DGG	Ramo Dirección General de Gobierno
DGIPS	Ramo Dirección General de Investigaciones Políticas y Sociales
JFK-NSF	John F. Kennedy Library, National Security Files
LBJ-NSF	Lyndon B. Johnson Library, National Security Files
LC	Lázaro Cárdenas
MAC	Manuel Ávila Camacho
NAW	U.S. National Archives at Washington
PEGJ-PC	Plutarco Emilio García Jiménez, Personal Collection

Introduction

1. This account of events is based on *Política*, 1 and 15 June 1962, and an interview by the author with Raquel Jaramillo, 3 September 1999, Colonia Rubén Jaramillo, Morelos.

2. Boyer, *Becoming Campesinos*, 3.

3. Some of these parallels may not be a coincidence, since Sandino spent time in Mexico among oil workers just after the revolution, where anarchist texts such as *Semilla Libertaria* continued to circulate. Even Sandino's spiritualism might share some characteristics with Jaramillo's Methodism, and both were members of Masonic lodges.

4. For example, Greg Grandin documents the life of such exceptional figures as José Angel Icó, Alfredo Cucul, Efraín Reyes Maaz, and Adelina Caal, who in Guatemala consistently challenged the authoritarian state structure from perspectives that ranged from the liberal notions espoused by the coffee elite at the beginning of the twentieth century, to Marxist analysis of dialectical materialism expressed through Mayan spirituality. Grandin, *The Last Colonial Massacre*. Closer to home, Lucio Cabañas, a rural schoolteacher who took up arms in the state of Guerrero in 1967, played a similar role by translating complex theory to concepts easily discernable to campesinos. His explanation of dialectical materialism through the growth cycle of corn is a particularly compelling example. See Luis Suárez, *Lucio Cabañas, el guerrillero sin esperanza*, 131–32. I thank Alex Aviña for bringing this last example to my attention.

5. Created by Plutarco Elías Calles in 1929, the National Revolutionary Party, or PRN, grouped various revolutionary leaders under one official party, often referred to as "the revolutionary family." In 1938 Cárdenas changed the name to the Mexican Revolutionary Party—PRM. Its final name change, to the PRI, came in 1946.

6. Brunk, "Remembering Three Moments in the Posthumous Career of the Martyr of Chinameca," 469.

7. Brunk, "Remembering Emiliano Zapata," 466.

8. Peruvian writer Mario Vargas Llosa used this term to refer to the PRI's ability to stay in power for so many decades while still holding presidential elections every six years. Made during a live national broadcast while visiting Mexico, these comments did not sit well with official circles, and Vargas Llosa left unexpectedly the next day.

9. For a pioneering study of everyday forms of peasant resistance see Scott, *Weapons of the Weak*.

10. Jeffrey Gould finds a similar dynamic in his case study of campesinos in Chinandega, Nicaragua, concluding that "the use of both proletarian and peasant tactics allowed the campesinos to enlarge the scope of their own demands and their recruitment base" and to "achieve a fuller understanding of themselves and

their class antagonists"; thus, "the combination of proletarian and peasant forms of consciousness and struggle led to the political maturation of the campesino movement." *To Lead as Equals*, 298.

11. Zolov, "Discovering a Land 'Mysterious and Obvious,'" 262.

12. Aguilar Camín and Meyer, *In the Shadow of the Mexican Revolution*, 164.

13. Bortz, "The Effects of Mexico's Postwar Industrialization on the U.S.-Mexico Price and Wage Comparison," 229.

14. Niblo, *Mexico in the 1940s*, 170 and 207–8. Mexican entrepreneurs continue to figure prominently among the world's wealthiest people. The August 2007 issue of *Fortune* magazine declared the Mexican telecommunications giant Carlos Slim Helú the richest man in the world.

15. Most of the scholarship on rural schoolteachers focuses on the resistance they met as agents of state consolidation. As with most historical works on twentieth-century Mexico, however, these studies conclude in 1940. The relationship between teachers and rural communities after 1940 has not received the same degree of attention. In spite of their tumultuous beginning, rural schools became a cornerstone of social justice when carried out in conjunction with other social reforms. For works on teachers and resistance to the revolutionary state's cultural project, see Vaughan, *Cultural Politics in Revolution*, and Rockwell, "Schools of the Revolution." For examples on teachers' activism in rural communities, see Blacker-Hanson, "La Lucha Sigue!" and Campos et al., *De las aulas a las calles*.

16. Genaro Vázquez, Lucio Cabañas, and Arturo Gámiz are some of the most famous examples of teachers turned guerrilla leaders and will be discussed briefly in the conclusion. Blacker-Hanson, in "La Lucha Sigue!" draws attention to the extent to which battles waged by educators in concert with other sectors of the population sought democratic transparency years before Mexico City students made demands of a similar nature in the 1968 student movement (p. 6). By showcasing teacher militancy in the post-1940 period, not only have recent works enriched the record of popular struggle during the Mexican Miracle, they have also "decentered" the focus on Mexico's capital and the struggles for democracy waged there. Rubin argues that to better understand Mexico's postrevolutionary regime, it is important to take "a decentered approach to power" that "illuminates both the origins and meanings of regional democratization and the workings of domination and resistance in Mexico"; *Decentering the Regime*, 9.

17. Reyna, "El conflicto ferrocarrilero," 211.

18. Revueltas, *Ensayo sobre un proletariado sin cabeza*, 196, 83. Revueltas especially criticized the opportunistic fashion with which the PCM acted, which led it to debate which elements of the national bourgeoisie it should support or combat, rather than stand "for, with, and alongside" the proletariat as the vanguard of revolution. Revueltas had himself been a two-time member of the PCM but had been expelled during the 1943 and 1960 purges.

19. Ravelo, *Los Jaramillistas*, 188.

20. Carr, *Marxism and Communism in Twentieth-Century Mexico*, 2. In one of the earlier historical studies to explore the decades beyond the 1940s, Carr analyzes precisely the role played by the PCM in relation to both popular social movements and the official party. By looking at these dissidents, Carr touches upon the most important popular mobilization in postrevolutionary Mexico, tracing the various challenges to the PRI's rule and the evolution of Mexico's Left, an evolution that marked a broadening of the Left itself.

21. A major breakthrough in understanding the attack at Tlatelolco itself came with the thirtieth anniversary of the massacre, as the government conceded to the declassification of official documentation. These documents suggest that it was members of the president's elite guard, the Estado Mayor Presidencial, who—dressed as civilians and interspersed among the protesters—opened fire on the soldiers, thus prompting the army to shoot into the crowd. See Scherer García and Monsiváis, *Parte de guerra*; Montemayor, *Rehacer la historia*; Aguayo, *Los archivos de la violencia*; Doyle, *Tlatelolco Massacre*.

22. The effects of this event extended to all sectors of Mexican society and soon found expression in Mexico's historiography. Moreover, in the decades that followed, a plethora of works compiling testimonies of participants and leaders' memoirs appeared. For example, Ascencio, *1968*; Campos Lemus and Sánchez Mendoza, *68*; Cázes, ed., *Memorial del '68*, Taibo, *68*; Bellinghausen, ed., *Pensar el 68*, Guevara Niebla, *La democracia en la calle*; González de Alba, *Los días y los años*; Poniatowska, *La noche de Tlatelolco*. To these works, scholars in the United States have added an analysis of the cultural production and gender dynamics in the student mobilization, for example, Carey, *Plaza of Sacrifices*; Frazier and Cohen, "Defining the Space of Mexico's '68"; and Zolov, *Refried Elvis*.

23. Luis González de Alba, CNH (Comité Nacional de Huelga; National Strike Committee), quoted in Poniatowska, *Massacre in Mexico*, 55. There are some accounts that Epifania Zúñiga, Jaramillo's wife, was pregnant at the time of their murder. However, I was unable to locate any evidence to prove or disprove this assertion.

24. For a brief discussion on the historiography of the Mexican Revolution, see Joseph and Nugent, "Popular Culture and State Formation in Revolutionary Mexico." For a discussion surrounding the debates about whether the Mexican Revolution qualifies as a revolution, see Knight, "The Mexican Revolution."

25. See Córdova, *La política de masas del cardenismo*; and Ruiz, *The Great Rebellion*. See also Hamilton, *The Limits of State Autonomy*, who argues that Cárdenas attempted to harness popular power under presidential leadership to mitigate the exploitation inherent in a capitalist system.

26. Postrevisionist scholars can be roughly divided into two categories. The first include broad socioeconomic histories of the revolution, such as Hart, *Revolu-*

tionary Mexico; Knight, *The Mexican Revolution*; and Tutino, *From Insurrection to Revolution*. This tradition has also produced a great number of regional case studies too extensive to list here. The second category, works in the cultural tradition that pay particular attention to state consolidation, include Vaughan, *Cultural Politics in Revolution*; Becker, *Setting the Virgin On Fire*; and Joseph and Nugent, *Everyday Forms of State Formation*.

27. See Joseph and Nugent, *Everyday Forms of State Formation*.

28. Ibid., 13, emphasis in original.

29. Vaughan, "Cultural Approaches to Peasant Politics in the Mexican Revolution," 275 and 274.

30. Knight, "The Peculiarities of Mexican History," 104.

31. Joseph, Rubenstein, and Zolov, *Fragments of a Golden Age*; Zolov, *Refried Elvis*; and Rubenstein, *Bad Language, Naked Ladies, and Other Threats to the Nation*. Other historical works dealing with this period but not in the realm of popular culture include Carey, *Plaza of Sacrifice*; Niblo, *Mexico in the 1940s*; Servín, *Ruptura y oposición*; Carr, *Marxism and Communism in Twentieth-Century Mexico*; and Loyola Díaz, *Ocaso del radicalismo revolucionario*.

32. Joseph, Rubenstein, and Zolov, *Fragments of a Golden Age*, 15, emphasis in original.

33. Loyo Brambila's work on the teachers' movement, for example, attempts to provide a "political memory" by reconstructing the key historical juncture that produced the "most important outbreak of rebellion against a union bureaucracy's control over organized labor groups." *El movimiento magisterial de 1958 en México*, 10. Studies of the railway workers' movement proposed a similar task, especially given the rapid triumph and decline of the 1958–59 rail movement. Gill, in *Los ferrocarrileros*, for example, dedicates his work to "those fallen in the railway workers' movement" and ends with an exhortation to "reconstruct a strong and democratic workers' movement and to end *charrismo*," 324. Alonso, in *El movimiento ferrocarrilero en México*, likewise states that his work aims to help "surpass the momentary crisis suffered by both labor leadership and the working class." Unless otherwise noted, all translations are my own.

34. Grandin, *The Last Colonial Massacre*, 14.

35. This is not to say that the levels of official violence in Mexico equaled those of the Argentine, Chilean, and Central American dictatorships for whom state terror was standard practice. Rather, it is to point to the existence of such methods in a country long hailed for its political stability.

36. Viotti da Costa, "New Publics, New Politics, New Histories," 20.

37. Cited in "Un día en la tierra de Zapata," *La cultura en México, Suplemento de Siempre!* 11 July 1962, no. 21.

38. José García, interview by Emilio Plutarco García, 1980, Ahuatlán, Morelos.

39. Aguayo, *La charola*, 203–5.

40. Joseph, "On the Trail of Latin American Bandits," 24. Joseph describes the way revisionist critics of social banditry—objecting to its overreliance on "popular" sources such as ballads, memory, and local legends—actually contribute to elite historiography in their own uncritical use of police and state records; ibid., 18–16 and 24.

41. To provide but one example of the contradictory and partial nature of written sources, one newspaper article described Jaramillo as both an enemy of the people of Morelos and, a few paragraphs later, stated that it was impossible to capture him because the population hid and protected him at all cost. This same article goes on to describes the women who are part of the movement as "old, ugly, and unspeakably dirty." *El Universal*, 9 March 1954. In fact, some written sources are even more unreliable than campesino memory. For example, one newspaper article placed the number of armed Jaramillistas at five hundred, an evident exaggeration. See the collection *Los Movimientos en Mexico, 1917–1994*, vol. 2 (El Universal: El Gran Diario de Mexico, 1994).

42. Daniel James writes, "Influenced by trends in literary criticism that emphasize the importance of narrative and the construction of texts—and that have tended by extension to see historical reality as another text—oral historians are increasingly aware of the limits of oral testimony as a source for expanding our stock of historical facts about the recent past. The form of oral narrative is often taken now to be as significant as the content." *Doña María's Story*, 123. The present study takes a different approach and is modeled on earlier uses of oral history, such as Gould's *To Lead as Equals* and Winn's *Weavers of Revolution*.

43. Portelli, *The Death of Luigi Trastulli and Other Stories*, 50.

44. Renato Ravelo, interview by the author, 20 October 1999, Chilpancingo, Guerrero.

45. Ibid.

46. Plutarco Emilio García Jiménez, interview by the author, 21 November 1999, Jiutepec, Morelos.

47. Pedro García, interview by the author, 5 May 1999, Cuautla, Morelos.

48. Groups throughout Mexico continued to use the figure of Zapata to legitimate demands they saw as stemming from his struggle. As his image spread to different corners of the country, it emerged infused in local cultural variants. See Stephen, *¡Zapata Lives!*.

49. José Allende, interview by Victor Hugo Sánchez Reséndiz, 1992, Jantetelco, Morelos.

50. Reyna Ortiz, 19 January 1991, cited in Guadalupe García, *Mis mejores soldados*, 43.

51. O'Malley, *The Myth of Revolution*, 7.

52. While racial mixing has indeed been extensive since the conquest, official rhetoric portraying all Mexicans as a product of both the Spanish and indigenous

population masks the racism that has historically existed and that, with few exceptions, continues to divide society along ethnic lines, with lighter skin consistently corresponding to higher socioeconomic class.

53. For the indigenous population, land is not only a source of livelihood; a community's relationship to the earth is a constituting element of their cosmology. This connection is sustained and renovated through religious ritual and practices. While this cultural element may not be as present for nonindigenous campesinos, the centrality of land as a source of production and reproduction accounts for the intrinsic overlap between race and class in Mexico's rural uprisings. Indigenous participation in Zapata's Army of the South still remains under-explored. López Austin's *Los manifiestos en náhuatl de Emiliano Zapata* provides an initial glimpse into this world.

54. Pedro Herminio, interview by the author, 25 May 1999, Xoxocotla, Morelos.

55. Plutarco Emilio García Jiménez's personal collection (PEG-PC). Here too Jaramillo is expressing himself through familiar dichotomies which, dating back to the origins of Mexico as a nation, were framed in terms of the Spanish Conquest and their ensuing colonial rule.

56. Ibid., capitals in original.

57. Félix Serdán, interview by author, 5 February 1999, Tehuixtla, Morelos.

58. "Encuentro entre Jaramillistas y Zapatistas," 27 March 1994, Zacatepec, Morelos (transcript on file with author). In their initial declaration, the EZLN demanded that President Carlos Salinas de Gortari (1988–94) step down and a transition government be set up.

Chapter 1: The Ghost of Zapata

1. Don Longino Rojas Alonso, in García Jiménez, *Cuatro testimonios de veteranos zapatistas*, 37–38 and 52.

2. Ibid., 38.

3. O'Malley argues that "the mystification of the revolution was guided by the government, [and] perpetuated the bourgeois character of the regime by utilizing deeper cultural constructs, and co-opt[ing] the revolutionary potential of the popular classes to the point that the Revolution became a counterrevolutionary myth." *The Myth of the Revolution*, 7.

4. Knight, *The Mexican Revolution*, 2:372.

5. Lomnitz-Adler, *Exits from the Labyrinth*, 123.

6. Womack, *Zapata and the Mexican Revolution*, 328.

7. De la Peña, *A Legacy of Promises*, 18.

8. Martin, "Hacendados and Villages in Late Colonial Morelos," 419.

9. Ibid., 420, 417, 426, and 421.

10. Tutino, *From Insurrection to Revolution in Mexico*, 190–91.

11. Hart, *Bitter Harvest*, 4.

12. Warman, *"We Come to Object,"* 78 and 94.

13. Ibid., 79–80.

14. Hart, *Bitter Harvest*, 43.

15. Mallon, *Peasant and Nation*, 170–74.

16. Ibid., 175.

17. Hart, *Bitter Harvest*, 5.

18. Mallon, "Peasants and State Formation in Nineteenth-Century Mexico," 23.

19. "Oficio del Subprefecto de Morelos al Prefecto del Distrito," Morelos, October 17, 1850, fols. 24–25; XI/481.3/3119, Archivo Histórico de la Defensa Nacional, Secretaría de la Defensa Nacional, Mexico City, cited in Mallon, "Peasant and State Formation in Nineteenth-Century Mexico," 17.

20. Domingo Diez, *Bibliografía del estado de Morelos*, 1: cxxviii, cited in Warman, *"'We Come to Object,'"* 79.

21. Archivo Judicial del Tribunal Superiores, doc. 17, cited in Hart, *Bitter Harvest*, 136.

22. Hart, *Bitter Harvest*, 139–40.

23. De la Peña, *A Legacy of Promises*, 54.

24. Womack, *Zapata and the Mexican Revolution*, 44–45. Womack defines ranchos as "little rural settlements that were independent but not incorporated as villages" (45). Pueblos, as opposed to ranchos, usually have a longer, more formal history as settlements, have local governance, and practice specific religious festivals.

25. Jiménez Guzmán, *La industria cañero-azucarero en México*, 16.

26. Hart, *Bitter Harvest*, 135.

27. Womack, *Zapata and the Mexican Revolution*, 63–64.

28. Sotelo Inclán, *Raíz y razón de Zapata*, 182–88, cited in Womack, *Zapata and the Mexican Revolution*, 63.

29. Katz, "Labor Conditions on Haciendas in Porfirian Mexico," 1.

30. On wages, see ibid.; on food prices, see Mayer and Sherman, *The Course of Mexican History*, 461.

31. Katz, "Labor Conditions on Haciendas in Porfirian Mexico," 22–23; and Gonzales, *The Mexican Revolution*, 32.

32. Brunk, *¡Emiliano Zapata!* 42.

33. Cited in Womack, *Zapata and the Mexican Revolution*, 197–98.

34. Knight, "The Mexican Revolution," 9.

35. Womack, *Zapata and the Mexican Revolution*, 393–404. "Científicos" were Díaz's advisors. They were characterized by a positivist, Social Darwinist ideology and offered technocratic solutions to bring modernity to Mexico.

36. Warman, "The Political Project of Zapatismo," 327; and Espejel López, Olivera de Bonfil, and Rueda Smithers, *Emiliano Zapata*, 47.

37. Warman, "The Political Project of Zapatismo," 322 and 334.

38. Womack, *Zapata and the Mexican Revolution*, 165.

39. Rosa King, *Tempest over Mexico*, 93, cited in Womack, *Zapata and the Mexican Revolution*, 168.

40. Ibid., 168 and 170.

41. Knight, *The Mexican Revolution*, 1:304.

42. Manuel Palafox, Zapatista leader, September 8, 1914, cited in Womack, *Zapata and the Mexican Revolution*, 234, translation in original. Womack's work continues to stand as the classic study on the Zapatista movement, and the present account of their struggle is based largely on his interpretation. In the forty years since Womack's publication, other studies based on documents and interviews unavailable in the 1960s have emerged and greatly expanded our understanding of the Zapatistas. Most famous in the United States is Samuel Brunk's biography of Zapata, which presents the Zapatista movement as more divided and conflict-ridden than does Womack's work. Such conflict appears at the level of leadership, within and between communities, between the military and civilian population, and among the urban intellectuals who became Zapata's advisers. However, while Brunk complicates some of our understandings of Zapatismo, his conclusions do not fundamentally contradict Womack's findings. In fact, in some ways they complement them. More importantly for the purposes of the present study, Brunk's interpretation leaves unchanged one of the fundamental aspects of the Zapatistas —the significance of their legacy for future generations of campesinos. For a good account of the historiography on the Zapatistas, see Ávila Espinosa, "La historiografía del zapatismo después de John Womack."

43. Womack, *Zapata and the Mexican Revolution*, 225, 240.

44. Ibid., 254.

45. Knight, *The Mexican Revolution*, 2:364.

46. Womack, *Zapata and the Mexican Revolution*, 218.

47. Gilly, *Chiapas, la razón ardiente*, 30.

48. Werner Tobler, "Peasants and the Shaping of the Revolutionary State," 499.

49. Womack, *Zapata and the Mexican Revolution*, 374.

50. Manuel Palafox, Zapatista leader, 8 September 1914, cited in Womack, *Zapata and the Mexican Revolution*, 234.

51. For a good discussion of this process, see Warman, *"We Come to Object,"* chap. 5.

52. Díaz, *Bibliografía del estado de Morelos* (Mexico City: Secretaria de Ralciones Exteriores, 1933), 1:ccxxi, cited in Warman, *"We Come to Object,"* 136.

53. Warman, *"We Come to Object,"* 141, 144, and 148.

54. Redfield, *Tepoztlán*, 201, 195, 194.

55. Sánchez Reséndiz, *De rebeldes fe*, 224–28.

56. Redfield, *Tepoztlán*, 199. Seventeen years later, Oscar Lewis, another U.S. anthropologist, studied this same village. Lewis's findings contradicted many of

Redfield's, who had emphasized local harmony and positive memories of the Zapatista struggle. Lewis instead focused on internal rivalry, competition, and the memories of devastation produced by the years of revolutionary fighting. Their differing accounts can, in part, be explained by the context in which each academic conducted his research. Redfield lived in Tepoztlán in 1926, the decade in which the federal government carried out an extensive land reform in the state. Lewis, on the other hand, lived there in 1943 when not only had agrarian reform long been declared completed in Morelos but demographic pressures were making themselves felt. See Coy, "A Watershed in Mexican Rural History."

57. Stephen, ¡Zapata Lives! 165. While Votán Zapata is in part a creation of EZLN spokesperson Subcomandante Marcos, the image is steeped in Tzeltal religious tradition and has been adopted more broadly in the region. As Stephen states, "Votán Zapata, as projected first by Marcos and then by others around him, is a unifying figure with local meaning that cuts across ethnic groups and helps bind together thousands waging the Zapatista struggle"; ibid., 164.

58. Brunk, "Remembering Emiliano Zapata," 464, 465.

59. For this process of state consolidation—and resistance to it—see Joseph and Nugent, *Everyday Forms of State Formation*.

60. Gilly, *Chiapas*, 30.

61. Félix Garduño, Anenecuilco, cited in *Historia y Libertad*, November 1994.

62. Bartra, *Los herederos de Zapata*, 91.

63. Lino Manzanares Tapia, interview by the author, 12 October 1999, Los Hornos, Morelos.

64. It is unclear whether Jaramillo was born in Morelos or the State of Mexico. In his autobiography he states that while he and his siblings' births were registered in Zacualpan, they were actually born in Tlaquiltenango, Morelos. See Jaramillo and Manjarrez, *Autobiografía y la matanza en Xochicalco*, 14.

65. Ibid., 14, 15.

66. Ibid., 13.

67. Jaramillo and Manjarrez, *Autobiografía y la matanza en Xochicalco*, 7.

68. Ibid., 56–57, 15.

69. Hermelinda Serdán, interview by Guadalupe García Velazco, 11 November 1990, cited in *Mis mejores soldados*, 30.

70. Baldwin, *Protestants and the Mexican Revolution*, xi.

71. Bastian, *Protestantes, liberales y francomasones*, 8.

72. Ruiz Guerra, *Hombres nuevos*, 125, 126, 129. The Catholic clergy and peasant communities in several parts of Mexico rebelled against the revolutionary government's anticlerical legislation. Known as the Cristero Revolt (1926–29), under the battle cry "Long Live Christ the King," participants resisted the consolidation of the revolutionary state, burned school buildings, and fought against the government's agrarian reform.

73. Baldwin, *Protestants and the Mexican Revolution*, 5. The progressive effects of Protestantism have also been noted in other parts of Mexico. For example, George Collier found that Protestantism was one of the factors that created a setting ripe for the Zapatista rebellion in many Chiapas communities, as it was less hierarchical than Catholicism and promoted active participation in group discussions. Such practices, contends Collier, promoted a critical assessment of the reality faced by Chiapanecans. Collier, *Basta*, 55–60.

74. Ruiz Guerra, *Hombres nuevos*, 13.

75. Jaramillo and Manjarrez, *Autobiografía y la matanza en Xochicalco*, 30, 31.

76. Reyes, "Freemasonry and Folklore in Mexican Presidentialism," 61.

77. Félix Serdán, interview by the author, 5 February 1999, Tehuixtla, Morelos. Félix was also a member of this society, but because of the secret nature of their organization, he strictly limited the information he provided on the Masons.

78. AGN-R, LC, 544.4/16.

79. Boyer, *Becoming Campesinos*, 3.

80. Renato Ravelo, interview by the author, 10 October 1999, Chilpancingo, Guerrero.

81. Lomnitz-Adler, *Exits from the Labyrinth*, 75, 76.

82. In Jiutepec, this ten-year exemption was granted to a cement factory in 1944; in 1953 it was applied to a plant for processing limes. In 1953 this exemption was extended a match-making plant for fifteen years. See Arias and Bazan, CIVAC, 31.

83. Arias and Bazan, CIVAC, 21.

84. See ibid.

85. See Murphy, "Links with an Agrarian Past," chap. 8.

86. See for example, *Periódico Oficial del Estado de Morelos*, 19 May 1940, 16 February 1941, 18 January 1942, 22 February 1942, 16 June 1946, 8 December 1946.

87. *Pequeñas propiedades* is a term in agrarian law applied to private landholdings in order to distinguish them from ejidos, communal landholdings.

88. *Presente!* (Cuernavaca), 15 March 1959.

89. *El Sol de Morelos*, 20 September 1965.

90. De la Peña, *A Legacy of Promises*, 114.

91. Livenais, *Peuplement et évolution agraire au Morelos (Mexique)*, 67.

92. Otero, *Farewell to the Peasantry?* 1, 26.

93. Longino Rojas, Alonso, quoted in Gacía Jiménez, *Cuatro testimonios de veteranos zapatistas*, 53.

Chapter 2: Jaramillo, Cárdenas, and the Cooperative

1. The Mexican business consortium "Escorpión" at the time owned one of the largest Pepsi-Cola bottling franchises in the world. In Morelos, when relating the

story of its privatization, people distinguish little between the two, stating simply that the mill was sold to Pepsi.

2. Bellingeri, "Los campesinos de Morelos y el proyecto cardenista," 85.

3. Ibid., 89; *El Nacional*, 2 February 1938; BMLT-AE "Ingenio Azucarero Construcción" 013509; *Excélsior*, 11 March 1938; BMLT-AE "Ingenio Azucarero Cooperativas" 013513.

4. Pointing to the complexities of how Cardenista policies unfolded throughout Mexico, recent studies on Cardenismo seek to dispel both the utopianism and black myth surrounding Cárdenas's legacy. See, for example, Fallaw, *Cárdenas Compromised*, and Bantjes, *As If Jesus Walked on Earth*. For a historiographic discussion of Cardenismo, see Knight, "Cardenismo."

5. See Fallaw, *Cárdenas Compromised*.

6. Even in areas that did not see significant uprisings during the revolution, one of the most important factors in eliciting agrarian reform was local mobilization. See Craig, *The First Agraristas*.

7. Singelmann and Tapia Santamaría, "La empresa cooperativa como medio de dominación," 123.

8. Ibid., 127.

9. Quote from Hellman, 90. The ejido especially suffered in its attempt to compete with large-scale enterprises that could produce goods at lower prices. Moreover, ejidatarios depended on government institutions for credit and technical assistance, but to the extent that subsequent administrations became increasingly allied with private capital, government officials were less interested in supporting the ejido, since it acted as a source of competition to capitalist entrepreneurs. See Hellman, *Mexico in Crisis*, 90–91.

10. Córdova, *La política de masas del cardenismo*, 16, 38.

11. Cárdenas, *Apuntes*, 1:440, cited in ibid., 41.

12. Córdova, *La política de masas del cardenismo*, 178.

13. See Hamilton, *The Limits of State Autonomy*, quote on p. 213.

14. See Quesada Aldana and Tapia Santamaría, "Mecanismos de dominación en un ejido cañero."

15. Félix Serdán, interview by the author, 5 February 1999, Tehuixtla, Morelos.

16. Comisarios ejidales to gobernador de Morelos, 8 Septiembre 1935, AGN-LC, 545.3/268.

17. Junta celebrada en el despacho del Sr. Presidente, 8 January 1936, AGN-LC, 545.3/268.

18. Gorgonio Alonso, interview by Plutarco Emilio García Jiménez, 1 September 1980, Emiliano Zapata, Morelos.

19. Ravelo, *Los Jaramillistas*, 37.

20. Benigno Coronel Miranda, interview by the author, 5 September 2000, Zacatepec, Morelos.

21. *El Universal*, 6 February 1938; BMLT-AE "Ingenio Azucarero Zacatepec Construcción" 013509.

22. *Revista del Banco Obrero*, January–February 1938; BMLT-AE "Ingenio Azucarero Zacatepec Construcción" 013509.

23. *El Nacional*, 15 January 1939; BMLT-AE "Ingenio Azucarero Cooperativas" 013513.

24. *Periódico Oficia de Morelos*, 25 December 1938.

25. Womack, *Zapata and the Mexican Revolution*, 374.

26. Presidente de la República to Banco Nacional Agrario, 30 September 1938, AGN-LC, 545.3/268.

27. Comité Ejecutivo Local to presidente de la república, 30 August 1939, AGN-LC, 545.3/268.

28. Pedro Castillo, interview by the author, 6 September 2000, Zacatepec, Morelos.

29. Singelmann and Tapia Santamaría, "La empresa cooperativa como medio de dominación," 141.

30. Roberto Orihuela, interview by the author, 8 December 1999, Altapalmira, Morelos.

31. *La Prensa*, 16 January 1938; BMLT-AE "Ingenio Azucarero Cooperativas" 013513.

32. *Excélsior*, 14 January 1938; *Excélsior*, 16 January 1938; BMLT-AE "Ingenio Azucarero Cooperativas" 013513.

33. Pablo Ortiz, interview by Plutarco Emilio García Jiménez, 1980, El Higuerón, Morelos.

34. Singelmann and Tapia Santamaría, "La empresa cooperativa como medio de dominación," 136.

35. Ravelo, *Los Jaramillistas*, 37.

36. Pedro Herminio, interview by the author, 25 May 1999, Xoxocotla, Morelos.

37. Singelmann and Tapia Santamaría, "La empresa cooperativa como medio de dominación," 134.

38. Rubén Jaramillo to presidente de la república, 13 August 1941, Tlaquiltenango, Morelos, AGN/P, Manuel Ávila Camacho (hereafter cited as MAC), 705.2/41.

39. See, for example, Rubén Jaramillo to presidente de la república, 13 August 1941 and 3 January 1942, Tlaquiltenango, Morelos, AGN/P-MAC, 705.2/41 and 521.3/13.1.

40. Singelmann and Santamaría, "La empresa cooperativa como medio de dominación," 135.

41. Representantes de las Sociedades de Tlaquiltenango, Galeana, Xoxocotla, Santa Rosa 30, Zacatepec, Tetelpa, Panchimalco, Higuerón, Amador Salazar, and Ticumán to presidente de la república, 24 September 1941, Zacatepec, Morelos, AGN/P-MAC, 523.1/13–1.

42. "Bases Constitutivas de la Sociedad Cooperativa de Ejidatarios, Obreros y Empleados del Ingenio 'Emiliano Zapata,'" S.C. de P.E. de R.S. Zacatepec, Morelos, Registro 494-P, 6 December 1939, PEGJ-PC.

43. Singelmann and Tapia Santamría, "La empresa cooperativa como medio de dominación," 136.

44. Cited Fuentes, *A New Time for Mexico*, 50–51, translation in original.

45. Roberto Orihuela Ochoa, interview by the author, 8 December 1999, Altapalmira, Morelos.

46. Singelmann and Tapia Santamaría, "La empresa cooperativa como medio de dominación," 129–30, quote on 137.

47. La Sociedad de Ejidatarios to presidente de la república, Tlatenchi, Morelos, October 1944, AGN/P-MAC, 202.2/317.

48. Ravelo, *Los Jaramillistas*, 40 and 40n.

49. Singelmann and Santamaría, "La empresa cooperativa como medio de dominación," 132.

50. Pablo Ortiz, interview by Plutarco Emilio García Jiménez, 1980, El Higuerón, Morelos.

51. Delegados Joaquín Rodríguez Rivero and Enrique Alba Calderón to director, 7 September 1948, AGN, Dirección General de Investigaciones Políticas y Sociales (hereafter cited as DGIPS), caja 103, vol. 2, 1/131/1033.

52. Benigno Coronel Miranda, interview by the author, 5 September 2000, Zacatepec, Morelos.

53. Comité de Defensa Cañera to presidente de la república, 11 February 1959, AGN/P, Adolfo López Mateos (hereafter cited as ALM), 703.4/15 (18). A permanent army dispatch was stationed in Zacatepec after the creation of the Emiliano Zapata sugar refinery.

54. Cited in Fuentes, *A New Time for Mexico*, 50.

55. Comité Ejecutivo de la Sección 72 to presidente de la república, 21 January 1943, Zacatepec, Morelos, AGN, Dirección General de Gobierno (hereafter cited as DGG), vol. 31-A, exp. 19, no. 2/331.8(14)25026; Comité Ejecutivo Nacional del Sindicato de Trabajadores de la Industria Azucarea y Similares al Gobernador del Estado, 7 April 1942, PEGJ-PC; *Novedades*, 15 July 1948.

56. Comité Ejecutivo de la Sección 72 to presidente de la república, 21 January 1943, AGN/P-DGG vol. 31-A Exp. 19 No. 2/331.8(14)25026.

57. Comité de Defensa Cañera to Adolfo López Mateos, 11 February 1959, AGN/P-ALM, 703.4/15.

58. Singelmann and Tapia Santamaría, "La empresa cooperativa como medio de dominación," 147.

59. Pliego de peticiones que presentan todos los obreros y campesinos que tienen relaciones con el ingenio de Zacatepec al C. Gerente del Propio Centro Industrial, April 1942, Zacatepec, Morelos, AGN/P-MAC, 523.1/13–1.

60. *Zacatepec, 60 años de vida municipal*, 19.

61. Presidente del Comisariado Ejidal to presidente de la república, 14 March 1942, El Higuerón, Morelos, AGN/P-MAC, 523.1/13–2.

62. Hamilton, *The Limits of State Autonomy*, 274–79.

63. Medin, *El sexenio alemanista*, 32–33, quote on 36.

64. *Diario Oficial de Morelos*, 11 February 1942.

65. Félix Valle, Antonio Becerra y 52 firmas más to presidente de la república, Cuautla, Morelos, 19 November 1942, AGN/P-MAC, 404.1/280.

66. Comité Ejidal to presidente, 15 November 1942, AGN/P-MAC, 404.1/3082.

67. "Cultivo Plantas Industriales," AGN/P-DGG, vol. 100, exp. 44, no. 2/300 (29)/2003; *Diario Oficial de Morelos*, 23 September 1943.

68. Diputado José Ramírez to presidente de la república, 13 March 1942, AGN/P-MAC, 523.1/13; Jaramillo and Manjarrez, *Autobiografía y la matanza en Xochicalco*, 45.

69. Jaramillo and Manjarrez, *Autobiografía y la matanza en Xochicalco*, 46.

70. Abel Oliván, interview by Plutarco Emilio García Jiménez, 1 September 1980, El Higuerón, Morelos.

71. Pablo Ortiz, interview by Plutarco Emilio García Jiménez, 1980, El Higuerón, Morelos.

72. Mónico Rodríguez, interview by Aura Hernández, 16 July 1997, Chiconcuac, Morelos. *El Machete* was a newspaper of the Mexican Communist Party.

73. Mónico Rodríguez, interview by Ricardo Montejano, "Ay Memoria," part 8, April 1999, Radio Educación.

74. Ibid., part 8 and 9. A thorough study of the workers at Zacatepec in general, and the communist organizing efforts in particular, still remains to be written. Aside from Mónico Rodríguez's testimony, the information here is drawn heavily from the campesino perspective, as well as Hodges, *Mexican Anarchism after the Revolution*, and Ronfeldt, *Atencingo*.

75. Mónico Rodríguez, interview by Ricardo Montejano, "Ay Memoria."

76. Some recall that Jaramillo carried the Bible in his satchel, and there are even a few accounts stating that he would lead prayers at certain meetings. But many of those closest to him maintain that, despite his religious background, he did not mix his faith with politics. Given the extent to which Jaramillo identified as an agrarista, a position that in Mexico was formally quite secular, it is unlikely that he alluded much to religion. Moreover, there is no mention of religion in any of the government reports by the agents who spied on him.

77. An updated version was put out in 1952 during the third armed uprising.

78. Hodges, *Mexican Anarchism after the Revolution*, 47.

79. Porfirio Jaramillo's real name was Salustio Jaramillo. He changed it when he fled his hometown of Tlaquiltenango in 1933 after killing a local cacique. Hodges, *Mexican Anarchism after the Revolution*, 38.

80. Ronfeldt, *Atencingo*, 10, 16, 37–38, quote on p. 16.

81. Collective interview with ejidatarios in San Nicolás Tolentino, 12 August 1969, quoted in ibid., 44.

82. Mónico Rodríguez, interview by Ricardo Montejano, "Ay Memoria," part 9 and 10, April 1999, Radio Educación.

83. Letter to Cárdenas, 19 May 1939, Field Notes from the Department of Agrarian Affairs and Colonization (DAAC), 14–16, cited in Ronfeldt, *Atencinco*, 42, translation in original.

84. Ronfeldt, *Atencingo*, 101, 221.

85. Ibid., 67. For a detailed account of the conflict, see chap. 4.

86. Ibid., 130–31.

87. Aurora Herrera (widow of Porfirio Jaramillo), interview by the author, 10 December 1999, Jiutepec, Morelos.

88. Ronfeldt, *Atencingo*, 100.

89. "Bases Constitutivas de la Sociedad Cooperativa de Ejidatarios, Obreros y Empleados del Ingenio 'Emiliano Zapata.'"

90. *Novedades*, 10 April 1942 and 28 April 1942; *El Popular*, 28 April 1942; BMLT-AC "Ingenio Azucarero Huelgas" 013515.

91. Diputado José Ramírez to presidente de la república, 13 March 1942, AGN/P-MAC, 523.1/13; Jaramillo and Manjarrez, *Autobiografía y la matanza en Xochicalco*, 46.

92. *El Popular*, 28 April 1942, 16; BMLT-AC "Ingenio Azucarero Huelgas" 013515.

93. Félix Serdán, interview by the author, 5 February 1999, Tehuixtla, Morelos.

94. Pliego de peticiones que presentan todos los obreros y campesinos que tienen relaciones con el ingenio de Zacatepec al C. Gerente del Propio Centro Industrial, April 1942, AGN/P-MAC, 523.1/13–1. This was a common retaliatory practice by the administration. Alberta Galarza, the wife of Mónico Rodríguez, recalls how when she went to the Zacatepec clinic, about to give birth, the doctors there had orders not to give Rodríguez's family any type of medical attention. Alberta Galarza, interview by the author, 9 March 1999, Chinconcuac, Morelos.

95. *El Nacional*, 11 June 1942; BMLT-AC "Ingenio Azucarero Zacatepec Huelgas" 013515.

96. *Novedades*, 28 April 1942, 15; BMLT-AC "Ingenio Azucarero Zacatepec Huelgas" 013515.

97. Ravelo, *Los Jaramillistas*, 42.

98. Félix Serdán, interview by the author, 19 December 2000, Cuernavaca, Morelos.

99. Jaramillo and Manjarrez, *Autobiografía y la matanza en Xochicalco*, 48.

100. Félix Serdán, interview by the author, 5 February 1999, Tehuixtla, Morelos.

101. Pedro Castillo, interview by the author, 6 September 2000, Zacatepec, Morelos.

102. Representantes del sector obrero y empleados to president, 4 November 1948, AGN-DGIPS, caja 795, vol. 2, no. 1/47/413.

103. *Novedades*, 15 July 1948.

104. *Prensa*, 5 March 1949; AGN-DGIPS, caja 801, vol. 2, no. 1/49/486.

105. "Morelos," 16 November 1948, AGN-DGIPS, caja 795, vol. 2. no. 1/47/413.

106. *Excélsior*, 25 November 1948. Unlike the 1942 strike, there is far less documentation about the 1948 labor mobilization. Oral histories as well as newspaper reports provide only vague descriptions of events. The information presented here is gleaned from a few testimonies in Ravelo's compilation and from *Excélsior*, 16, 17, 19, and 25 November 1948.

107. Ravelo, *Los Jaramillistas*, 105–8.

108. Gomezjara, *La lucha por la tierra debe ser contra el capital*, 357; Ravelo, *Los Jaramillistas*, 111.

109. Ravelo, *Los Jaramillistas*, 111–12.

110. *Excélsior*, 19 November 1948; Ravelo, *Los Jaramillistas*, 112.

111. Comisariados ejidales to secretario de la presidencia de la república, 26 March 1953, AGN/P-ARC, 710.12, exp. 5.

112. Sociedades Cañeras del Ingenio "Emiliano Zapata" to presidente, 21 December 1958, AGN/P-ALM, 703.4/15.

113. Comisariados ejidales to secretario de la presidencia de la república, 26 March 1953, AGN-P, Adolfo Ruiz Cortines (hereafter cited as ARC), 710.12, exp. 5.

114. Memorandum, 13 March 1958, AGN/P-ARC, 710.12/5.

115. Jaramillo and Manjarrez, *Autobiografía y la matanza en Xochicalco*, 51.

Chapter 3: The Agrarista Tradition

1. Jaramillo and Manjarrez, *Autobiografía y la matanza en Xochicalco*, 16.

2. Knight, *The Mexican Revolution*, 2:372.

3. Scott, "Foreword," ix.

4. Purnell, *Popular Movements and State Formation in Revolutionary Mexico*, 110.

5. See, for example, Larín, *La rebelión de los cristeros*; Meyer, *La cristeada*; Butler, *Popular Piety and Political Identity in Mexico's Cristero Rebellion*; Purnell, *Popular Movements and State Formation in Revolutionary Mexico*.

6. Purnell, *Popular Movements and State Formation in Revolutionary Mexico*, 5; Bartra, *Los herederos de Zapata*, 39–40.

7. Aguilar and Zermeño, "Ensayo introductorio," 19–20.

8. Meyer, *El sinarquismo, el cardenismo y la iglesia (1937–1947)*, 9, 24, 162, 178–79.

9. Recent studies on religious movements in Mexico have noted not only the important role of Catholicism but the extent to which the particular understanding of religion determined people's involvement. Mathew Butler, for example, found

that support for Cristeros was stronger "where orthodox forms of Catholicism were inseparable from a sense of community identity." *Popular Piety and Political Identity in Mexico's Cristero Rebellion*, 217. Likewise, Pablo Serrano Álvarez situates the Sinarquista movement in the Bajío as part of a continuation of the Cristero movement and states that it expressed an "ultra-Catholic, nationalist, provincial, authoritarian, millenarian, anticommunist, anti-Yanqui and Hispanist" ideology. *La batalla del espíritu*, 16. Tapia Santamaría identifies a "diversified Catholicism" in the Bajío that mediated both expressions of domination and confrontation. For popular groups, concludes Tapia Santamaría, religion holds a multiplicity of cultural traditions, including a re-elaboration of the dominant culture. *Campo religioso y evolución política en el Bajío zamorano*, 237–38.

10. Newcomer, *Reconciling Modernity*, 12–14; Aguilar and Zermeño, "Ensayo introductorio," 28.

11. Ramírez Melgarejo, "La bola chiquita, un movimiento campesino," 176, 181.

12. Lino Manzanares Tapia, interview by the author, 12 October 1999, Los Hornos, Morelos.

13. 14 January 1943, AGN-DGIPS, vol. 94, exp 2. no. 1/131/806.

14. 4 October 1943, AGN-DGIPS, vol. 775, exp. 2, no. 1/43/238.

15. Ibid.

16. 1 March 1943, AGN-DGIPS, vol. 775, exp. 2. no. 1/43/238.

17. "Plan de Cerro Prieto," Point 6, CCJM, exp. 34/945/mesa penal, julio 1945.

18. Ibid., Point 1.

19. Bartra, *Los herederos de Zapata*, 73.

20. 25 November 1944, AGN-DGIPS, caja 783, exp. 2, no. 1/44/308.

21. Bartra, *Los herederos de Zapata*, 71.

22. 4 November 1943, AGN-DGIPS, caja 775, exp. 2, no 1/43/238.

23. 6 March 1944, AGN-DGIPS, caja 95, exp. 2, no. 1/131/810.

24. 24 April 1944, AGN-DGIPS, caja 95, exp. 2, no. 1/131/810.

25. 25 January 1943, AGN-DGIPS, caja 93, exp. 2, no. 1/131/784.

26. Jaramillo and Manjarrez, *Autobiografía y la matanza en Xochicalco*, 57–58.

27. Pedro García, interview by the author, 5 May 1999, Cuautla, Morelos.

28. José Rodríguez, interview by Salvador Núñez, 14 July 1979, Nepatlán, Puebla.

29. José Rodríguez, interview by Salvador Núñez, 16 July 1979, Nepatlán, Puebla.

30. Plan de Cerro Prieto, Point 19.

31. Ibid., Point 7.

32. Ibid.

33. Jaramillo and Manjarrez, *Autobiografía y la matanza en Xochicalco*, 24.

34. Plan de Cerro Prieto, Point 9.

35. Ibid., Point 17.

36. Ibid., Point 18.

37. Ibid., Point 11.

38. Ibid., Point 14.

39. José Rodríguez, interview by Salvador Núñez, 16 June 1979, Nepatlán, Puebla.

40. The Plan de Ayala, for example, established that two-thirds of the landlords' expropriated wealth be used as indemnification for victims of the war. Moreover, the Plan the Ayala actually embraced many aspects of nineteenth-century liberalism, unlike the positivists; however, it did so with a sense of social responsibility.

41. Plan de Cerro Prieto, Point 5.

42. Palacios, "Postrevolutionary Intellectuals, Rural Readings and the Shaping of the 'Peasant Problem' in Mexico," 325.

43. Raby, *Educación y revolución social en México*, 106–7.

44. Doña Socorro Meléndez, quoted in Vaughan, "The Implementation of National Policy in the Countryside: Socialist Education in Puebla in the Cárdenas Period" (paper presented to the 7th Conference of Mexican and U.S. Historians, Oaxaca, October 1985), 7, cited in Alan Knight, "Popular Culture and the Revolutionary State in Mexico, 1910–1940," 430.

45. Knight, "Popular Culture and the Revolutionary State in Mexico, 1910–1940," 430.

46. Raby, *Educación y revolución social en México*, 107.

47. José Faria, interview by Plutarco Emilio García Jiménez, 1981, Cuernavaca, Morelos.

48. See, for example, Schell, *Church and State Education in Revolutionary Mexico City*; Rockwell, "Schools of the Revolution"; and Vaughan, *Cultural Politics in Revolution*.

49. Raby, *Educación y revolución social en México*, 245.

50. Bartra, *Los Herederos de Zapata*, 76, 68.

51. Jaramillo and Manjarrez, *Autobiografía y la matanza en Xochicalco*, 51.

52. Cirilo García, interview by the author, 12 February 1999, Jojutla, Morelos.

53. The terms *compadre* and *comadre* denotes a bond of fictive kin established between the godparents and parents of a child.

54. Samuel Piedra, interview by the author and Victor Hugo Sánchez Reséndiz, 6 December 1999, El Higuerón, Morelos.

55. Pedro Herminio, interview by the author, 25 May 1999, Xoxocotla, Morelos.

56. Montemayor, *Chiapas, la rebelión indígena de México*, 72.

57. Lino Manzanares Tapia, interview by the author, 12 October 1999, Los Hornos, Morelos.

58. Crescencio Castillo interview by the author and José Ramón Corona, 18 September 1999, San Roque, Puebla.

59. CCJM, Ramo Penal, exp. 25/943.

60. Ravelo, *Los Jaramillistas*, 140.

61. CCJM, Ramo Penal, exp. 25/943. Of the remaining four, one was listed as deceased and there was no information for the other three.

62. Felix Serdán, interview by the author, 5 February 1999; and Jaramillo and Manjarrez, *Autobiografía y la matanza en Xochicalco*, 88–89.

63. Cirilo García, interview by the author, 12 February 1999, Jojutla, Morelos.

64. Crescencio Castillo interview by the author and José Ramón Corona, 18 September 1999, San Roque, Puebla.

65. *Constitución Política de los Estados Unidos Mexicanos*, 26.

66. Jaramillo and Manjarrez, *Autobiografía y la matanza en Xochicalco*, 96.

67. Ibid.

Chapter 4: "Like Juárez, with Our Offices on the Run"

1. Jaramillo and Manjarrez, *Autobiografía y la matanza en Xochicalco*, 106.

2. De Grammont, "La Unión General de Obreros y Campesinos," 229.

3. Bantjes, *As If Jesus Walked on Earth*, 212.

4. For a discussion on the effects of this policy on the countryside, see Sanderson, *The Transformation of Mexican Agriculture*; Barkin and Suárez, *El fin de la autosuficiencia alimentaria*; Adler Hellman, *Mexico in Crisis*, chap. 4; and Hewitt de Alcántara, *La modernización de la agricultura mexicana, 1940–1970*.

5. Sanderson, *Agrarian Populism and the Mexican State*, 144.

6. Sanderson, *The Transformation of Mexican Agriculture*, 44.

7. Adler Hellman, *Mexico in Crisis*, 95.

8. Warman, "*We Come to Object*," 194–95.

9. Cirilo García, interview by the author, 12 February 1999, Jojutla, Morelos.

10. Brunk, *¡Emiliano Zapata!* 9.

11. See Womack, *Zapata and the Mexican Revolution*, chap. 8. Illustrative of this process is the incident recounted by Womack where Zapata, mediating between village elders and the agronomist assigned to draw the boundary between Yautepec and Anenecuilco, instructed, "The pueblos say that this tecorral [stone wall] is their boundary and that's where you are going to trace me your marks. You engineers sometimes get stuck on straight lines, but the boundary is going to be the stone wall, even if you have to work six months measuring all its ins and outs." 227.

12. Brunk, *¡Emiliano Zapata!* 9.

13. Womack, *Zapata and the Mexican Revolution*, 228.

14. PAOM stationery, PEGJ-PC.

15. PAOM bond courtesy of Guadalupe García.

16. Bernabel Subdía Galindo, interview by the author, 12 October 1999, Los Hornos, Morelos.

17. Since PAOM members were known as Jaramillistas and also identified themselves as such, I use the term Jaramillistas interchangeably with PAOM members and supporters.

18. Gorgonio Alonso, interview by Plutarco Emilio García Jiménez, 1 September 1980, Emiliano Zapata, Morelos.

19. "Al Campesinado de Morelos," 25 September 1945, AGN-DGIPS, caja 788, exp. 2, no. 1/45/312.

20. Boyer, *Becoming Campesino*, 4.

21. AGN-DGIPS, caja 102, no. 2–1/131/1028.

22. "Programa Mínimo de Acción Política y de Gobierno," 10 November 1945. PEGJ-PC.

23. Partido Agrario-Obrero Morelense, "Declaración de Principios," n.d. PEGJ-PC.

24. "Programa Mínimo de Acción Política y de Gobierno."

25. In this way it differed from their proposed reforms for the countryside, which emphasized campesino ownership and administration of the land and the tools to work it. It also differed from the vision put forth in the Plan de Cerro Prieto.

26. Partido Agrario-Obrero Morelense, "Declaración de Principios."

27. This demand reflected the frustrations of campesinos as they faced the time-consuming and costly bureaucracy, including that of the Department of Agriculture.

28. "Programa Mínimo de Acción Política y de Gobierno."

29. Ibid.

30. Ibid.

31. Ibid.

32. Ibid.

33. Ibid.

34. Ravelo, *Los Jaramillistas*, 83. This campesino is also expressing the general dissatisfaction at president Ávila Camacho's 1942 decree that forced campesinos in the Zacatepec zone to farm sugarcane.

35. José Urbán to Jefe del Departamento de Gobierno, 23 March 1946, AGN-DGG, vol. 265, exp. 2/311.G(14)2.

36. Ibid.

37. *Periódico Oficial de Morelos*, 7 April 1946.

38. Comité Municipal y Representantes Generales to presidente de la república, 21 April 1946, AGN-DGG, vol. 265, exp. 2/311.G(14)2.

39. Representantes Generales to presidente de la república, 21 April 1946, AGN-DGG, vol. 265, exp. 2/311.G(14)2.

40. José Rodríguez and four other signatures to presidente de la república, 26 April 1946, AGN-DGG, vol. 265, exp. 2/311.G(14)2.

41. To the ministro de la Suprema Corte de Justicia de la Nación, 2 August 1946, AGN-DGG, Vo1.100, exp. 2/311P(14)1.

42. "Memorandum," 22 April 1946, AGN-DGG, vol. 265, exp. 2/311.G(14)2.

43. Rubén Jaramillo to presidente de la república, 29 April 1946, AGN-DGG, vol. 264, exp. 2/311.G(14)2.

44. President of Executive Committee to secretario de gobernación, 6 May 1946, AGN-DGG, vol. 264, exp. 2/311.G(14)2.

45. José Urbán Casas to procurador general de la justicia, 7 May 1946, AGN-DGG vol. 264, exp. 2/311.G(14)2, tomo 3.

46. Ravelo, *Los Jaramillistas*, 84, 86.

47. Garrido, *El partido de la revolución institucionalizada*, 294.

48. Vaughan, "Transnational Processes and the Rise and Fall of the Mexican Cultural State," 474.

49. Ravelo, *Los Jaramillistas*, 84.

50. In the 1988 elections, Cuauhtémoc Cárdenas (son of Lázaro Cárdenas) split from the PRI and formed a political party which would later become the Democratic Revolutionary Party (Partido de la Revolución Democrática or PRD). His candidacy achieved an unprecedented level of popular support. Amidst numerous accounts of fraud, the government declared their candidate Carlos Salinas de Gortari the winner. But in Mexico, popular memory holds that Cárdenas received the majority of the votes. While a PRI-PAN congressional decree ordered the 1988 ballots burned in 1991, the extent of official fraud in 1988 continues to be revealed. See, for example, "Elecciones sin huella: El 88 crimen electoral impute," *Proceso*, 6 July 2003. See also de la Madrid Hurtado, *Cambio de Rumbo*; Castañeda, *La herencia*; and Barberán, Cárdenas, López Monjardín, and Zavala, *Radiografía de un fraude*. The vast number of irregularities against the left-leaning candidate Andrés Manuel López Obrador in the 2006 presidential elections have made the 1988 fraud all the more present in people's minds.

51. Langston, "Three Exits from the Mexican Institutional Revolutionary Party," 18.

52. Pellicer de Brody and Reyna, *El afianzamiento de la estabilidad política (1952–1960)*, 53.

53. Reyna, "Las elecciones en el México institucionalizado, 1946–1976," 106.

54. Servín, *Ruptura y oposición*, 135.

55. Estrada Correa, *Henriquismo*; and Muñoz Cota, *Aquí está Miguel Henríquez Guzmán*.

56. Carr, *Marxism and Communism in Twentieth-Century Mexico*, 190.

57. 11 May 1952, AGN-DGIPS, caja 27, no. 2–1/061.8/15, tomo 9.

58. José Rodríguez, interview by Salvador Núñez, 16 June 1979, Nepatlán, Puebla.

59. Gomezjara, *El movimiento campesino en México*, 173.

60. PAOM, "El Pueblo de Morelos Frente a la Sucesión Presidencial," 5 February 1951, "Rubén Jaramillo" Museum, Tlaquiltenango, Morelos.

61. PAOM to comisariados ejidales, 10 July 1951. EPGJ-PC.

62. Ravelo, *Los Jaramillistas*, 125–26.

63. Jaramillo and Manjarrez, *Autobiografía y la matanza en Xochicalco*, 110.

64. Ravelo, *Los Jaramillistas*, 139.

65. Cited in Jaramillo and Manjarrez, *Autobiografía y la matanza en Xochicalco*, 101.

66. "El Pueblo de Morelos Frente a la Sucesión Presidencial."

67. Pedro García, interview by the author, 5 May 1999, Cuautla, Morelos.

68. January 1950, AGN-DGIPS, caja 807, Campaña Presidencial, enero 1951.

69. "A Participar en la Campaña Electoral: Hablan las Mujeres que militan en el Partido Agrario Obrero Morelense," 10 February 1951, PEGJ-PC.

70. *El Universal*, 13 May 1952.

71. *Séptimo Censo General de Población*, 6 June 1950.

72. Roxborough, "Mexico," 214.

73. Medina, *Civilismo y modernización del autoritarismo 1940–1952*, 93–94.

74. *El Universal*, 8 August 1951. The article itself is a letter from Jorge Prieto Laurens, president of the Mexican Popular Anticommunist Front, questioning the FPPM's moral right to challenge the ruling party, since the Henriquista leadership was made up of disaffected PRI members. The letter ends by reproaching Henríquez Guzmán's words of praise for Lombardo Toledano, whom the writer condemns for his communism and links to Stalin. What is significant here is the newspaper's choice of a headline that first and foremost implicated Henríquez Guzmán as a communist. For an account of the way the national press fomented the Red scare, see Servín, "Proganda y Guerra Fría," 9–39.

75. N.d., AGN-DGIPS, caja 27, exp. 2–1/061.8/15.

76. 14 May 1952, AGN-DGIPS, caja 27, exp. 2–1/061.8/15, tomo 9.

77. *El Universal*, 13 May 1952.

78. 12 May 1952, AGN-DGIPS, caja 27, exp. 2–1/061.8/15, tomo 9.

79. Ibid.

80. 13 February 1951, AGN-DGIPS, caja 807, Campaña Presidencial, February 1951. A document put forth by this federation described the miserable situation in the countryside and criticized government policy that forced thousands of campesinos into the bracero ranks. It also condemned the state for jailing campesinos whose only crime was "wanting to own their own land." Finally, it blamed the CNC for creating a division in the countryside by maintaining "false apolitical pretenses which only denied the rural population their civic rights." *El Universal*, 31 May 1951.

81. *La Prensa*, 12 May 1952.

82. José Rodríguez to presidente municipal, 10 April 1952, AGN-DGG, vol. 100, exp. 2/311P.(14)2; and *Excélsior*, 12 May 1952.

83. José Rodríguez, interview by Salvador Núñez, 14 July 1979. During the French invasion, Benito Juárez fled Mexico City but did not resign as president. With the French army pursuing him, he escaped with his cabinet first to San Luis Potosí, then to Chihuahua and later to El Paso del Norte (today Ciudad Juárez).

84. Informe Confidencial sobre las actividades Henriquistas en el Estado de Morelos, n.d., PEGJ-PC.

85. Servín, *Ruptura y oposición*, 288, 293, and 315.

86. Alicia Pérez Salazar, interview by the author, 3 August 2000, Mexico City.

87. Pedro Herminio, interview by the author, 25 May 1999, Xoxocotla, Morelos.

88. Pedro García, interview by the author, 5 May 1999, Cuautla, Morelos, and *La Prensa*, 31 July 1952.

89. Ravelo, *Los Jaramillistas*, 121–33.

90. Servín, *Ruptura y oposición*, 321, 334.

91. Cirilo García, interview by Plutarco Emilio García Jiménez, 29 July 1981, Acapulco, Guerrero.

92. Samuel Piedra, interview by the author and Víctor Hugo Sánchez Reséndiz, 6 December 1999, El Higuerón, Morelos.

93. Pablo Ortiz, interview by Plutarco Emilio García Jiménez, 1980, El Higuerón, Morelos.

94. Langston, "Thee Exits from the Mexican Institutional Revolutionary Party," 23.

95. *La Prensa*, 8 July 1952.

96. *Excélsior*, 8 July 1952; and *El Nacional*, 8 July 1952.

97. National Archives and Records Service, RG 59, 712.00/7–2952, 29 July 1952, cited in Servín, 350n45.

98. Langston, "Thee Exits from the Mexican Institutional Revolutionary Party," 23.

99. "Sobre el Henriquismo: El populismo de derecha y la historia escamoteada," *La cultura en México/Suplemento de Siempre*, 557, 11 October 1972, 3–8.

100. Ravelo, *Los Jaramillistas*, 127, 188.

101. Eliut Hernández, interview by the author, 15 December 1999, Tlaquiltenango, Morelos.

102. Pedro García, interview by the author, 5 May 1999, Cuautla, Morelos.

103. Cirilo García, interview by Plutarco Emilio García Jiménez, 6 June 1981, Acapulco, Guerrero.

104. PAOM, "Libro Segundo de Registro," "Rubén Jaramillo" Museum. Compiled seven years after their last participation in the elections, this registry was an attempt to formalize the membership of what the Jaramillistas would call a party of "permanent struggle." The number of Jaramillista supporters was far greater. In

1959, for example, when Jaramillo solicited the land of Michapa and Guarín, he did so at the head of six thousand campesinos.

105. Jaramillo and Manjarrez, *Autobiografía y la matanza en Xochicalco*, 108.

106. Samuel Piedra, interview by the author and Víctor Hugo Sánchez Reséndiz, 6 December 1999, El Higuerón, Morelos.

107. Langston, "Thee Exits from the Mexican Institutional Revolutionary Party," 24.

108. Pellicer de Brody and Reyna, *El afianzamiento de la estabilidad política*, 59–60.

Chapter 5: "They Made Him into a Rebel"

1. José Aguero, interview by Plutarco Emilio García Jiménez, 1980, Cuernavaca, Morelos.

2. Ibid. and Jaramillo and Manjarrez, *Autobiografía y la matanza en Xochicalco*, 110.

3. Jaramillo and Manjarrez, *Autobiografía y la matanza en Xochicalco*, 110. See also José Hernández to Ernesto Escobar Muñoz, 28 August 1946, PEGJ-PC; José Hernández Rodríguez to Juez Mixto de Primera Instancia, 28 August 1946, PEGJ-PC; "El Informador" 29 Agosto 1946, PEGJ-PC; and "La Hora" 1 September 1946. These sources also recount the incident, although they report only two dead and one wounded. It is unclear from the sources, but perhaps the injured person later died from his wounds.

4. CCJM, exp. 34/945/mesa penal Julio 1945.

5. *Siempre!* 2 July 1953, 8–9.

6. Ibid., 246; oficial mayor to secretario de gobernación, 5 August 1949, AGN-DGG, vol. 109, exp. 2/300(29)2530, doc. 31; Torres Ramírez, *Hacia la utopía industrial*, 261–66.

7. 16 September 1947, AGN-DGIPS, caja 84, exp. 2–1/131/655, tomo 3.

8. Agustín Leyva, interview by the author, 25 May 1999, Coatetelco, Morelos.

9. Cited in Torres, *Hacia la utopía industrial*, 267.

10. Meyer, *El sinarquismo, el cardenismo y la iglesia*, 231.

11. The most detailed accounts of this conspiracy come from Pedro García, interview by the author, 5 May 1999, Cuautla, Morelos; and José Rodríguez, interview by Salvador Núñez, 14 July 1979, Nepatlán, Puebla.

12. Jaramillo and Manjarrez, *Autobiografía y la matanza en Xochicalco*, 113. Overall, the rifle sanitario elicited so much discontent that the government was forced to take alternative measures within a couple of years. It gradually decreased the number of cattle it killed and instead applied a policy of quarantine and vaccination. During his last state of the union address in 1952, Alemán declared victory over the disease, thus celebrating the end of the embargo by the United States of certain Mexican products.

13. Reyes Aranda, interview by Plutarco Emilio García Jiménez, 1978, Jojutla, Morelos.

14. Ravelo, *Los Jaramillistas*, 81.

15. "Partido Agrario Obrero Morelense: De Lucha y Acción Permanente," 1 September 1953, AGN/P-ARC, 606.3/3–16.

16. Rodolfo López de Nava to presidente de la república, 4 October 1953, AGN/P-ARC, 606.3/3–16.

17. "Ultimátum dirigido al Gral. Rodolfo López de Nava," 24 September 1953, AGN/P-ARC, 606.3/3–16.

18. Rodolfo López de Nava to presidente de la república, 4 October 1953, AGN/P-ARC, 606.3/3–16.

19. Ravelo, *Los Jaramillistas*, 132.

20. Ibid., 130.

21. AGN-DGIPS, caja 102, 2–1/131/1028.

22. Terán, "El levantamiento de los campesinos gasquistas," 127.

23. Ravelo, *Los Jaramillistas*, 132.

24. Terán, "El levantamiento de los campesinos gasquistas," 136.

25. José Rodríguez, interview by Salvador Núñez, 14 July 1979, Nepatlán, Puebla.

26. Unidad Investigaciones Campesinos, "Los movimientos guerrilleros rurales en el México contemporaneo," 18.

27. Hermilo Montes y demás firmantes to presidente de la república, 11 April 1954, AGN/P-ARC, 606.3/3–16.

28. Pedro Almanza y demás firmantes to Adolfo Ruíz Cortines, 29 August 1956, AGN/P-ARC, 606.3/3–16.

29. Ricarda Juárez, interview by the author, 1 May 1999, Ahuatepec, Morelos.

30. Ravelo, *Los Jaramillistas*, 134.

31. Félix Serdán, interview by the author, 1 August 2000, Tehuixtla, Morelos.

32. C. E. Fisher, ed., "The World Over," 8 March 1954, AGN/P-ARC, 606.3/3–16.

33. Hodges, *Mexican Anarchism after the Revolution*, 61.

34. Foreign Service Despatch, U.S. National Archives at College Park, 712.00/5–2962, Despatch 1482.

35. *Polígrafo*, 21 September 1954, in AGN/P-ARC, 606.3/3–16.

36. Ibid.

37. Elisa Servín, "Proganda y Guerra Fría," 24.

38. *El Universal*, 9 March 1954.

39. *El Universal*, 9 and 11 March 1954.

40. *El Universal*, 14 March 1954.

41. *El Universal*, 9 March 1954.

42. *El Excélsior*, 10 March 1954.

43. *El Universal*, 9 March 1954.

44. *Excélsior*, 9 and 12 March 1954. These newspaper reports do not actually use the term "guerrilla" but describe precisely this strategy by noting that the Jaramillistas attacked targets such as local and state police forces and then dispersed quickly into the sierra, rather than taking the army on in direct battle.

45. Womack, *Zapata and the Mexican Revolution*, 100–101.

46. *Excélsior*, 9 March 1954.

47. *Excélsior*, 13 March 1954.

48. *El Sol de Morelos*, 16 February 1950.

49. Batalla, *Donde quiera que me paro soy yo*, 79.

50. Sindicato Nacional Azucarero to Miguel Alemán, 15 June 1942, AGN-DGIPS, caja 62, exp. 82, no. 2/331.9(14)25026; 6 March 1946, AGN-DGIPS, caja 96, exp. 2, no. 1/131/841; Pedro García, interview by the author, 5 May 1999, Cuautla, Morelos.

51. *El Sol de Morelos*, 6 April 1950.

52. Pedro García, interview by the author, 5 May 1999, Cuautla, Morelos.

53. *El Sol de Morelos*, 12 April 1950.

54. Ravelo, *Los Jaramillistas*, 142.

55. Crescencio Castillo, interview by the author and José Ramón Corona, 1 September 1999, San Roque, Puebla. Campesinos in Mexico refer to soldiers as "gobierno"—government. The judicial police, or *judiciales*, are a federal police force. Castillo's interchangeable use of soldiers, government, and judicial police reveals how campesinos witnessed little difference between various elements of the state enforcement agencies.

56. Cirilo García, interview by the author, 12 February 1999, Jojutla, Morelos.

57. Ibid.

58. José Rodríguez, interview by Salvador Núñez, 14 July 1979, Nepatlán, Puebla.

59. "Plan de Cerro Prieto," courtesy of Plutarco Emilio García Jiménez. An English translation appears in Hodges, *Mexican Anarchism after the Revolution*, 68–72. Hodges explains that the year was missing from the Plan de Cerro Prieto given to him by Renato Ravelo. But, through an analysis of some of the plan's points, Hodges places the year at 1952 (pp. 72–73). He explains that the document had to have been drafted before President Ruiz Cortines took office: "The reference in Point 11 of the Plan to 'revolutionary chiefs . . . trying to make a new revolution, but whose program, if they have any, we ignore' is clearly to the leaders grouped around General Henríquez, who were preparing for an armed uprising" (p. 73). The year of the Plan de Cerro Prieto in García's collection is also missing. However, this same version is published in *Cuadernos Agrarios* 5, no. 10/11 (1980), and the year given there is 1957. Given that Henriquistas such as Celestino Gasca continued to talk of an armed uprising even after Ruiz Cortines assumed the presidency, the 1957 date cannot be discarded completely, but most likely Hodges is correct in arguing

for the 1952 date, since the general fervor and prospects of an armed uprising were higher in the months after the elections. Also, it makes sense that the Jaramillistas would write this version of the plan immediately after they took up arms, rather than waiting five years.

60. Plan de Cerro Prieto, PEGJ-PC.

61. Ibid., Point 14.

62. Ibid., Point 9.

63. Ibid., Point 6.

64. Ibid., Point 5.

65. Ibid., Points 4 and 9.

66. Hodges, *Mexican Anarchism after the Revolution*, 55.

67. Plan de Cerro Prieto, Point 14, PEGJ-PC.

68. Armando Bartra writes, "From the political point of view, the [Magonist] position represents the conception of a truly revolutionary process for the masses, since it put forth the notion that the masses, the people in arms, had the power and democratically carried out the social transformation." *Regeneración*, 30.

69. Plan de Cerro Prieto, Point 2 (capitals in original).

70. The word *acarreado* literally meaning "to be carried" or "taken," is used to describe those who are recruited by local officials to attend rallies in support of official candidates. The people taken to these rallies are offered free transportation to and from the site, a meal, drinks, and PRI paraphernalia. If people are inclined not to attend they are often threatened with a cut in material subsidies or the loss of their job, since official unions are often in charge of much of the logistics.

71. "Manifiesto: A la Opinión Pública de la República," November 1956. Document given to the author by Jesús Flores, a Jaramillista from Mitepec, Puebla.

72. Rodolfo Lopez de Nava to Adolfo Ruiz Cortines, 18 November 1953, AGN/ P-ARC, 606.3/3–16.

73. Anonymous interview in Carlos Fuentes, "Dicen que Rubén Jaramillo . . . ," *Punto Crítico* 1, no. 6 (June 1972): 42.

Chapter 6: Gender, Community, and Struggle

1. Hermelinda Serdán, interview by Guadalupe García Velazco, 20 November 1990, quoted in *Mis mejores soldados*, 60–61.

2. Raquel Jaramillo, interview by the author, 3 September 1999, Colonia Rubén Jaramillo, Morelos.

3. José Allende, interview by the author, 18 May 1999, Jantetelco, Morelos; Crescencio Castillo, interview by the author and José Ramón Corona, 18 September 1999, San Roque, Puebla; and Mónico Rodríguez, interview by Ricardo Montejano, *La Jornada*, 23 May 1999.

4. García, *Mis mejores soldados*, 62.

5. The Zapatista movement in Chiapas is really one of the first rural-based struggles in Mexico to underscore, tactically and programmatically, the importance of women's participation in social movements, as well as the various layers of exploitation to which they are subjected.

6. McGee Deutsch, "Gender and Sociopolitical Change in Twentieth-Century Latin America," 267–68.

7. Olcott, *Revolutionary Women in Postrevolutionary Mexico*, 91–92.

8. Antonio Luna Arroyo, *La mujer mexicana en la lucha social* (Mexico City: PNR, 1936), 19, cited in ibid., 20.

9. Vaughan, "Rural Women's Literacy and Education during the Mexican Revolution," 118.

10. Ibid., 113–14; Vaughan, "Modernizing Patriarchy," 202.

11. Vaughan, "Rural Women's Literacy and Education during the Mexican Revolution," 117.

12. *Orientaciones para las Ligas Femeniles de Lucha Social en los ejidos* (Mexico City: n.p., 1938), cited in Olcott, *Revolutionary Women in Postrevolutionary Mexico*, 140, Olcott's translation.

13. See Olcott, *Revolutionary Women in Postrevolutionary Mexico.*

14. Pablos Tuñón's *Mujeres que se organizan* is one of the few exceptions.

15. Ibid., 162–63.

16. Warman, *"We Come to Object,"* 253 and 278.

17. Arizpe and Botey, "Mexican Agricultural Development Policy and Its Impact on Rural Women," 75.

18. Arturo Warman, *"We Come to Object,"* 281.

19. Ibid., 253.

20. McGee Deutsch, "Gender and Sociopolitical Change in Twentieth-Century Latin America," 304.

21. Ibid., 305.

22. Maxine Molyneux develops these categories in "Mobilization without Emancipation?"

23. Ibid., 240.

24. Ibid.

25. Ibid., 240, 241.

26. Plan de Cerro Prieto, CCJM, Point 17. Of the plan's one hundred signatures, only two are women's names. Two more are ambiguous (the name Guadalupe could be either male or female), and two others signatories supplied only their first initial.

27. Bartra, *Regeneración*, 235.

28. Ibid., 236–37.

29. Plan de Cerro Prieto, CCJM, Point 11.

30. Ibid., Point 18.

31. Ravelo, *Los Jaramillistas*, 131.

32. Pedro García, interview by the author, 5 May 1999, Cuautla, Morelos.

33. Apolinar Ramírez to gobernador constitucional del Estado de Morelos, 13 August 1946, courtesy of Plutarco Emilio García Jiménez.

34. Kaplan, "Female Consciousness and Collective Action," 566.

35. Margarita García, interview by the author and José Ramón Corona, 18 September 1999, San Roque, Puebla.

36. Batalla, *Donde quiera que me paro, soy yo*, 79–80.

37. Paula Batalla, interview by Plutarco Emilio García Jiménez, 12 May 1981, Atlacomulco, Morelos.

38. This form of female participation in strikes is common and has been noted in works such as Weber, *Dark Sweat, White Gold*; and Ruiz, *Cannery Women, Cannery Lives*.

39. Ravelo, *Los Jaramillistas*, 108–9.

40. Ibid., 109.

41. *Excélsior*, 25 November 1948.

42. Alberta Galarza, interview by the author, 9 March 1999, Chinconcoac, Morelos.

43. Batalla, *Donde quiera que me paro, soy yo*, 91.

44. "A Participar en la Campaña electoral: Hablan las mujeres que militan en el Partido Agrario Obrero Morelense," 10 February 1951, PEGJ-PC.

45. Ibid.

46. Boyer, *Becoming Campesinos*, 235–36.

47. "A Participar en la Campaña electoral: Hablan las mujeres que militan en el Partido Agrario Obrero Morelense," 10 February 1951, PEGJ-PC.

48. Ibid.

49. Ibid.

50. José Rodríguez, interview by Salvador Núñez, 14 July 1979, Nepatlán, Puebla.

51. Point 10, "PAOM, Declaración de Principios," n.d., PEGJ-PC.

52. Batalla, *Donde quiera que me paro, soy yo*, 83.

53. Natividad Guzmán, interview by Guadalupe García, 30 August 1994, Alpuyeca, Morelos.

54. *El Universal*, 14 May 1952.

55. "Estado de Morelos," 26 April 1961, AGN-DGIPS, caja 1980 2–1/G1/17.

56. "Acción Popular Morelense," 15 May 1953, Cuernavaca, Morelos, courtesy of Guadalupe García.

57. Ibid.

58. "Al Pueblo de Morelos," courtesy of Plutarco Emilio García Jiménez.

59. Kaplan, "Community and Resistance in Women's Political Cultures," 259.

60. Interview by Guadalupe García, 4 December 1990, El Higuerón, Morelos, quoted in Guadalupe García, *Mis mejores soldados*, 26.

61. Margarita Hernández, interview by the author, 21 July 2007, Temixco, Morelos.

62. Ricarda Juárez, interview by the author, 17 May 1999, Ahuatepec, Morelos.

63. Natividad Guzmán, interview by Guadalupe García, 30 August 1994, Alpuyeca, Morelos.

64. Ravelo, *Los Jaramillistas*, 30.

65. Paula Batalla, interview by Guadalupe García, 19 October 1990, cited in *Mis mejores soldados*, 59.

66. Jaramillo and Manjarrez, *Autobiografía y la matanza en Xochicalco*, 118.

67. Ravelo, *Los Jaramillistas*, 149.

68. Soto, *Emergence of the Modern Mexican Woman*, 43.

69. Jaramillo and Manjarrez, *Autobiografía y la matanza en Xochicalco*, 118 (as stated earlier, Jaramillo wrote his autobiography in the third person).

70. Batalla, *Donde quiera que me paro, soy yo*, 121.

71. See Olcott, *Revolutionary Women in Postrevolutionary Mexico*.

72. García, *Mis mejores soldados*, 62.

Chapter 7: Judas's Embrace

1. Anastasia L. Vda. Anzures to President Adolfo Ruiz Cortines, 3 February 1958; "Manifiesto al Estado de Morelos y a la Nación," 6 February 1958; Pedro Ortiz et al. to President Adolfo Ruiz Cortines, 8 February 1958; El Pueblo de Morelos to Angel Carabajal [*sic*], 24 February 1958, all located in AGN-DGG, vol. 265, 2/311G(14) 5, tomo 3.

2. Anastasia L. Vda. Anzures to President Adolfo Ruiz Cortines.

3. Ravelo, *Los Jaramillistas*, 168; Rubén Jaramillo to director del DAAC, 29 September 1959, Nuevo Centro de Población "Otilio Montaño," AGA, 22/5568.

4. Nuevo Centro de Población "Otilio Montaño," AGA, 22/5568.

5. Rubén Jaramillo to presidente de la República, 27 January 1959, AGN/P-ALM, 111/348.

6. Salvador González Lazcona to Rubén Jaramillo, 31 March 1960, AGA, Dotación de Ejidos, Apatzingo de Michapa, Morelos, 23/3130.

7. Nuevo Centro de Población "Otilio Montano," 10 Agosto 1960, AGA, 22/5568.

8. Comité Particular Ejecutivo del Nuevo Centro de Población Agraria Profesor y General Otilio Montano to Presidente Adolfo López Mateos, 10 September 1960, AGN/P-ALM, 111/348.

9. José Rodríguez, interview by Salvador Núñez, 14 July 1979, Nepatlán, Puebla.

10. Cited in Womack, *Zapata and the Mexican Revolution*, 240–41.

11. Ibid., 235.

12. José Rodríguez, interview by Salvador Núñez, 14 July 1979, Nepatlán, Puebla.

13. Federico Tafoya ingeniero postulante to jefe del DAAC, 3 October 1960, AGA, 22/5586.

14. Rubén Jaramillo to jefe del DAAC, 3 August 1960, AGA, 22/5568.

15. Ravelo, *Los Jaramillistas*, 170.

16. Comité Ejecutivo del Nuevo Centro de Población Otilio Montaña to presidente de la República, 20 November 1961, AGA, 22/5568; Ravelo, *Los Jaramillistas*, 180.

17. 21 February 1961, AGN/P-ALM; Salvador Lazcona to director general de asuntos jurídicos, 24 February 1961, AGA, 22/5568, Nuevos Centros de Población Otilio Montaña.

18. Rubén Jaramillo to delegado agrario en el Estado, 23 August 1961, AGN-DGIPS, caja 2916, exp. 1/148.

19. Secretario ejecutivo de asuntos agrarios to Rubén Jaramillo, Felix Serdán, José Solís Suárez, 8 May 1961, AGA, 22/5568.

20. Comité Ejecutivo del Nuevo Centro de Población Otilio Montaña to presidente de la república, 20 November 1961, AGA 22/5568; Ravelo, *Los Jaramillistas*, 172.

21. Ravelo, *Los Jaramillistas*, 171.

22. Jaramillo and Manjarrez, *Autobiografía y matanza en Xochicalco*, 152.

23. Rubén Jaramillo to presidente de la República, 12 February 1962, AGA 22/5560.

24. José Rodríguez, interview by Salvador Núñez, 14 July 1979, Nepatlán, Puebla.

25. Wenceslao Velasco Ayala to presidente de la república, 18 January 1951, AGN-DGG, vol. 265, exp. 2/311G(14)5.

26. Formally reintroduced to Gustavo Díaz Ordaz in 1964, the proposal had been developed and introduced for processing in 1959. Filemón Vega to presidente de la República, 20 December 1964, AGN-DGIPS, 2916.

27. Ravelo, *Los Jaramillistas*, 168.

28. For a detailed account of this process in Morelos's *oriente*, see Warman, *"We Come to Object,"* chap. 5.

29. *Presente!* 25 February 1962.

30. 19 February 1962, DFIPS, 2916, exp. 1/148. The Estado Mayor Presidencial is a body made up of representatives of the three armed forces which protects and advises the president.

31. Jucio de Amparo 80/962, 15 February 1962, CCJM.

32. Mallon, "Local Intellectuals, Regional Mythologies, and the Mexican State, 1840–1994," 68.

33. Ibid.

34. Pellicer de Brody, *México y la revolución Cubana*, 90.

35. Cited in ibid., 21.

36. In the late 1960s and early 1970s, a few other Latin American countries began to renew ties with Cuba.

37. U.S. Embassy in Mexico, Proposal to tie loans to anti-communist measures, secret telegram, 17 July 1961, John F. Kennedy Library, National Security Files (hereafter cited as JFK-NSF).

38. U.S. Embassy in Mexico, Memo of conversation with President López Mateos, secret telegram, 18 December 1961, JFK-NSF, CO-Mexico, General 1/61–5/62, box 141.

39. Lopez Mateos Visit, 2/20–2/22/64, 18 February 1964, Lyndon B. Johnson Library, National Security Files (hereafter cited as LBJ-NSF), CO-Mexico. Emphasis in original.

40. See, for example, U.S. Embassy in Mexico, Confidential Telegram, 8 September 1967, LBJ-NSF, CO-Mexico, Memos and Miscellaneous, vol. 3, 3/67–11/67 (2 of 3).

41. Buchenau, "Por una guerra fría más templada," 145; U.S. Embassy in Mexico, Secret Telegram, 28 June 1967, NAW, RG 59, CFPC 67–69, POL Cuba–A.

42. For a good discussion of this policy in light of the recently declassified documents, see Kate Doyle, "Double Dealing: Mexico's Foreign Policy toward Cuba," 2 March 2003, http://www.gwu.edu/%7Ensarchiv/NSAEBB/NSAEBB83/press.htm, accessed July 15, 2005.

43. Pellicer, *México y la revolución Cubana*, 103.

44. *Política*, 1 July 1960, cited in ibid., 23; *Política*, 15 June 1961, cited in ibid., 104.

45. Pellicer, *México y la revolución Cubana*, 104.

46. *La Voz de México* (Mexico), 30 May 1961.

47. Pedro García, interview by the author, 5 May 1999, Cuautla, Morelos.

48. Investigaciones Politicas y Sociales, 26 April 1961, Estado de Morelos, AGN-DGIPS, caja 1980, no. 2–1/G1/17.

49. President's Trips to Mexico, 26 May 1962, National Security Archives JFK-NSF, Trips and Conferences, 5/11/62–5/31/62, box 237.

50. Central Intelligence Agency, "Meeting at National University of Mexico in protest against visit of president," 24 June 1962, EO-1999–00042 [available online at www.foia.cia.gov/search.asp].

51. Batalla, *Donde quiera que me paro soy yo*, 103.

52. *La Cultura en Mexico, Suplemento de Siempre!* no. 21, 11 July 1962.

53. José Aguero, interview by Emilio Plutarco García, 1981, Cuernavaca, Morelos.

54. Ravelo, *Los Jaramillistas*, 186.

55. Ravelo, *Los Jaramillistas*, 178.

56. José Rodríguez, interview by Salvador Núñez, 16 June 1979, Nepatlán, Puebla.

57. Ibid.

58. Ravelo, *Los Jaramillistas*, 190.

59. Ibid.

60. Ibid.

61. Ibid.

62. Ravelo, *Los Jaramillistas*, 193–94.

63. Based on an interview with Mónico Rodríguez, Hodges placed the number at 220; *Mexican Anarchism after the Revolution*, 66. In the CEMOS archives, membership cards exist for Jaramillo, his wife, their three sons, and thirteen other PAOM members.

64. May 1, 1962, CEMOS, caja 46, folder 90.

65. Interview published posthumously, *Impacto*, 6 June 1962, no. 640.

66. *La Voz de México*, 10 June 1962.

67. Carr, *La izquierda mexicana a través del siglo XX*, 189–90.

68. See Hodges, *Mexican Anarchism after the Revolution*, intro. and chap. 3.

69. Bartra, *Los herederos de Zapata*, 91.

70. *La Cultura en Mexico, Suplemento de Siempre!* no. 21, 11 July 1962.

71. Cited in Jaramillo and Manjarrez, *Autobiografía y la matanza en Xochicalco*, 155. Arturo Orona and Jacinto López were both prominent campesino organizers. Orona was a member of the CNC and the Communist Party (until his expulsion in 1972), and the López was a founding member of the General Union of Workers and Campesinos of Mexico (UGOCM) and a principal leader in many land struggles in northern Mexico.

72. "Recent Developments—Garzón and the Movimiento de Liberación Nacional," 24 September 1962, National Archives, RG 59, 1960–63, box 1510, folder 712.00/9–162.

73. Ibid.

74. Articles expressing this shock appeared in *La Prensa, Novedades, Impacto, Excélsior, Siempre! Presente!* and *Política*. See Jaramillo and Manjarrez *Autobiografía y la matanza en Xochicalco*, 155–62.

75. Grupo de vecinos de la Colonia Moderna de Monterrey to presidente de la república, 6 June 1962, AGN/P-ALM, 541/531.

76. Alberto Larios to jefe de la Oficina de Quejas de la Presidencia, 25 May 1962, AGN/P-ALM, 541/531.

77. Confederación de Supremos Consejos del Rito Primitivo Universal de Cuba to presidente de la República, 29 May 1962, AGN/P-ALM, 541/531; Jaramillo and Manjarrez, *Autobiografía y la matanza en Xochicalco*, 159.

78. *Excélsior*, 28 May 1962.

79. Crescencio Castillo, interview by the author, 18 September 1999, San Roque, Puebla.

80. *La Cultura en Mexico, Suplemento de Siempre!* no. 21, 11 July 1962.

81. Ibid.

82. Informa sobre la muerte del líder campesino Rubén Jaramillo y Familia, 24 May 1962, Dirección Federal de Seguridad (DFS), vol. 36–62–62, H 1–6 L1.

83. Carlos Montemayor, *Chiapas*, 67.

84. Aura Hernández, "Librepensamiento," *La Jornada Morelos*, supplement, 23 May 2000.

85. *Política*, 15 June 1962.

86. José Rodríguez, interview by Salvador Nuñez, 16 June 1979, Nepatlán, Puebla.

87. National Archives at College Park, 712.00/5–2962, Despatch # 1482.

88. National Archives at College Park, 712.00/6–562, box 1510.

Conclusion

1. Scholars, too, have flocked to study the causes, demands, and tactics of the Zapatistas, producing a lively debate on the origins, nature, and tactics of the Chiapas rebels. The movement has been variously characterized as a class-based revolt, an uprising for indigenous revival, a postmodern movement, and an example of the crisis over citizenship in the wake of the global restructuring of capital. For a good synthesis on the scholarly debate surrounding the EZLN's rebellion, see Berger, "Romancing the Zapatistas," 149–70. Castañeda's *Utopia Unarmed*, published just before the Zapatista uprising, states, "For the left, the fall of socialism in the Soviet Union and Eastern Europe represents the end of a stirring, effective, nearly century-old utopia. Indeed, the very notion of an overall alternative to the status quo has been severely questioned. It is now practically impossible for the left to think outside the existing parameters of present-day Latin American reality. . . . The idea of revolution has withered and virtually died because its outcome has become either unwanted or unimaginable."

2. "Estatuto de las Fuerzas de Liberación Nacional," cited in Womack, *Rebellion in Chiapas*, 196, translation in original.

3. García Jiménez, *Cuatro testimonios de veteranos zapatistas*, 97.

4. Known as the "National Consultation for Indigenous Rights and Culture and for the End of the War of Extermination," in 1999, five thousand Zapatistas dispersed to every municipality in the nation promoting this referendum. Beginning in February 2001, EZLN commanders traveled throughout southern Mexico. They arrived in Mexico City and on March 3 addressed Congress, urging the implementation of the law protecting indigenous rights and culture as established by San Andrés Accords. These agreements, the first in a series of proposals for negotiation, had been signed but never implemented by the administration of President Ernesto Zedillo (1994–2000). In April 2001, the Mexican Senate, including members of the left-leaning Party of the Democratic Revolution, approved a heavily watered-down

version of the bill, which the Zapatistas rejected as it disavowed the main points of the San Andrés Accords.

5. Skocpol, *States and Social Revolution*; Scott, *The Moral Economy of the Peasant*; Wolf, *Peasant Wars of the Twentieth Century*; and Moore, *Social Origins of Dictatorship and Democracy*. Other important works focusing on peasant consciousness (but not necessarily rebellions or revolutions) include Scott, *Weapons of the Weak*; and Popkin, *The Rational Peasant*.

6. Stern, "New Approaches to the Study of Peasant Rebellion and Consciousness," 9 (emphasis in original).

7. Ibid.

8. Bellingeri's *Del agrarismo armado a la guerra de los pobres*, Montemayor's *La guerrilla recurrente*, Bartra's *Guerrero Bronco* and Hodges's *Mexican Anarchism after the Revolution* are the exceptions.

9. AGN-DFS, exp. 11–4–69 H 59–63 L 79.

10. AGN-DFS, exp. 100–10–16/4 H 26 L 6.

11. Bartra, *Guerrero Bronco*, 139.

12. Pedro García, interview by the author, 10 October 1999, Cuautla, Morelos.

13. Cabañas extended this request to Raquel Jaramillo, the only surviving daughter of the Jaramillo's family, but, to his and the Jaramillistas' dismay, she became a staunch supporter of President López Mateos and in 1999 remained an avid *Priísta*. AGN-DFS, exp. 100–15–1 H 82 L 11.

14. Pedro García, interview by the author, 10 October 1999, Cuautla, Morelos.

15. AGN-DFS, exp. 11–4–68 H 306–307 L 42.

16. AGN-DFS, exp. 100–15–1 H 82 L 11.

17. The Revolutionary Teachers' Movement (Movimiento Revolucionario del Magisterio or MRM) originated in 1956 when teachers throughout Mexico attempted to organize an independent union. The MRM was linked to the Communist Party.

18. Emilio Plutarco García, interview by the author, 21 November 1999, Jiutepec, Morelos.

19. "Actividades Subversivas en el Estado de Morelos," 14 April 1969, AGN-DFIPS, caja 2951, exp. Morelos.

20. "Honremos las Luchas Vallejista y Jaramillista," 27 March 1969, AGN-DFIPS, caja 2951, exp. Morelos. The Term "Vallejistas" refers to the railway workers' union—and their leader Demetrio Vallejo—whose massive strike in 1958–59 was severely repressed by the government.

21. Ibid.

22. Aguayo observes this same tendency in infiltrators' reports from the 1970s. See *La charola*, 203–5.

23. Ibid., 124.

24. Ibid., 203.

25. José Allende, interview by the author, 18 May 1999, Jantetelco, Morelos.

26. "Genaro Vázquez Rojas y Gavillas Existentes en el Estado de Guerrero," 7 May 1968, AGN-DGIPS, caja 2938.

27. Arturo Warman, "El problema del campo," in Pablo González Casanova and Enrique Florescano, *Mexico Hoy* (Mexico City: Siglo XXI, 1979), 117–18, cited in Adler Hellman, *Mexico in Crisis*, 171.

28. Unión de Pueblos de Morelos—CNPA, *Breve historia de una larga lucha*, 4.

29. Ibid.

30. Purnell, *Popular Movements and State Formation in Revolutionary Mexico*, 196.

31. As previously noted, bottom-up scholarship for this period is slowly emerging, especially in the realm of popular culture. See, for example, Joseph, Rubenstein, and Zolov, eds., *Fragments of a Golden Age*; Zolov, *Refried Elvis*. Others include Rubin, *Decentering the Regime*; and Rus, "The Comunidad Revolucionaria Institucional."

BIBLIOGRAPHY

Archives and Personal Collections

Archivo General Agrario (AGA)
Archivo General de la Nación (AGN):
    Ramo Dirección Federal de Seguridad (DFS)
    Ramo Dirección General de Investigaciones Políticas y Sociales (DGIPS)
    Ramo Dirección General de Gobierno (DGG)
    Ramo Presidentes (AGN/P):
        Lázaro Cárdenas (LC)
        Manuel Ávila Camacho (MAC)
        Adolfo Ruiz Cortines (ARC)
        Adolfo López Mateos (ALM)
Biblioteca Miguel Lerdo de Tejada, Archivo Económico (BMLT-AE)
Casa de la Cultura Jurídica de Morelos (CCJM)
Centro de Estudios del Movimiento Obrero y Socialista (CEMOS)
John F. Kennedy Library, National Security Files (JFK-NSF)
Lyndon B. Johnson Library, National Security Files (LBJ-NSF)
Plutarco Emilio García Jiménez, Personal Collection (PEGJ-PC)
"Rubén Jaramillo" Museum, Tlaquiltenango, Morelos
U.S. National Archives at College Park
U.S. National Archives at Washington (NAW)

Interviews

Aguero, José. Teacher Interview by Plutarco Emilio García Jiménez, 1980, Cuernavaca, Morelos.

Alberto, Ricardo. Campesino. Interview by Plutarco Emilio García Jiménez, 1980, Xoxocotla, Morelos.

Allende, José. Campesino. Interview by the author, 18 May 1999, Jantetelco, Morelos.

Allende, José. Interview by Victor Hugo Sánchez Reséndiz, 1992, Jantetelco, Morelos.

Alonso, Gorgonio. Campesino. Interview by Plutarco Emilio García Jiménez, 1 September 1980, Emiliano Zapata, Morelos.

Aranda, Reyes. Campesino. Interview by Plutarco Emilio García Jiménez, 1978, Jojutla, Morelos.

Campos, Pablo. Campesino. Interview by the author, 25 October 1999, Tetelcingo, Morelos.

Castillo, Crescencio. Campesino. Interview by the author and José Ramón Corona, 18 September 1999, San Roque, Puebla.

Castillo, Pedro. Worker at the Zacatepec sugar refinery. Interview by the author, 6 September 2000, Zacatepec, Morelos.

Coronel Miranda, Benigno. Campesino. Interview by the author, 5 September 2000, Zacatepec, Morelos.

Faria, José. Rural School Teacher. Interview by Plutarco Emilio García, 1981, Cuernavaca, Morelos.

Flores, Jesús. Campesino. Interview by the author, 7 November 1999, Mitepec, Puebla.

Herminio, Pedro. Campesino. Interview by the author, 25 May 1999, Xoxocotla, Morelos.

Herrera, Aurora. Campesina and widow of Porfirio Jaramillo, agrarian leader at Atencingo and brother of Rubén Jaramillo. Interview by the author, 10 December 1999, Jiutepec, Morelos.

Jaramillo, Raquel. Stepdaughter of Rubén Jaramillo. Interview by the author, 3 September 1999, Colonia Rubén Jaramillo, Morelos.

Jiménez, Miguel. Campesino. Interview by the author, 19 September 1999, Tetelcingo, Morelos.

Juárez, Ricarda. Campesina. Interview by the author, 1 May 1999, Ahuatepec, Morelos.

Galarza, Alberta. Housewife. Interview by the author, 9 March 1999, Chinconcuac, Morelos.

García, Margarita. Campesina. Interview by the author and José Ramón Corona, 18 September 1999, San Roque, Puebla.

García Jiménez, Plutarco Emilio. Teacher, activist, CNPA delegate, and former Morelos state Representative with the Party of the Democratic Revolution (PRD). Interview by the author, 21 November 1999, Jiutepec, Morelos.

García, Cirilo. Campesino. Interview by the author, 12 February 1999, Jojutla, Morelos.

———. Interview by Plutarco Emilio García Jiménez, 29 July 1981, Acapulco, Guerrero.

García, José. Interview by Plutarco Emilio García Jiménez, 1980, Ahuatlán, Morelos.

García, Margarita. Campesina. Interview by the author and José Ramón Corona, 18 September 1999, San Roque, Puebla.

García, Pedro. Campesino. Interview by the author, 5 May, 12 May, and 10 October 1999, Cuautla, Morelos.

Guzmán, Natividad. Campesina. Interview by Guadalupe García, 30 August 1994, Alpuyeca, Morelos.

Hernández, Eliut. Teacher, daughter of Eleuterio Sánchez, Jaramillista tortured and killed by Morelos police chief. Interview by the author, 15 December 1999, Tlaquiltenango, Morelos.

Hernández, Margarita. Teacher. Interview by the author, 20 July 2007, Temixco, Morelos.

Leyva, Agustín. Campesino. Interview by the author, 25 May 1999, Coatetelco, Morelos.

Manzanares Tapia, Lino. Campesino. Interview by the author, 12 October 1999, Los Hornos, Morelos.

Oliván, Abel. Campesino. Interview by Plutarco Emilio García Jiménez, 1 September 1980, El Higuerón, Morelos.

Orihuela, Roberto. Zone inspector for the Zacatepec sugar refinery. Interview by the author, 8 December 1999, Altapalmira, Morelos.

Ortiz, Pablo. Campesino. Interview by Plutarco Emilio García Jiménez, 1980, El Higuerón, Morelos.

Pérez Salazar, Alicia. High ranking FPPM member. Interview by the author, 3 August 2000, Mexico City.

Piedra, Samuel. Campesino. Interview by the author and Victor Hugo Sánchez Reséndiz, 6 December 1999, El Higuerón, Morelos.

Ravelo, Renato. Activist, scholar, and professor at the Universidad Autónoma de Guerrero. Interview by the author, 10 October 1999, Chilpancingo, Guerrero.

Rodríguez, José. Rural teacher. Interviews by Salvador Núñez, 16 June 1979 and 14 July 1979, Nepatlán, Puebla.

Rodríguez, Mónico. Interview by Aura Hernández, 16 July 1997, Chinconcuac, Morelos.

Serdán, Felix. Campesino. Interviews by the author, 5 February 1999, 1 August 2000 and 19 December 2000, Tehuixtla, Morelos.

Subdía Galindo, Bernabel. Campesino. Interview by the author, 12 October 1999, Los Hornos, Morelos.

Newspapers and Magazines

Excélsior (Mexico City)
Historia y Libertad (Morleos)
La Hora (Morelos)
Impacto (Mexico City)
La Jornada (Mexico City)
El Nacional (Mexico City)
Novedades (Mexico City)
Periódico Oficial (Mexico City)
Periódico Oficial de Morelos (Morelos)
Polígrafo (Morelos)
Política (Mexico City)
Proceso (Mexico City)
La Prensa (Mexico City)
Presente! (Morelos)
Punto Crítico (Mexico City)
Revista del Banco Obrero (Mexico City)
Siempre! (Mexico City)
El Sol de Morelos (Morelos)
El Universal (Mexico City)
La Voz de México (Mexico City)

Published Primary Sources

Acosta Chaparro, Mario A. *Movimientos subversivos en México*. Mexico City, 1990.

Bases Constitutivas de la Sociedad Cooperativa de Ejidatarios, Obreros y Emplea- dos del Ingenio "Emiliano Zapata." Zacatepec, Morelos, 1950.

Batalla, Paula. *Donde quiera que me paro, soy yo.* Edited by Carola Carbajal Ríos and Ana Victoria Jiménez A. Cuernavaca: CIDAHL, 1988.

Constitución Política (1917). Mexico City: Ediciones Andrade, 1964.

Estados Unidos Mexicanos Sexto Censo de Población, 1940. Mexico City: Secre- taría de la Economía Nacional Dirección General de Estadística, 1943.

Estrada Correa, Francisco. *Henriquismo: El arranque del cambio.* Mexico City: Costa-Amic Editores, 1988.

García Velazco, Guadalupe. *Mis mejores soldados*. Morelos: Culturas Populares, 1994.

García Jiménez, Plutarco Emilio. *Cuatro testimonios de veteranos zapatistas*. Mexico City: Dirección General de Culturas Populares Unidad Regional Morelos / UPM-CNPA, 1995.

Jaramillo, Rubén M., and Froylán C. Manjarrez. *Autobiografía y La matanza de Xochicalco*. 4th ed. 1967. Mexico City: Editorial Nuestro Tiempo, 1981.

Montejano, Ricardo. "Ay memoria: Raíz y razón de Mónico Rodríguez." *XEEP Radio Educación*, 1060, March–June 1999.

Muñoz Cota, José. *Aquí está Miguel Henríquez Guzmán*. Mexico City: Costa Amic Editores, 1978.

Plan de Cerro Prieto [Spanish]. *Cuadernos Agrarios* 5, nos. 10–11 (1980): 197–201.

Plan de Cerro Prieto [English]. In Donald Hodges, *Mexican Anarchism after the Revolution*, 68–72. University of Texas Press, 1995.

Ravelo, Renato. *Los Jaramillistas*. Mexico City: Editorial Nuestro Tiempo, 1978.

Ravelo Lecuona, Renato. *Félix Serdán: Memorias de un guerrillero*. Mexico City: Editorial Rizoma, 2000.

Séptimo Censo General de Población, 6 de junio de 1950. Mexico City: Secretaría de Economía, Dirección General de Estadística, 1953.

Suárez, Luis, ed. *Lucio Cabañas, el guerrillero sin esperanza*. Mexico City: ROCA, 1976.

Unión de Pueblos de Morelos—CNPA. *Breve historia de una larga lucha*. Mexico City: Coordinadora Naciónal Plan de Ayala, 2000.

Zacatepec, 60 años de vida municipal. Morelos: Ediciones del H. Congreso del Estado de Morelos, 1998.

Secondary Sources

Aguayo, Sergio. *La charola: Una historia de los servicios de inteligencia en México*. Mexico City: Editorial Grijalbo, 2001.

———. *Los archivos de la violencia*. Mexico City: Grijalbo, 1998.

Aguilar Camín, Héctor, and Lorenzo Meyer. *In the Shadow of the Mexican Revolution*. Austin: University of Texas Press, 1993.

Aguilar Mora, Manuel, and Carlos Monsiváis. "Sobre el henriquismo: El populismo de derecha y la historia escamoteada." *La cultura en México*, supplement of *Siempre*, 557, October 11, 1972: 3–8.

Aguilar, Rubén, and Guillermo Zermeño. "Ensayo introductorio: La iglesia y el sinarquismo en México." In *Religion, política y sociedad: El sinarquismo y la iglesia en México*, ed. Ruben Aguilar y Guillermo Zermeño. Mexico City: Universidad Iberoamericana, 1992.

Alonso, Antonio. *El movimiento ferrocarrilero en México, 1958–1959.* Mexico City: Ediciones Era, 1972.

Alvarez, Sonia E., Evelina Dagnino, and Arturo Escobar, eds. *Culture of Politics, Politics of Culture: Re-Visioning Latin American Social Movements.* Boulder: Westview, 1998.

Arias, Patricia, and Lucia Bazan. CIVAC: *Un proceso de industrialización en una zona campesina.* 2nd ed. Mexico City: Cuadernos de la Casa Chata, 1980.

Arizpe, Lourdes, and Carlota Botey. "Mexican Agricultural Development Policy and Its Impact on Rural Women." *Rural Women and State Policy: Feminist Perspectives on Latin American Agricultural Development,* ed. Carmen Diana Deere and Magdalena León. Boulder: Westview, 1987.

Ascencio, Esteban. *1968: Más allá del mito.* Mexico City: Ediciones del Milenio, 1998.

Ávila Espinosa, Felipe. "La historiografía del zapatismo después de John Womack." In *Estudios sobre el zapatismo,* 31–55, ed. Laura Espejel. Mexico City: Instituto Nacional de Antropología e Historia, 2000.

Baldwin, Deborah J. *Protestants and the Mexican Revolution: Missionaries, Ministers, and Social Change.* Urbana: University of Illinois Press, 1990.

Bantjes, Adrian A. *As If Jesus Walked on Earth: Cardenismo, Sonora, and the Mexican Revolution.* Wilmington, Del.: Scholarly Resources, 1998.

Barberán, José, Cuauhtémoc Cárdenas, Adriana López Monjardín, and Jorge Zavala. *Radiografía de un fraude.* Mexico City: Editorial Nuestro Tiempo, 1988.

Barkin, David, and Blanka Suárez. *El fin de la autosuficiencia alimentaria.* Mexico City: Centro de Ecodesarrollo, 1985.

Bartra, Armando. *Guerrero Bronco.* Mexico City: Ediciones sinfiltro, 1996.

———. *Los herederos de Zapata.* Mexico City: Ediciones Era, 1985.

———. "Movimientos obreros y populares a fines de los 50s." *Cien años de lucha de clases en México (1876–1976),* vol. 2, ed. Ismael Colmenares et al. Mexico City: Ediciones Quinto Sol, 1985.

———. *Regeneración.* Mexico City: Ediciones Era, 1977.

Bastian, Jean-Pierre, ed. *Protestantes, liberales y francomasones.* Mexico City: Fondo de Cultura Económica, 1990.

Becker, Marjorie. *Setting the Virgin On Fire: Lázaro Cárdenas, Michoacán Campesinos, and the Redemption of the Mexican Revolution.* Berkeley: University of California Press, 1995.

Bellingeri, Marco. *Del agrarismo armado a la guerra de los pobres: Ensayos de guerrilla rural en el México contemporáneo, 1940–1974.* Mexico City: Ediciones Casas Juan Pablos / Gobierno del Distrito Federal / Secretaría de Cultura de la Ciudad de México, 2003.

———. "Los campesinos de Morelos y el proyecto cardenista: Alianza, subordinación y ruptura (1935–1943)." *Historia* 11 (Oct.–Dec. 1985): 85–93.

Bellinghausen, Hermann, ed. *Pensar el 68*. Mexico City: Cal y Arena, 1988.

Berger, Mark T. "Romancing the Zapatistas: International Intellectuals and the Chiapas Rebellion." *Latin American Perspectives* 28, no. 2 (2001): 149–70.

Bortz, "The Effects of Mexico's Postwar Industrialization on U.S.-Mexico Price and Wage Comparisons." In *U.S.-Mexico Relations: Labor Market Interdependence*, ed. Jorge A. Bustamante, Clark W. Reynolds, and Raúl A. Hinojosa Ojeda, 214–34. Stanford: Stanford University Press.

Boyer, Christopher. *Becoming Campesinos: Politics, Identity, and Agrarian Struggle in Postrevolutionary Michoacán, 1920–1935*. Stanford: Stanford University Press, 2003.

Blacker-Hanson, O'Neill. "La Lucha Sigue! ('The Struggle Continues!'): Teacher Activism in Guerrero and the Continuum of Democratic Struggle in Mexico." PhD diss., University of Washington, 2005.

Brunk, Samuel. "Remembering Emiliano Zapata: Three Moments in the Posthumous Career of the Martyr of Chinameca." *Hispanic American Historical Review* 78, no. 3 (1998): 457–90.

———. *Emiliano Zapata!* Albuquerque: University of New Mexico, 1995.

Buchenau, Jürgen. "Por una guerra fría más templada: México entre el cambio revolucionario y la reacción estadounidense en Guatemala y Cuba." *Espejos de la guerra fría: México, América Central y el Caribe*, ed. Daniela Spenser. Mexico City: CIESAS, 2004.

Butler, Matthew. *Popular Piety and Political Identity in Mexico's Cristero Rebellion: Michoacán, 1927–1929*. Oxford: Oxford University Press, 2004.

Campbell, Hugh G. *La derecha radical en México, 1929–1949*. Translated by Pilar Martínez Negrete. Mexico City: Secretaría de Educación Pública, 1976.

Campos, Juan Luís, Arturo Cano, Luis Hernández, Francisco Pérez Arce, Carlos Rojo, Gisela Salinas, Susan Street, Paco Ignacio Taibo II, Rosa Elvira Vargas, and Pilar Vázques. *De las aulas a las calles*. Mexico City: Equipo Pueblo and Información Obrera, 1990.

Campos Lemus, Sócrates A., and Juan Sánchez Mendoza. *68: Tiempo de hablar*. Mexico City: Sansores y Aljure, 1998.

Carr, Barry. *La izquierda mexicana a través del siglo XX*. Translated by Paloma Villegas. Mexico City: Ediciones Era, 1996.

———. *Marxism and Communism in Twentieth-Century Mexico*. Lincoln: University of Nebraska Press, 1992.

Castañeda, Jorge. *La herencia: Arqueología de la sucesión presidencial en México*. Mexico City: Aguilar, 1999.

———. *Utopia Unarmed: The Latin American Left after the Cold War*. New York: Alfred A. Knopf, 1993.

Carey, Elaine. *Plaza of Sacrifices: Gender, Power, and Terror in 1968 Mexico*. Albuquerque: University of New Mexico Press, 2005.

Cázes, Daniel, ed. *Memorial del '68: Relato a muchas voces.* Mexico City: La Jornada, 1993.

Collier, George. *Basta! Land and the Zapatista Rebellion in Chiapas.* Oakland: Food First, 1999.

Córdova, Arnaldo. *La política de masas del cardenismo.* Mexico City: Ediciones Era, 1974.

Coy, Peter. "A Watershed in Mexican Rural History: Some Thoughts on the Reconciliation of Conflicting Interpretations." *Journal of Latin American Studies* 3, no. 1 (1971): 39–75.

Craig, Ann. *The First Agraristas: An Oral History of a Mexican Agrarian Reform Movement.* Berkeley: University of California Press, 1983.

De la Madrid Hurtado, Miguel. *Cambio de Rumbo: testimonio de una presidencia, 1982–1988.* Mexico City: Fondo de Cultura Económica, 2004.

Doyle, Kate. "Double Dealing: Mexico's Foreign Policy toward Cuba." National Security Archives, March 2, 2003. *http://www.gwu.edu/%7Ensarchiv/NSAEBB/NSAEBB83/press.htm* (accessed July 15, 2005).

———. *Tlatelolco Massacre: Declassified U.S. Documents on Mexico and the Events of 1968.* Washington: National Security Archives, 1998.

Escobar, Arturo, and Sonia Alvarez, eds. *The Making of Social Movements in Latin America.* Boulder: Westview, 1992.

Espejel López, Laura, Alicia Olivera de Bonfil, and Salvador Rueda Smithers, eds. *Emiliano Zapata: Antologia.* Mexico City: Instituto Nacional de Estudios Históricos de la Revolución de México, 1988.

Fallaw, Ben. *Cárdenas Compromised: The Failure of Reform in Postrevolutionary Yucatán.* Durham: Duke University Press, 2001.

Fein, Seth. "Myths of Cultural Imperialism and Nationalism in Golden Age Mexican Cinema." *Fragments of a Golden Age: The Politics of Culture in Mexico Since 1940*, ed. Gilbert Joseph, Anne Rubenstein, and Eric Zolov, 159–98. Durham: Duke University Press, 2001.

Foweraker, Joe, and Ann L. Craig, eds. *Popular Movements and Political Change in Mexico.* Boulder: Lynne Rienner, 1990.

Fowler-Salamini, Heather, and Mary Kay Vaughan, eds. *Creating Spaces, Shaping Transitions: Women of the Mexican Countryside (1850–1990).* Tucson: University of Arizona Press, 1994.

Frazier, Lessie Jo, and Deborah Cohen. "Defining the Space of Mexico '68: Heroic Masculinity in the Prison and 'Women' in the Streets." *Hispanic American Historical Review* 83, no. 4 (2003): 617–60.

Fuentes, Carlos. *A New Time for Mexico.* Translated by Marina Gutman Castañeda and Carlos Fuentes. Berkeley: University of California Press, 1997.

García Jiménez, Plutarco. "Lucha electoral y autodefensa en el jaramillismo." *Cuadernos Agrarios* 10 (July–Dec. 1994): 95–116.

————. "El movimiento jaramillista una experiencia de lucha campesina y popular del periodo post-revolucionario en México." In *Morelos: Cinco siglos de historia regional*, ed. Horacio Crespo, 301–10. Cuernavaca: Centro de Estudios Históricos del Agrarismo en México, 1984.

Garrido, Luis Javier. *El partido de la revolución institucionalizada*. Mexico City: Siglo XXI, 1982.

Gill, Mario. *Los ferrocarrileros*. Mexico City: Editorial Extemporaneos, 1971.

Gilly, Adolfo. *Chiapas, la razón ardiente*. Mexico City: Ediciones Era, 1997.

————. *La revolución interrumpida*. Rev. ed. Mexico City: Ediciones Era, 1998.

————. *Nuestra caída en la modernidad*. Mexico City: Joan Boldó Climent, 1988.

Giménez, Catalina H. *Así cantaban la revolución*. Mexico City: Grijalbo & Conaculta, 1990.

Gomezjara, Francisco. *La lucha por la tierra debe ser contra el capital*. Mexico City: Ediciones Sociología, 1982.

————. *El movimiento campesino en México*. Mexico City: Editorial Campesina, 1970.

González de Alba, Luis. *Los días y los años*. Mexico City: Ediciones Era, 1971.

Gonzales, Michael J. *The Mexican Revolution, 1910–1940*. Albuquerque: University of New Mexico Press, 2002.

Gould, Jeffrey. *To Lead as Equals: Rural Protest and Political Consciousness in Chinandega, Nicaragua, 1912–1919*. Chapel Hill: University of North Carolina Press, 1990.

Grammont, Hubert C. de. "La Unión General de Obreros y Campesinos." In *Historia de la cuestión agraria mexicana*, vol. 8, *Política estatal y conflictos agrarios, 1950–1970*, 222–60. Mexico City: Siglo XXI, 1989.

Grandin, Greg. *The Last Colonial Massacre: Latin America in the Cold War*. Chicago: University of Chicago Press, 2004.

Guevara Niebla, Gilberto. *La democracia en la calle: Crónica del movimiento estudiantil mexicano*. Mexico City: Siglo XXI, 1988.

Hamilton, Nora. *The Limits of State Autonomy*. Princeton: Princeton University Press, 1981.

Hansen, Roger. *The Politics of Mexican Development*. Baltimore: Johns Hopkins University Press, 1971.

Hart, John Mason. *Revolutionary Mexico*. Berkeley: University of California Press, 1987.

Hart, Paul. *Bitter Harvest: The Social Transformation of Morelos, Mexico, and the Origins of the Zapatista Revolution, 1840–1910*. Albuquerque: University of New Mexico Press, 2005.

Harvey, Neil. *The Chiapas Rebellion: The Struggle for Land and Democracy*. Durham: Duke University Press, 1998.

Hellman, Judith Adler. *Mexico in Crisis*. 2nd ed. New York: Homes & Meier, 1983.

Hewitt de Alcántara, Cynthia. *La modernización de la agricultura mexicana, 1940–1970*. Mexico City: Siglo XXI, 1978.

Hodges, Donald. *Mexican Anarchism after the Revolution*. Austin: University of Texas Press, 1995.

Huitzer, Gerrit. "Land Invasions as Non-Violent Strategy of Peasant Rebellion: Some Cases from Latin America." *Journal of Peace Research* 9, no. 2 (1972): 121–32.

Human Rights Commission. *The Political Violence in Mexico: A Human Rights Affair*. Mexico City: Partido de la Revolución Democrática, Human Commission and Parliamentary Group, 1992.

James, Daniel. *Doña María's Story: Life History, Memory, and Political Identity*. Durham: Duke University Press, 2000.

Joseph, Gilbert, Anne Rubenstein, and Eric Zolov, eds. *Fragments of a Golden Age: The Politics of Culture in Mexico Since 1940*. Durham: Duke University Press, 2001.

Joseph, Gilbert, and Daniel Nugent, eds. *Everyday Forms of State Formation*. Durham: Duke University Press, 1994.

———. "Popular Culture and the State Formation in Revolutionary Mexico." *Everyday Forms of State Formation*, ed. Gilbert Joseph and Daniel Nugent. Durham: Duke University Press, 1994.

———. "On the Trail of Latin American Bandits: A Reexamination of Peasant Resistance." *Latin American Research Review* 25, no. 3 (1990): 7–53.

Jiménez Guzmán, Lucero. *La industria cañero-azucarero en México*. Mexico City: Universidad Nacional Autónoma de Mexico City / Centro de Investigaciones Multidiciplinarias, 1986.

Katz, Friedrich, ed. *Riot, Rebellion, and Revolution*. Princeton: Princeton University Press, 1988.

———. *The Secret War in Mexico*. Chicago: University of Chicago Press, 1981.

———. "Labor Conditions on Haciendas in Porfirian Mexico: Some Trends and Tendencies." *Hispanic American Historical Review* 54, no. 1 (1974): 1–47.

Kaplan, Temma. "Community and Resistance in Women's Political Cultures." *Dialectical Anthropology* 15 (1990): 259–67.

———. "Female Consciousness and Collective Action: The Case of Barcelona, 1910–1918." *Signs* 7, no. 3 (1982): 545–67.

Knight, Alan. "Weapons and Arches in the Mexican Revolutionary Landscape." *Everyday Forms of State Formation*, ed. Gilbert Joseph and Daniel Nugent, 24–66. Durham: Duke University Press, 1994.

———. "Cardenismo: Juggernaut or Jalopy?" *Journal of Latin American Studies* 26, no. 1 (1994): 73–107.

———. "Popular Culture and the Revolutionary State in Mexico, 1910–1940." *Hispanic American Historical Review* 74, no. 3 (August 1994): 393–444.

———. "The Peculiarities of Mexican History: Mexico Compared to Latin America, 1821–1992." *Journal of Latin American Studies* 24 (1992): 99–144.

————. "Historical Continuities in Social Movements." In *Popular Movements and Political Change in Mexico*, ed. Joe Foweraker and Ann Craig, 78–102. Boulder: Lynne Rienner, 1990.

————. *The Mexican Revolution*. Cambridge: Cambridge University Press, 1986.

————. "The Mexican Revolution: Bourgeois? Nationalist? Or Just a 'Great Rebellion.'" *Bulletin of Latin American Research* 4, no. 2 (1985): 1–37.

Langston, Joy. "Thee Exits from the Mexican Institutional Revolutionary Party: Internal Ruptures and Political Stability." Mexico City: Centro de Investigación y Docencia Económica, 1993.

Larín, Nicolás. *La rebelión de los cristeros, 1926–1929*. Translated by Angel C. Tomás. Mexico: Ediciones Era, 1968.

Livenais, Patrick. *Peuplement et évolution agraire au Morelos (Mexique)*. Paris: L'Harmattan, 2001.

López Austin, Miguel. *Los manifiestos en náhuatl de Emiliano Zapata*. Mexico City: UNAM, 1996.

Lomnitz-Adler, Claudio. *Exits from the Labyrinth: Culture and Ideology in the Mexican National Space*. Berkeley: University of California Press, 1992.

Loyo Brambila, Aurora. *El movimiento magisterial de 1958 en México*. Mexico City: Ediciones Era, 1979.

Loyola Díaz, Rafael. *Ocaso del radicalismo revolucionario*. Mexico City: Instituto de Investigaciones Sociales de la UNAM, 1991.

Macín, Raúl. *Un profeta olvidado*. Montevideo: Tierra Nueva, 1970.

Mallon, Florencia. *Peasant and Nation: The Making of Postcolonial Mexico and Peru*. Berkeley: University of California Press, 1995.

————. "Local Intellectuals, Regional Mythologies and the Mexican State, 1840–1994: The Many Faces of Zapatismo." In Legislating Culture, special issue, *Polygraph* 10 (1998): 39–77.

————. "Peasant and State Formation in Nineteenth-Century Mexico: Morelos, 1848–1858." *Political Power and Social Theory* 7 (1988): 1–54.

Martin, Cheryl English. *Rural Society in Colonial Morelos*. Albuquerque: University of New Mexico, 1985.

————. "Hacendados and Villages in Late Colonial Morelos." *Hispanic American Historical Review* 63, no. 3 (1982): 407–27.

Martin, Jo Ann. "Antagonisms of Gender and Class in Morelos." *Creating Spaces, Shaping Transitions: Women of the Mexican Countryside (1850–1990)*, ed. Heather Fowler-Salamini and Mary Kay Vaughan. Tucson: University of Arizona Press, 1994.

Mayer, Michael C., and William L. Sherman. *The Course of Mexican History*. 5th edition. Oxford: Oxford University Press, 1995.

McGee Deutsch, Sandra. "Gender and Sociopolitical Change in Twentieth-Century Latin America." *Hispanic American Historical Review* 71, no. 2 (1991): 259–306.

Medin, Tzvi. *El sexenio alemanista*. Mexico City: Ediciones Era, 1990.

Medina, Luis. *Civilismo y modernización del autoritarismo 1940–1952*, vol. 20 of *Historia de la Revolución mexicana*. Mexico City: El Colegio de México, 1979.

Meyer, Jean A. *El sinarquismo, el cardenismo y la iglesia (1937–1947)*. 2nd ed. Mexico City: Tusquets Editores, 2003.

———. *La cristeada*. 3 vols. Mexico City: Siglo XXI, 1973.

Molyneux, Maxine. "Mobilization without Emancipation? Women's Interests, State and Revolution in Nicaragua." In *New Social Movements and the State in Latin America*, ed. David Slater, 233–59. CEDLA Latin American Studies no. 29, Amsterdam: CEDLA, 1985.

Montemayor, Carlos. *Rehacer la historia: Análisis de los nuevos documentso del 2 de octubre de 1968 en Tlatelolco*. Mexico City: Editorial Planeta, 2000.

———. *La guerrilla recurrente*. Mexico City: Universidad Autónoma de Ciudad Juárez, 1999.

———. *Chiapas, la rebelión indígena de México*. 2nd ed. Mexico City: Joaquín Mortiz, 1998.

———. *Guerra en el paraiso*. Mexico City: Seix Barral, 1997.

Moore, Barrington, Jr. *Social Origins of Dictatorship and Democracy: Lord and Peasant in the Making of the Modern World*. Boston: Beacon, 1966.

Murphy, Douglas. "Links with an Agrarian Past: The Hotel Hacienda Cocoyoc and Four Centuries of Estate Continuity and Change." PhD diss., University of North Carolina, 1998.

Newcomer, Daniel. *Reconciling Modernity: Urban State Formation in 1940s León, México*. Lincoln: University of Nebraska Press, 2004.

Niblo, Stephen. *Mexico in the 1940s: Modernity, Politics, and Corruption*. Wilmington, Del.: Scholarly Resources, 1999.

O'Malley, Ilene V. *The Myth of the Revolution: Hero Cults and the Institutionalization of the Mexican State, 1920–1940*. New York: Greenwood, 1986.

Olcott, Jocelyn. *Revolutionary Women in Postrevolutionary Mexico*. Durham: Duke University Press, 2005.

Otero, Gerardo. *Farewell to the Peasantry? Political Class Formation in Rural Mexico*. Boulder: Westview, 1999.

Pablos Tuñón, Esperanza. *Mujeres que se organizan*. Mexico City: Grupo Editorial Miguel Ángel Porrúa, 1992.

Palacios, Guillermo. "Postrevolutionary Intellectuals, Rural Readings and the Shaping of the 'Peasant Problem' in Mexico: El Maestro Rural, 1932–34." *Journal of Latin American Studies* 30, no. 2 (1998): 309–39.

Pellicer de Brody, Olga, and José Luis Reyna. *El afianzamiento de la estabilidad política (1952–1960)*, vol. 22 of *Historia de la Revolución mexicana*. Mexico City: Colegio de México, 1978.

Pellicer de Brody, Olga. *México y la revolución cubana*. Mexico City: El Colegio de México, 1972.

Peña, Guillermo de la. *A Legacy of Promises: Agriculture, Politics, and Ritual in the Morelos Highlands of Mexico*. Austin: University of Austin Press, 1981.

Poniatowska, Elena. *Fuerte es el silencio*. Mexico City: Ediciones Era, 1980.

———. *Massacre in Mexico*. Translated by Helen R. Lane. New York: Viking, 1975.

———. *La noche de Tlatelolco: testimonios de historia oral*. Mexico City: Ediciones Era, 1971.

Popkin, Samuel L. *The Rational Peasant: The Political Economy of Rural Society in Vietnam*. Berkeley: University of California Press, 1979.

Portelli, Alessandro. *The Death of Luigi Trastulli and Other Stories: Form and Meaning in Oral History*. Albany: State University of New York Press, 1991.

Posas Horcasitas, Ricardo. *La democracia en blanco: El movimiento médico en México, 1964–1965*. Mexico City: Siglo XXI, 1993.

Purnell, Jennie. *Popular Movements and State Formation in Revolutionary Mexico*. Durham: Duke University Press, 1999.

Quesada Aldana, Sergio, and Jesús G. Tapia Santamaría. "Mecanismos de domicanción en un ejido cañero: El caso de Tlaquiltenango, Morelos." Licenciatura thesis, Universidad Iberoamericana, 1977.

Raby, David L. *Educación y revolución social en México*. Translated by Roberto Gómez Ciriza. Mexico City: Secretaría de Educación Pública, 1974.

Ramírez Melgarejo, Ramón. "La bola chiquita, un movimiento campesino." In *Los campesinos en la tierra de Zapata*, ed. Arturo Warman, 2:165–221. Tlalpan: Centro de Investigaciones Superiores, Instituto Nacional de Antropología e Historia, 1976.

Redfield, Robert. *Tepoztlán: A Mexican Village*. Chicago: University of Chicago Press, 1930.

Revueltas, José. *Ensayo sobre un proletariado sin cabeza*. 1962. Mexico City: Ediciones Era, 1980.

Reyes, Guillermo de los. "Freemasonry and Folklore in Mexican Presidentialism." *Journal of American Culture* 20, no. 2 (1997).

Reyna, José Luis. "Las elecciones en el México institucionalizado, 1946–1976." *Las elecciones en México*, ed. Pablo González Casanova, 101–18. Mexico City: Siglo Veintiuno Editores, 1985.

———. "El conflicto ferrocarrilero: De la inmovilidad a la acción." In *Historia de la Revolución Mexicana*, vol. 22. Mexico City: Colegio de México, 1978.

Rockwell, Elsie. "Schools of the Revolution: Enacting and Contesting State Forms in Tlaxcala, 1910–1930." *Everyday Forms of State Formation*, ed. Gilbert Joseph and Daniel Nugent. Durham: Duke University Press, 1994.

Ronfeldt, David. *Atencingo, the Politics of Agrarian Struggle in a Mexican Ejido.* Stanford: Stanford University Press, 1973.

Roxborough, Ian. "Mexico." In *Latin America between the Second World War and the Cold War, 1944–1948,* ed. Leslie Bethell and Ian Roxborough, 190–216. Cambridge: Cambridge University Press, 1992.

Rubenstein, Anne. *Bad Language, Naked Ladies, and Other Threats to the Nation: A Political History of Comic Books in Mexico.* Durham: Duke University Press, 1998.

Rubin, Jeffrey W. *Decentering the Regime: Ethnicity, Radicalism, and Democracy in Juchitán, Mexico.* Durham: Duke University Press, 1997.

Ruiz Guerra, Rubén. *Hombres nuevos: Metodismo y modernización en México (1873–1930).* Mexico City: Centro de Comunicación Cultural, 1992.

Ruiz, Ramón E. *The Great Rebellion.* New York: W. W. Norton, 1980.

Ruiz, Vicki. *Cannery Women, Cannery Lives.* Albuquerque: University of New Mexico, 1987.

Rus, Jan. "The Comunidad Revolucionaria Institucional: The Subversion of Native Government in Highland Chiapas, 1936–1968." *Everyday Forms of State Formation,* ed. Gilbert Joseph and Daniel Nugent, 265–300. Durham: Duke University Press, 1994.

Sánchez Reséndiz, Víctor Hugo. *De rebeldes fe: Identidad y formación de la conciencia zapatista.* Cuernavaca: Instituto de Cultura de Morelos, 2003.

Sanderson, Steve. *The Transformation of Mexican Agriculture.* Princeton: Princeton University Press, 1986.

——. *Agrarian Populism and the Mexican State.* Berkeley: University of California Press, 1981.

Schmidt, Arthur. "Making It Real Compared to What? Reconceptualizing Mexican History since 1940." *Fragments of a Golden Age: The Politics of Culture in Mexico Since 1940,* ed. Gilbert Joseph, Anne Rubenstein, and Eric Zolov, 23–70. Durham: Duke University Press, 2001.

Schell, Patience A. *Church and State Education in Revolutionary Mexico City.* Tucson: University of Arizona Press, 2003.

Scherer García, Julio, and Carlos Monsiváis. *Parte de guerra: Tlatelolco 1968.* Mexico City: Nuevo Siglo / Aguilar, 1999.

Scott, James. Foreword. *Everyday Forms of State Formation,* ed. Gilbert Joseph and Daniel Nugent, vii–xii. Durham: Duke University Press, 1994.

——. *Weapons of the Weak: Everyday Forms of Peasant Resistance.* New Haven: Yale University Press, 1985.

——. *The Moral Economy of the Peasant: Rebellion and Subsistence in Southeast Asia.* New Haven: Yale University Press, 1976.

Skocpol, Theda. *States and Social Revolution: A Comparative Analysis of France, Russia and China.* New York: Cambridge University Press, 1979.

Semo, Ilan. *El ocaso de los mitos, (1958–1968)*. Vol. 6 of *México, un pueblo en la historia*, ed. Enrique Semo. Mexico City: Alianza Editorial Mexicana, 1989.

Serrano Álvarez, Pablo. *La batalla por el espíritu: El movimiento sinarquista en el Bajío (1932–1951)*. Mexico City: Consejo Nacional para la Cultura y las Artes, 1992.

Servín, Elisa. "Proganda y Guerra Fría: La campaña anticomunista en la prensa mexicana del medio siglo." *Signos Históricos* 11 (Jan.–June 2002): 9–39.

———. *Ruptura y oposición: El movimiento henriquista, 1945–1954*. Mexico: Ediciones Cal y Arena, 2001.

Singelmann, Peter, and Jesús Santamaría. "La empresa cooperativa como medio de dominación: el caso de un ingenio azucarero." *Dinámica de la empresa mexicana: Perspectivas políticas, económicas y sociales*, ed. Viviane B. de Márquez, 121–49. Mexico City: El Colegio de México, 1979.

Soto, Shirlene. *Emergence of the Modern Mexican Woman*. Denver: Arden, 1990.

Stern, Steve J. "New Approaches to the Study of Peasant Rebellion and Consciousness." *Resistance, Rebellion, and Consciousness in the Andean Peasant World, 18th to 20th Centuries*, 3–25. Madison: University of Wisconsin Press, 1987.

Stephen, Lynn. *¡Zapata Lives! Histories and Cultural Politics in Southern Mexico*. Berkeley: University of California Press, 2002.

Tapia Santamaría, Jesús. *Campo religioso y evolución política en el Bajío zamorano*. Michoacán: Colegio de Michoacán, 1986.

Taibo II, Paco Ignacio. *68*. Mexico City: Joaquín Mortiz, 1991.

Tarrow, Sidney. *Power in Movement: Social Movements and Contentious Politics*. Cambridge: Cambridge University Press, 1998.

Terán, Martha. "El levantamiento de los campesinos gasquistas." *Cuadernos Agrarios* 5, nos. 10–11 (1980): 115–38.

Torres Ramírez, Blanca. *Hacia la utopía industrial (1940–1952)*. Vol. 21 of *Historia de la Revolución Mexicana*. Mexico City: Colegio de México, 1984.

Tuñón Pablos, Esperanza. *Mujeres que se organizan*. Mexico City: UNAM / Miguel Ángel Porrúa, 1992.

Tutino, John. *From Insurrection to Revolution*. Princeton: Princeton University Press, 1986.

Unidad de Investigaciones Campesinas. "Los movimientos guerrilleros rurales en el México contemporaneo (1943–1973)." *Estudios Contemporaneos* 1, no. 2 (1980): 7–26.

Vaughan, Mary Kay. "Cultural Approaches to Peasant Politics in the Mexican Revolution." *Hispanic American Historical Review* 79, no. 2 (1999): 269–305.

———. "Transnational Processes and the Rise and Fall of the Mexican Cultural State: Notes from the Past." *Fragments of a Golden Age: The Politics of Culture in Mexico Since 1940*, ed. Gilbert Joseph, Anne Rubenstein, and Eric Zolov, 471–87. Durham: Duke University Press, 2001.

———. "Modernizing Patriarchy: State Policies, Rural Households, and Women in Mexico, 1930–1940." *Hidden Histories of Gender and the State in Latin America*, ed. Elizabeth Dore and Maxine Molyneux. Durham: Duke University Press, 2000.

———. *Cultural Politics in Revolution: Teachers, Peasants, and Schools in Mexico (1930–1940)*. Tucson: University of Arizona Press, 1997.

———. "Rural Women's Literacy and Education during the Mexican Revolution: Subverting a Patriarchal Event?" *Creating Spaces, Shaping Transitions: Women of the Mexican Countryside (1850–1990)*, ed. Heather Fowler-Salamini and Mary Kay Vaughan. Tucson: University of Arizona Press, 1994.

Viotti da Costa, Emilia. "New Publics, New Politics, New Histories: From Economic Reductionsm to Cultural Reductionism—in Search of Dialectics." *Reclaiming the Political in Latin American History: Essays from the North*, ed. Gilbert Joseph. Durham: Duke University Press, 2001.

Warman, Arturo. "The Political Project of Zapatismo." Translated by Judith Brister. Katz, *Riot, Rebellion, and Revolution*, ed. Friedrich Katz, 321–37. Princeton: Princeton University Press, 1988.

———. *"We Come to Object": The Peasants of Morelos and the National State*. Translated by Stephen K. Ault. Baltimore: Johns Hopkins University Press, 1980.

———. "El problema del campo." *Mexico Hoy*, ed. Pablo González Casanova and Enrique Florescano. Mexico City: Siglo XXI, 1979.

Weber, Devra. *Dark Sweat, White Gold*. Berkeley: University of California Press, 1994.

Werner Tobler, Hans. "Peasants and the Shaping of the Revolutionary State, 1910–1940." *Riot, Rebellion, and Revolution*, ed. Friedrich Katz, 487–518. Princeton: Princeton University Press, 1988.

Winn, Peter. *Weavers of Revolution*. Oxford: Oxford University Press, 1986.

Wolf, Eric. *Peasant Wars of the Twentieth Century*. New York: Harper and Row, 1969.

Womack, John, Jr. *Rebellion in Chiapas: An Historical Reader*. New York: New Press, 1999.

———. *Zapata and the Mexican Revolution*. New York: Vintage, 1968.

Zolov, Eric. "Discovering a Land 'Mysterious and Obvious': The Renarrativizing of Postrevolutionary Mexico." *Fragments of a Golden Age: The Politics of Culture in Mexico Since 1940*, ed. Gilbert Joseph, Anne Rubenstein, and Eric Zolov, 234–72. Durham: Duke University Press, 2001.

———. *Refried Elvis: The Rise of the Mexican Counterculture*. Berkeley: University of California Press, 1999.

INDEX

Institutional Revolutionary Party. *See* Partido Revolucionario Institucional (PRI)

intelligence, 203

James, Daniel, 230 n. 42

Jaramillistas: armed hiding, 141–45; armed uprisings, 86–87, 139–49, 209; army pursuit of, 101–5; campaigns, 108, 112–13, 123–34; characteristics of, 20–22; and draft resistance, 90–94; on education, 49–50, 53, 97, 116–17; elections, *110*, 119–23, 134–35; extent of movement, 12; ideology, 5–6, 97–101; land rights, 2, 100, 184–86, 216; mobilizations, 108, 146; and moral legitimacy, 5; origins of, 2, 3; radicalization, 139–40, 215–17, 221–24; source materials, 16–20; tactics, 6–7; women, 4, 20, 24, *130*, 161, 168–83; and Zapata legacy, 23, 27, 43, 54, 85; on Zapata's remains, 26

Jaramillo, Atanasio, 43

Jaramillo, Porfirio, 76, 78

Jaramillo, Rubén, 43–50, *126*, *131*, *179*, *191*, *204*; amnesty, 24, 105–7, 141, 146; assassination of, 1, 7, 24, 153, 162, 201, 207–8, 209–10, 215, 218; on Bay of Pigs, 199; on class structure, 96; and Emiliano Zapata Cooperative, 56–58, 60–66, 73–75, 83; gubernatorial campaign, 108, 112–13, 142; gubernatorial election, 119–23, 134–35, 140–41; as leader, 48–49, 73–75, 148; legacy of, 24–25, 211–24; Marxist/Maoist influences, 49; as Mason, 47; as Methodist pastor, 44–47; on military draft, 93, 95–96; pardons, 1, 4, 162, 184, 201; in Partido Comunista Mexicano, 10; portrayal of, 150, 151–55, 172; as rice farmer, 48; and

Rodríguez, 74–75; on sanitary rifle, 145; wives, 162; on women, 181–82; Zapata comparison, 49–50

Jaúrigui, Eusebio, 72

Jenkins, William, 76–77

Juárez, Benito, 44

Juárez, Ricarda, 149

Kaplan, Temma, 171, 180

Knight, Alan, 27, 38

labor unions, 63, 65, 80, 157–58

land distribution/reform, 32, 34–35, 37; ejidos, 37, 40, 41, 52, 85–86, 115–16, 148; Jaramillistas on, 2, 100, 184–86, 216; long-term effect, 13; loss of, 26; Madero on, 36; in Morelos, 27; movements, 40; post-revolution, 40–41; Zapatistas on, 38–40, 211, 214. *See also* Plan de Ayala

laws: Jaramillistas on, 27; reform, 32

League of Agrarian Communities, 48, 65, 133

Legorreta, Agustín, 52, 53

Lewis, Oscar, 233 n. 56

Leyva, Agustín, 144

Liberal Party, 32

López Avelar, Norberto, 184

López de Nava, Rodolfo, 146, 178

López Mateos, Adolfo, 1, 184, 197, 198, 201

López Obrador, Andrés Manuel, 223

López Portillo, José, 26

Lumumba, Patrice, 218

Madero, Francisco I., 27, 35–37

Manzanares, Lino, 91, 103

Marcos, Subcomandante, 20, 234 n. 57

Martinez, José, 1

Masons, 47

Maximilian (emperor), 31

McGee Deutsch, Sandra, 167

TANALÍS PADILLA

is an Assistant Professor in the Department

of History at Dartmouth College.

Library of Congress Cataloging-in-Publication Data
Padilla, Tanalís
Rural resistance in the land of Zapata : the Jaramillista
Movement and the myth of the Pax-Priísta, 1940–1962 /
Tanalís Padilla.
p. cm.
Includes bibliographical references and index.
ISBN 978-0-8223-4337-0 (cloth : alk. paper)
ISBN 978-0-8223-4319-6 (pbk. : alk. paper)
1. Mexico—Politics and government—1946–1970.
2. Jaramillo, Rubén M., d. 1962. 3. Morelos (Mexico :
State)—Politics and government—20th century. 4. Morelos
(Mexico : State)—History—Autonomy and independence
movements. 5. Land reform—Mexico—History—20th
century. I. Title.
F1235.5.P33 2008
972'.49082—dc22   2008019638